Love in the Time of Communism

In the aftermath of the reunification of Germany one former dissident recalled nostalgically that under the East German regime 'we had more sex and we had more to laugh about'. *Love in the Time of Communism* is a fascinating history of the GDR's forgotten sexual revolution and its limits. Josie McLellan shows that under communism divorce rates soared, abortion became commonplace, and the rate of births outside marriage was amongst the highest in Europe. Nudism went from ban to state-sponsored boom, and erotica became common currency in both the official economy and the black market. Public discussion of sexuality was, however, tightly controlled, and there were few opportunities to challenge traditional gender roles or sexual norms. Josie McLellan's pioneering account questions some of our basic assumptions about the relationship between sexuality, politics, and society and is a major contribution to our understanding of the everyday emotional lives of postwar Europeans.

JOSIE MCLELLAN is Senior Lecturer in Modern European History at the University of Bristol. Her previous publications include *Antifascism and Memory in East Germany: Remembering the International Brigades 1945–1989* (2004).

T0371473

Love in the Time of Communism

Intimacy and Sexuality in the GDR

Josie McLellan

CAMBRIDGE
UNIVERSITY PRESS

CAMBRIDGE
UNIVERSITY PRESS

University Printing House, Cambridge CB2 8BS, United Kingdom

One Liberty Plaza, 20th Floor, New York, NY 10006, USA

477 Williamstown Road, Port Melbourne, VIC 3207, Australia

314-321, 3rd Floor, Plot 3, Splendor Forum, Jasola District Centre, New Delhi - 110025, India

79 Anson Road, #06-04/06, Singapore 079906

Cambridge University Press is part of the University of Cambridge.

It furthers the University's mission by disseminating knowledge in the pursuit of education, learning and research at the highest international levels of excellence.

www.cambridge.org
Information on this title: www.cambridge.org/9780521727617

First published 2011

A catalogue record for this publication is available from the British Library

Library of Congress Cataloging in Publication data
McLellan, Josie.
  Love in the time of communism : intimacy and sexuality in the GDR /
Josie McLellan.
    p. cm.
  Includes bibliographical references and index.
  ISBN 978-0-521-89891-1 – ISBN 978-0-521-72761-7 (pbk.)
  1. Sex–Germany (East)–History.   2. Communism and love–
Germany (East)–History.   3. Germany (East)–Social conditions
4. Germany (East)–History.   I. Title.
  HQ18.G3M39   2011
  306.70943´109045–dc23
  2011026302

ISBN 978-0-521-89891-1 Hardback
ISBN 978-0-521-72761-7 Paperback

Contents

Figures

Every effort has been made to contact the copyright holders of the images reproduced in this book. In the event of any error, please inform the publisher who will be glad to correct future editions of the work.

Tables

Acknowledgements

My first thanks go to the people who agreed to be interviewed for this project. Without their willingness to talk about their lives, this book would have been a far poorer one. I am also enormously grateful to Angela Brock, who carried out and transcribed the bulk of the interviews. Angela's tact and empathy make her an ideal interviewer, and she was a model of efficiency throughout, not letting even the arrival of her son Wieland put her off her stride.

The research for this book would not have been possible without funding from the following sources: the Alexander von Humboldt Foundation, the British Academy, the Leverhulme Trust, and the University of Bristol Faculty of Arts Research Fund. I am very thankful for their support.

In Germany, Birke and Ulrike Urban-Stahl and Sophia New and Dan Belasco Rogers made both short and long research visits possible with practical help and peerless hospitality. Regina Vogel was an ideal sounding board for ideas, and a constant source of enthusiasm and fun. I owe a huge amount to Siegfried Lokatis and the late Simone Barck, who patiently schooled me in the ways of the censors. Simone is sadly missed by all who knew her. Erasmus Schroeter and T. O. Immisch went above and beyond the call of duty in offering friendly advice and assistance on East German photography. My research was greatly helped by scores of archivists and librarians who went out of their way to find relevant material and track down missing files and books.

At the University of Bristol, I am extremely lucky to have colleagues who are supportive and sharp in equal measure: thanks in particular to Robert Bickers, Tim Cole, Juliane Fürst, Anke Holdenried, Chris McLeod, Chris Pearson, Kirsty Reid, James Thompson, and Ian Wei. A series of conversations with Richard Sale helped the writing process immeasurably. I have enjoyed discussing this topic with students, particularly in the second-year units 'German Bodies' and 'Behind the Wall' and the MA unit 'Everyday Life Under Dictatorship'. It has been a real pleasure to see how thoughtfully students engage with the primary source material, and this book has been greatly enriched by their insights.

Numerous colleagues in the UK and the United States have been generous with their time and expertise. I would particularly like to thank Paul Betts, Mary Fulbrook, Lisa Heineman, Dagmar Herzog, and Bob Moeller for their support and advice along the way. I am especially grateful to Mark Fenemore and Jennifer Evans for casting an expert eye on the chapters on young people and homosexuality.

At Cambridge University Press, Michael Watson has been a reassuring and patient editor. The two anonymous readers' reports were perceptive and constructive: their advice improved the manuscript considerably. Chloe Howell and Jo Breeze were invaluable guides to the production process. Karen Anderson Howes, copy-editor *extraordinaire*, not only saved my blushes on numerous points, but also actually made the whole process a pleasure. Cameron Duder took on the indexing at short notice, with efficiency and expertise.

A number of people provided childcare so that I had time and peace of mind to work. For this, I thank Nancy Irwin, Leon Quinn, Sonia McLellan, and Anna Hraboweckyj.

I have spent many happy hours throughout this period with friends both new and old, in particular Tanya Barman, Emily Fletcher, Anke Holdenried, Claire Spencer, and Zoe Waxman. My parents, Sonia and Ian, and my sister, Alice, have been wonderful companions, and excellent hosts. Leon Quinn has read everything from early scribblings to a complete draft. His enthusiasm for the book never flagged, in good times and in bad. Finally, this book is dedicated to my daughter Rosanna, whose arrival made the past few years busy but very happy ones.

Some of the material in this book previously appeared elsewhere. Chapter 6 is a substantially revised version of my article 'State Socialist Bodies: East German Nudism from Ban to Boom', *Journal of Modern History* 79 (March 2007), 48–79; ©2007 by the University of Chicago. Parts of Chapter 7 have appeared as 'Visual Dangers and Delights: Nude Photography in East Germany', *Past and Present* 205 (2009), 143–174, © the Past and Present Society, 2009; and as ' "Even Under Socialism, We Don't Want to Do Without Love": East German Erotica', in David Crowley and Susan Reid (eds.), *Pleasures in Socialism: Leisure and Luxury in the Eastern Bloc* (Evanston: Northwestern University Press, 2010), 218–237, © Northwestern University Press. My thanks to all of the above for their kind permission to reproduce this material.

1 Introduction: the East German sexual revolution

'We had more sex, and we had more to laugh about', said the actress Katharina Thalbach in November 2008, reflecting on her life in East Germany.[1] A startling conclusion, not least because Thalbach, an opponent of the communist regime, left East Germany in the midst of a political storm in 1976 and was banned from returning for the next decade. Nevertheless, in her memories of life under communism, political repression coexists with sexual liberation. This is echoed by the novelist Thomas Brussig, who paints an enviable picture of East German relationships based on love and mutual respect. East Germans, he argues, were 'generous and tolerant', 'freer and more cooperative', and less 'watchful and mistrusting' than West Germans.[2] Such interpretations are by no means the preserve of the eastern German chattering classes. Ordinary East Germans interviewed in 2007 and 2008 spontaneously offered similar memories of the 'lightheartedness of those years' and 'a sexuality without taboos'. One concluded: 'not everything was good in East Germany, but in principle you could live out your sexuality freely'.[3]

There is something unsettling about these statements. They contradict the idea that life in the Eastern bloc was grey and joyless, and that between the assembly line and the bread queue opportunities for happiness were few. They also suggest a surprising degree of autonomy in private life, at odds with twentieth-century imaginings of authoritarian regimes as fundamentally hostile to sex. Not for nothing does O'Brien, Winston Smith's torturer in *Nineteen Eighty-Four*, boast that: 'We shall abolish the orgasm. Our neurologists are at work upon it

---

[1] Irene Bazinger, 'Im Gespräch: Katharina Thalbach. Wir im Osten hatten mehr Sex und mehr zu lachen', *Frankfurter Allgemeine Zeitung*, 21.11.2008, 42. I'm very grateful to Til von Rahmen for this reference. All translations from the German are my own, unless otherwise indicated.
[2] Thomas Brussig, 'Aber der Sex war schöner', *Vanity Fair* [Germany] 17 (2007), 98.
[3] Quotes are from Frau V, Herr P, and Herr D. Details of interviewees can be found in the Appendix.

now ... There will be no love, except the love of Big Brother.'⁴ Orwell's
Anti-Sex League, it seems, failed to find its realisation in the GDR.
But many accounts go even further than this to suggest that in some
ways life behind the Iron Curtain was more enjoyable than life in the
West. According to many, East German socialism produced conditions
that actually encouraged and optimised intimacy, for example wom-
en's financial independence and the dearth of sexual consumer goods
and pornography.⁵ Freed from economic and ideological oppression,
women were able to build relationships with men based on mutual trust
and respect. As Wolfgang Engler wrote in a widely read book on *The
East Germans*, 'seldom was love more socially unburdened'.⁶

The idea that communism encouraged and even enabled intimacy
is, however, highly contested. Others hold equally strong views that life
under communism was profoundly repressive in sexual matters. Letters
written to the German sex shop magnate Beate Uhse after the fall of
the Berlin Wall complained bitterly of lives blighted by prudishness
and rhapsodised about the potential sexual liberation made possible by
communism's collapse.⁷ The East German regime did not hesitate to
prescribe moral standards, and was quick to intervene in relationships
that were seen to threaten the social order. Stasi surveillance could completely shatter the private sphere, most famously in cases such as that
of Vera Wollenberger, who was systematically spied upon by her own
husband.⁸ Even after the decriminalisation of homosexuality, same-sex
relationships remained almost completely invisible, with gay men and
lesbians dependent on fragile private networks for support, advice, and
contact with like-minded people.⁹

So on the one hand we have a narrative of repression which stresses
a lack of privacy, and a consequently inhibiting effect on personal

⁴ George Orwell, *Nineteen Eighty-Four* (Harmondsworth: Penguin, 1989), p. 280.
⁵ For a scholarly statement of this position, see Dagmar Herzog, *Sex After Fascism: Memory and Morality in Twentieth-Century Germany* (Princeton: Princeton University Press, 2005), p. 188.
⁶ Wolfgang Engler, *Die Ostdeutschen. Kunde von einem verlorenen Land* (Berlin: Aufbau, 2000), p. 258.
⁷ Dorothee Wierling, 'Vereinigungen. Ostdeutsche Briefe an Beate Uhse', *BIOS: Zeitschrift für Biographieforschung, Oral History und Lebensverlaufsanalysen* 20 (special issue, 2007), 146–155.
⁸ Vera Wollenberger, *Virus der Heuchler. Innenansicht aus Stasi-Akten* (Berlin: Espresso/ Elefanten Press, 1992).
⁹ Christina Karstädt and Anette von Zitzewitz (eds.), *... viel zu viel verschwiegen. Eine historische Dokumentation von Lebensgeschichten lesbischer Frauen in der Deutschen Demokratischen Republik* (Berlin: Hoho Verlag Christine Hoffmann, 1996); Jürgen Lemke, *Gay Voices from East Germany* (Bloomington: Indiana University Press, 1991).

relationships. On the other hand, a 'romantic' narrative insists that state interference in private lives was negligible, and that 'top-down' influence was in any case largely benign. But trying to ascertain whether East German sexuality was 'good' or 'bad' is something of a reductive exercise.[10] A more pressing task is to explain the dramatic changes that took place in East German (hetero)sexual mores. Between the foundation of the German Democratic Republic in 1949 and its collapse in 1989, divorce and abortion rates soared, as did the rate of births outside marriage. Nude bathing moved from the preserve of a few to an almost universal fact of life. Nude photography, all but banned in the early years of the Cold War, became the subject of state-sponsored courses and large-scale exhibitions. The central aim of this book is to explain this transformation, and explore its limits.

The changes in East German attitudes towards sexuality and the body challenge some of our wider assumptions about the relationship between sexuality, politics, and society. We still know far too little about the everyday emotional lives of Europeans after 1945.[11] As Dagmar Herzog has pointed out in a brilliant recent essay, 'one of the areas that we still understand the least is the long sexual revolution of the second half of the twentieth century'.[12] This book aims to contribute to this budding historiography which should, as Herzog urges, pay attention both to national peculiarities and to transnational trends and influences. The Western sexual revolution is usually linked to liberalising tendencies within government and civil society. As twentieth-century societies became more democratic, so the theory goes, attitudes towards sexuality became increasingly permissive. A similar liberalisation of sexuality in East Germany, however, calls into question the link with democratisation, particularly in the absence of many of the things which are assumed to have driven the sexual revolution in the West – a free press, the sex industry, the student movement, an independent judiciary. Despite their very different political systems, were the post-war histories of Eastern and Western Europe, particularly their social

---

[10] On this point, see Mark Fenemore, 'The Recent Historiography of Sexuality in Twentieth-Century Germany', *Historical Journal* 52 (2009), 773; and more broadly Victoria Harris, 'Sex on the Margins: New Directions in the Historiography of Sexuality and Gender', *Historical Journal* 53 (4) (2010), 1085–1104.

[11] For some early results of a number of ongoing projects on women's lives in Eastern Europe, see Shana Penn and Jill Massino (eds.), *Gender Politics and Everyday Life in State Socialist Eastern and Central Europe* (New York: Palgrave Macmillan, 2009).

[12] Dagmar Herzog, 'Syncopated Sex: Transforming European Sexual Cultures', *American Historical Review* 114 (2009), 1295. See also Dagmar Herzog, 'Sexuality in the Postwar West', *Journal of Modern History* 78 (2006), 144–171.

histories, more similar than they appear at first glance? On either side of the Iron Curtain, Europeans shared comparable social experiences of growing prosperity, urbanisation, secularisation, and increased mobility. What were the effects of such upheavals on intimate relationships? Was there something distinctive about East German intimacy? What does it tell us about what it was really like to live under communism, and what light does it shed on how and why attitudes towards sexuality change? Understanding East German difference, and East German commonality, will help us to understand more fully the history of postwar intimacy.

Sex and love in postwar East Germany

It is impossible to grasp the extent of change without understanding the conditions in East Germany during the early years of the GDR. The first years of German communism were inauspicious ones for sex and intimacy. The end of the Second World War was accompanied by sexual violence and familial upheaval on an unprecedented scale.[13] Millions of German women and girls were raped by Red Army soldiers during the last months of the war and the first years of the occupation period.[14] Millions of families found themselves on the move, forcibly resettled from Germany's eastern territories or having lost their homes in Allied bombing raids. Millions of German men remained in prisoner-of-war camps in the Soviet Union, returning only years after the war had ended.[15] Millions of women, unsure whether their husbands would ever come home again, faced years of 'standing alone'.[16] For

---

[13] Atina Grossmann, *Jews, Germans and Allies: Close Encounters in Occupied Germany* (Princeton: Princeton University Press, 2007); see also Jennifer Evans, 'Reconstruction Sites: Sexuality, Citizenship, and the Limits of National Belonging in Divided Berlin, 1944–1958', unpublished Ph.D. dissertation, Binghamton University, State University of New York (2001). Evans' monograph *Life Among the Ruins: Cityscape and Sexuality in Cold War Berlin* will be published by Palgrave Macmillan in September 2011.

[14] Norman Naimark, *The Russians in Germany* (Cambridge, MA: Harvard University Press, 1995), ch. 2; Atina Grossman, 'A Question of Silence: The Rape of German Women by Occupation Soldiers', in Robert Moeller (ed.), *West Germany Under Construction: Politics, Society and Culture in the Adenauer Era* (Ann Arbor: University of Michigan Press, 1997), pp. 33–52; Hsu-Ming Two, 'The Continuum of Sexual Violence in Occupied Germany, 1945–1949', *Women's History Review* 5 (1996), 191–218; Annette Timm, *The Politics of Fertility in Twentieth-Century Berlin* (New York: Cambridge University Press, 2010), pp. 268–272.

[15] Frank Biess, *Homecomings: Returning POWs and the Legacies of Defeat in Postwar Germany* (Princeton: Princeton University Press, 2006).

[16] Elizabeth Heineman, *What Difference Does a Husband Make? Women and Marital Status in Nazi and Postwar Germany* (Berkeley: University of California Press, 1999).

some, prostitution was the only way to make ends meet.[17] Even families who were reunited struggled to readjust: husbands and wives had often grown apart during the war years and cramped living conditions made it hard to re-establish intimacy. Nor did the state do much to help such couples. The East German regime's emphasis on ideological and economic regeneration above all else was encapsulated in the opening lines of its national anthem: 'risen from the ruins and facing the future'. The establishment of communism would, Marxist orthodoxy suggested, inevitably lead to private happiness – until then, citizens were expected to defer individual pleasures and devote themselves to the massive task of building the 'better Germany'.

The subject of sex was further problematicised by the events of the recent past. The unique sexual culture of the Weimar Republic had been partially tolerated and even supported by German communists, who had campaigned for the reform of laws forbidding abortion and homosexuality.[18] There was a certain amount of overlap between the KPD (Communist Party of Germany) and the Weimar sex reform movement, and social democrats in particular had been involved with the left wing of the nudist movement.[19] But such activities had always caused unease, and many communists remained deeply uncomfortable with the subject of sex and the body. This tendency was reinforced by the reactionary turn in Soviet policy in the mid 1930s, which reversed the liberal reforms that had followed the October Revolution in Russia. Abortion and homosexuality were recriminalised, and the open discussion of alternative forms of family life and sexuality came to an end.[20]

---

[17] Uta Falck, *VEB Bordell. Geschichte der Prostitution in der DDR* (Berlin: Ch. Links Verlag, 1998), pp. 22–36; Annamarie Troeger, 'Between Rape and Prostitution: Survival Strategies and Chances of Emancipation for Berlin Women After World War II', in Judith Friedlander (ed.), *Women in Culture and Politics: A Century of Change* (Bloomington: Indiana University Press, 1986), pp. 97–117.

[18] Atina Grossman, *Reforming Sex: The German Movement for Birth Control and Abortion Reform, 1920–1950* (Oxford: Oxford University Press, 1995); Eric D. Weitz, *Creating German Communism, 1890–1990: From Popular Protests to Socialist State* (Princeton: Princeton University Press, 1997), esp. ch. 6; Manfred Herzer, 'Communists, Social Democrats, and the Homosexual Movement in the Weimar Republic', *Journal of Homosexuality* 29 (1995), 197–226; Cornelie Usborne, *Cultures of Abortion in Weimar Germany* (Oxford: Berghahn Books, 2007).

[19] Giselher Spitzer, '"Nackt und frei". Die proletarische Freikörperkulturbewegung', in Hans Joachim Teichler and Gerhard Hauk (eds.), *Illustrierte Geschichte des Arbeitersports* (Berlin and Bonn: J. H. W. Dietz Nachf., 1987), pp. 174–181; Giselher Spitzer, 'Die "Adolf-Koch-Bewegung". Genese und Praxis einer proletarischen Selbsthilfe-Organisation zwischen den Weltkriegen', in Hans Joachim Teichler (ed.), *Arbeiterkultur und Arbeitersport* (Clausthal-Zellerfeld: Deutsche Vereinigung für Sportwissenschaft, 1985), pp. 77–104.

[20] Janet Evans, 'The Communist Party of the Soviet Union and the Woman's Question: The Case of the 1936 Decree "In Defense of Mother and Child"', *Journal of*

Given that many of the leaders of the East German state had spent the majority of the Nazi period in Soviet exile, it was inevitable that some of these attitudes returned with them to Germany in 1945.

The Third Reich had also left an uneasy legacy with regard to sexuality. Its peculiar mixture of licentiousness and repression had glorified the heterosexual naked body, and allowed a certain degree of permissiveness with regard to unmarried sex between Germans.[21] Sex without procreative potential or between racial groups, however, was penalised with massive brutality.[22] There is little direct evidence as to how this experience was remembered or received in East Germany. No doubt the fact that Nazism was explained in strictly Marxist terms, as a product of monopoly capitalism, made it easier for East Germans to ignore or forget its other aspects. What is striking is the unwillingness of the East German regime to overhaul legislation in this area. Although the ban on abortion was temporarily lifted in the wake of the Red Army rapes, the 1950 Law for the Protection of Mother and Child allowed abortion only in cases where the mother's health was severely threatened or there were eugenic grounds for a termination.[23] Male homosexuality also remained illegal, as paragraph 175a of the legal code, introduced by Nazi legislators, was retained on the East German statute books. Homosexuality was not persecuted on anything like the same scale as under the Nazis, but the retention of this paragraph was nevertheless a

Contemporary History 16 (1981), 757–775; Daniel Healey, *Homosexual Desire in Revolutionary Russia: The Regulation of Sexual and Gender Dissent* (Chicago: University of Chicago Press, 2001). On the persistence of prudish official attitudes in the late Stalinist period (and the rather more permissive attitudes of young people), see Juliane Fürst, *Stalin's Last Generation: Soviet Post-War Youth and the Emergence of Mature Socialism* (Oxford: Oxford University Press, 2010), pp. 250–291. On the Khrushchev period, see Deborah Field, *Private Life and Communist Morality in Khrushchev's Russia* (New York: Peter Lang, 2007).

[21] Herzog, *Sex After Fascism*, ch. 1; Dagmar Herzog (ed.), *Sexuality and German Fascism* (Oxford: Berghahn, 2004).

[22] On sex between racial groups, see especially Birthe Kundrus and Patricia Szobar's contributions to Herzog, *Sexuality and German Fascism* (Kundrus, 'Forbidden Company: Romantic Relations Between Germans and Foreigners, 1939 to 1945', pp. 201–222, and Szobar, 'Telling Sexual Stories in the Nazi Courts of Law: Race Defilement in Germany, 1933 to 1945', pp. 131–160). On the persecution of homosexuals, see Günter Grau, *Hidden Holocaust? Gay and Lesbian Persecution in Nazi Germany 1933–1945* (London: Routledge, 1995); Harry Oosterhuis, 'Medicine, Male Bonding and Homosexuality in Nazi Germany', *Journal of Contemporary History* 34 (1997), 187–205.

[23] Kirsten Poutrus, 'Von den Massenvergewaltigungen zum Mutterschutzgesetz. Abtreibungspolitik und Abtreibungspraxis in Ostdeutschland, 1945–1950', in Richard Bessel and Ralph Jessen (eds.), *Die Grenzen der Diktatur. Staat und Gesellschaft in der DDR* (Göttingen: Vandenhoeck und Ruprecht, 1996), pp. 170–198; the text of the 1950 legislation can be found at www.verfassungen.de/de/ddr/mutterkindgesetz50.htm.

deliberate decision to ignore calls for a change in the law and continue the criminalisation of gay men.[24]

The 1950s were not a time of unrelieved repression.[25] The state attempted to incorporate women's rights into both legislation and daily practice (with mixed success).[26] The sex reform movement continued to have a muted influence in the world of publishing, particularly in the lists of the Greifenverlag.[27] A new publication, *Das Magazin*, was launched in 1954, with a cheery mix of literature, features, and erotica that was both to shape and to reflect East Germans' attitudes towards sexuality. By and large, though, the state tended to act in a morally prohibitive way. Attempts to revive the Weimar popular nudist tradition were met with incomprehension and moral panic. 'Protect the eyes of the nation!' implored Johannes R. Becher, the East German minister for culture.[28] Reproductive heterosexuality was handed down from the highest levels. The Ten Commandments of Socialist Ethics and Morals, unveiled by East German leader Walter Ulbricht in 1958, left little doubt as to how citizens should lead their lives (see Figure 1.1). 'You should live cleanly and decently and respect your family', thundered commandment number nine.[29] In some ways, the gap between regime and population was not so wide. By and large, most East Germans aspired to be 'clean' and 'decent', and disapproved of those who were not. But what was meant

---

[24] Günter Grau, 'Liberalisierung und Repression. Zur Strafrechtsdiskussion zum §175 in der DDR', *Zeitschrift für Sexualforschung* 15 (2002), 323–340; Günter Grau, 'Return of the Past: The Policy of the SED and the Laws Against Homosexuality in Eastern Germany Between 1946 and 1968', *Journal of Homosexuality* 37 (1999), 1–29.

[25] Herzog, *Sex After Fascism*, 193; Mark Fenemore, 'The Growing Pains of Sex Education in the German Democratic Republic', in Lutz D. H. Sauerteig and Roger Davidson (eds.), *Shaping Sexual Knowledge: A Cultural History of Sexuality in Twentieth-Century Europe* (London: Routledge, 2009), pp. 71–90.

[26] Ina Merkel, ... *und Du Frau an der Werkbank* (Berlin: Elefantenpress, 1990); Heineman, *What Difference Does a Husband Make?*, ch. 7; Donna Harsch, *Revenge of the Domestic: Women, the Family and Communism in the German Democratic Republic* (Princeton and Oxford: Princeton University Press, 2007). Heike Trappe, *Emanzipation oder Zwang? Frauen in der DDR zwischen Beruf, Familie und Sozialpolitik* (Berlin: Akademie Verlag, 1995), is an excellent sociological account of these and subsequent policies on women's fertility choices and working lives.

[27] Carsten Wurm, Jens Henkel and Gabriele Ballon, *Der Greifenverlag zu Rudolstadt 1919–1993. Verlagsgeschichte und Bibliographie* (Wiesbaden: Harrassowitz Verlag, 2001), p. 135.

[28] In a classic case of communist paternalism, Becher was himself a practising nudist, but opposed its dissemination to the wider population: Lutz Thormann, ' "Schont die Augen der Nation!" Zum Verhältnis vom Nacktheit und Öffentlichkeit in der DDR', unpublished MA thesis, University of Jena (2007), p. 20.

[29] *Protokoll der Verhandlungen des V. Parteitages der Sozialistischen Einheitspartei Deutschlands. 10. bis 16. Juli 1958 in der Werner-Seelenbinder-Halle zu Berlin* (Berlin: Dietz, 1959), p. 159.

Figure 1.1: Abisag Tüllmann: 'Ten Commandments for the new socialist people and a declaration of love to the [German Democratic] Republic on the stairs of a school'. The banner below the 'Ten Commandments' reads: 'We love our Republic with Walter Ulbricht for Germany's happiness.' Photo taken in 1963 in Schenkenberg, Brandenburg.

by these terms would shift quite considerably over the following thirty years, transforming the landscape of intimacy in the process.

The East German sexual revolution

At first glance, East Germany seems like an unlikely place for a sexual revolution. Many of the key tropes of the Western sexual revolution were simply not present in the East, in particular erotica entrepreneurs such as Beate Uhse or Hugh Hefner, radical feminist statements like the 'Myth of the Vaginal Orgasm', and widespread media discussion of sex. Indeed Dagmar Herzog suggests that, unlike West Germany, the East did not experience a sexual revolution.[30] Her term 'sexual evolution' emphasises the gradual, undramatic nature of change and also implies that these developments were very different to the sudden and public changes in the West. Although Herzog acknowledges that East Germans 'carved out their own freedoms', her account tends to emphasise the evolution of official attitudes towards sex, particularly the role played by progressive sexologists and the state-led spread of women's rights.[31] There is no doubt that official attitudes towards sex evolved – and that sexologists had a role to play in this. But the social history of sexuality shows that change also happened from the bottom up, and that these changes resembled and, in some cases, exceeded Western sexual revolutions. The sexual evolution from above needs to be understood alongside the revolution from below: these two developments intertwined with and fed off each other.

By insisting that a 'sexual revolution' did not take place in East Germany, we risk drawing a false dichotomy between East and West. It is true that public discussion of sexuality was much more circumscribed than in the West and, as we shall see, this had important implications for the nature of East German intimacy. But in other respects, the Eastern and Western sexual revolutions were surprisingly similar. It is inarguable that fundamental changes took place in the choices people made about their private lives and that these changes took place over a relatively short period of time. And, in some cases, changes in East German sexual behaviour were more radical than those that took place in West Germany and elsewhere in the developed world.

---

[30] Herzog, *Sex After Fascism*, p. 192; Dagmar Herzog, 'The East German Sexual Evolution', in Katherine Pence and Paul Betts (eds.), *Socialist Modern: East German Everyday Culture and Politics* (Ann Arbor: University of Michigan Press, 2008), pp. 71–95.

[31] Herzog, 'The East German Sexual Evolution', p. 83.

Denying East German developments the label 'sexual revolution' also makes claims for Western sexual revolutions that they simply cannot bear. Change everywhere was patchy and often highly localised. Much of the sound and fury of the sexual revolution took place in the metropolis and was communicated to the wider population only at second hand. Leicester was not London, Poitiers was not Paris, Braunschweig was not Berlin. Beth Bailey's study of Lawrence, Kansas, points out that most Americans lived away from the cutting edge, in towns and cities without gay saunas, red-light districts, or singles bars.[32] Nonetheless, this did not mean that the sexual revolution passed them by; in fact, their changing attitudes towards sex were an integral part of it. As Bailey points out, metropolitan radicals and sexual entrepreneurs alone could not transform sexual behaviour. It was also shaped by 'people who had absolutely no intention in abetting a revolution in sex'.[33]

Bailey's findings raise an important point about the causation of sexual change, which challenges the existing literature's emphasis on the public discussion and commodification of sex. Herzog, writing about West Germany, points to a combination of commercialised sexuality, legislative reform, and the New Left's interest in, and obsessive discussion of, sexuality.[34] Jeffrey Weeks' work on Britain argues that increasing affluence destabilised existing sexual norms and encouraged a more market-driven sexuality to come to the fore.[35] Sheila Jeffreys, in contrast, describes a patriarchal counter-revolution based on the sexual domination of women. Drawing mostly on evidence from the UK, she paints a picture of elite sexual radicals whose work shored up male supremacy.[36] These scholars do not agree on the causes of the sexual revolution; they do, however, all focus on discourses about, and discussions of, sexuality.

Bailey, on the other hand, describes the ways in which individuals' decisions about their own sexual behaviour also played an important role. Similarly, Hera Cook's account of a 'long sexual revolution' in British women's control of their fertility, culminating with the introduction of the Pill, stresses technological and social factors over cultural ones.[37] Rather than simply being led by the radicals of the revolution,

---

[32] Beth Bailey, *Sex in the Heartland* (Cambridge, MA: Harvard University Press, 1999), p. 5.
[33] *Ibid.*   [34] Herzog, *Sex After Fascism*, pp. 141–142.
[35] Jeffrey Weeks, *Sex, Politics and Society: The Regulation of Sexuality Since 1800*, 2nd edn (London: Longman, 1989), pp. 250–251.
[36] Sheila Jeffreys, *Anticlimax: A Feminist Perspective on the Sexual Revolution* (London: Women's Press, 1990), pp. 91–144.
[37] Hera Cook, *The Long Sexual Revolution: English Women, Sex, and Contraception 1800–1975* (Oxford: Oxford University Press, 2004).

ordinary people made changes in their lives for private, often practical reasons. Together, these accumulated into an unintended mass movement.

The idea that a sexual revolution can take place, at least in part, 'from below', rather than being shaped only by legislators, entrepreneurs, radicals, and sexual theorists, is highly relevant to the East German case. Here, although a lack of freedom of speech prevented unfettered discussion of sexuality, popular pressure was often an important spur to change. A bottom-up model of the sexual revolution also allows us to think about the role played by socio-economic factors. Improved housing and the increasing availability of contraception had a profound impact on people's sexual behaviour. Shorter working weeks and increased disposable income also changed the ways in which people spent their leisure time. On the whole, individuals growing up in the postwar period had more choice about who they met, more privacy in which to meet them, and more control over their fertility. This experience was shared, to different degrees, by both East and West Europeans.

As important as the why and when of the East German sexual revolution is the question of its limits. Attitudes changed dramatically, but we should not assume that all these developments signalled a sexually permissive society. Nude photographs, for example, could underline rather than undermine conservative ideas about gender and the family. A thaw in official attitudes towards homosexuality did not necessarily lead to popular tolerance or acceptance. The unevenness of the East German sexual revolution not only illuminates the workings of socialist society, but also acts as a valuable comparison with the West. Particularly significant here is the fact that the East German sexual revolution took place in the absence of either a free market or freedom of speech. Both of these factors, as we shall see, had important implications for the form and timing of sexual change.

My use of the term 'revolution' should not be taken to mean either that attitudes were utterly transformed or that East Germany became a sexually liberal society. But neither was this the case in any Western country. Like all sexual revolutions, the East German one involved elements of evolution and, like all revolutions, it was unfinished, uneven, and stunted in places. Change took place at different speeds in different areas. As Bailey puts it: 'In order to make sense of "the sexual revolution", we need to sort out its various strands. They do not all have to stand – or fall – together.'[38] It is important not only to highlight

---

[38] Bailey, *Sex in the Heartland*, p. 2.

the differences between the 1950s and the 1980s, but also to try to pinpoint when things changed. At first glance the late 1960s and early 1970s seem to be a key period: the decriminalisation of homosexuality and abortion (in both cases earlier than in many West European countries), a marked rise in the availability of nude photographs, the establishment of nudism as a mass pursuit. This was in part a result of political change afoot in the highest echelons of East German governance: Walter Ulbricht's replacement as first secretary of the SED (Sozialistische Einheitspartei Deutschlands, the Socialist Unity Party of Germany) by Erich Honecker in 1971. After the economic and social experimentation of the previous two decades, Honecker's coronation began a less obviously ideological period in SED rule. Not only did the cultural sphere see a partial thaw, but the party increasingly made concessions to its citizens' individualism.[39] Nevertheless, we should not place too much importance on the change in leadership. Many trends had begun in the 1960s or even the 1950s. And nor did social change culminate in the 1970s. For example, decriminalisation had little immediate impact on most gay and lesbian lives, and homosexuality became publicly visible only in the mid to late 1980s. Equally, many trends in heterosexual behaviour peaked in the 1980s. The 1960s and 1970s are usually considered to be the key decades in the development of East German society: the uneven pace of sexual change raises some questions about the universality of that conclusion.[40]

Sex, society, and the state

Recent scholarship has challenged the myth of a monolithic communist dictatorship, showing that regime priorities were often unclear, subject to change, and hotly disputed both within the state apparatus and from below.[41] This is certainly true of matters sexual, where moral conviction was often trumped by a need to win over the population, or attempts to project a progressive image to the world outside the GDR's borders, or simply by pragmatic economic and social considerations. For all its

[39] Paul Betts, *Within Walls: Private Life in the GDR* (Oxford: Oxford University Press, 2010), p. 12.
[40] See for example Mary Fulbrook (ed.), *Power and Society in the GDR, 1961–1979: The 'Normalisation of Rule'?* (Oxford: Berghahn, 2009).
[41] On the development of the historiography on this topic, see Corey Ross, *The East German Dictatorship: Problems and Perspectives in the Interpretation of the GDR* (London: Arnold, 2002); Mary Fulbrook, 'Putting the People Back In? The Contentious State of GDR History', *German History* 24 (2006), 609–620. On the influence of ordinary female citizens on family policy, see especially Harsch, *Revenge of the Domestic*.

moral rhetoric, particularly in the 1950s and 1960s, the SED's chief concerns in this area were practical ones: the birth rate; the inclusion and retention of women in the workforce; and the international and domestic reputation of the GDR. As was the norm in all industrialised countries, the East German birth rate was in decline, a trend that accelerated in the 1960s and 1970s. This was a particularly serious matter in a country that had already seen substantial population depletion in the 1950s and that could not expect to see substantial immigration. Halting the decline in the birth rate was crucial in practical terms, in order to provide the state with the workers of the future. But it was also an important Cold War battleground, as Annette Timm points out: 'To be able to show that East Germans were willing to have more children than their West German counterparts was, after all, to be able to argue that they had more confidence in the future, lived in a more socially equitable society, and were supported by a health care system that allowed them to make rational reproductive decisions.'[42] Encouraging women to take up paid employment, and to remain in the workforce once they had children, was another fundamental plank of East German labour policy. The tensions between pro-natalism and female employment were to prove central to the development of family and sexual policy. Finally, the SED was acutely aware of its image – at home and abroad. As the ideological fervour of the GDR's early years dissipated, increased sexual autonomy and the growing importance of the private sphere were to become a central part of the 'social contract' between the state and the population.[43] The party was keen to project an image of a modern, forward-looking East German state, which took the lead in progressive policy making. This desire to be 'world-leading' – or at least to keep pace with the times – played an important role in the decisions to decriminalise abortion and homosexuality and significantly shaped changing attitudes towards nudism and young people's sexuality.

State policy was also subject to a considerable amount of pressure from below in the form of petitions, complaints, and feedback to lower-level functionaries. This aspect of socialist rule has been the subject of much research over the past ten years, and it is particularly interesting to see how these processes worked away from the familiar arenas of the workplace, the housing office, and the shops.[44] Sexuality (as opposed to

---

[42] Timm, *The Politics of Fertility*, pp. 289–290.
[43] Betts, *Within Walls*, p. 13.
[44] See for example Sheila Fitzpatrick, 'Supplicants and Citizens: Public Letter-Writing in Soviet Russia in the 1930s', *Slavic Review* 55 (1996), 78–105. There is a rich literature on petitioning in the GDR including Young-sun Hong, 'Cigarette Butts and the Building of Socialism in East Germany', *Central European History* 35(3) (2002),

14 Introduction

the sexual act) involves the private world of bodies and emotions *and* the public world of politics, economics, and social policy. As we shall see, these two worlds were not discrete. Nor should we assume that regime and popular agendas were always mutually exclusive. At times they diverged radically, but the most popular and enduring changes were based on the overlap between state and individual interests. The decriminalisation of abortion and the introduction of a year's maternity leave were popular policies with women, who welcomed the increased control over their own fertility and the opportunity to spend time with their young children. But the two policies also worked together to further the regime's aims of keeping mothers in work while maintaining the birth rate. The marginalisation of same-sex relationships can also be seen as a result of overlapping priorities on the part of the regime and the heterosexual majority. Neither group had an interest in the quality of life of homosexual citizens and in some cases shared frankly homophobic values. Furthermore, an open discussion of homosexuality threatened to destabilise many of the gender norms on which East German society was built.

East German socialism oversaw quite fundamental changes in female – and to a lesser extent – male behaviour, but an almost complete silence on what this meant for gender identity. Women's changing role in society was endlessly discussed – with one of the highest rates of female paid employment in the world, it could hardly have been otherwise.[45] The challenges and rewards of balancing work, children, and political engagement were never knowingly underplayed. Men's role in all this, however, was often passed over in silence, despite the fact that many men took a more active role in the household than either their fathers or their Western counterparts.[46] What is particularly noticeable is the extent to which East German public discourse avoided any discussion of how changing gender roles challenged traditional notions of masculinity and femininity. This was especially true for men: images of men changing nappies now coexisted alongside the more usual images

---

327–344; Peter Becker and Alf Lüdtke (eds.), *Akten. Eingaben. Schaufenster. Die DDR und ihre Texte* (Berlin: Akademie Verlag, 1997); Ina Merkel (ed.), *'Wir sind doch nicht die Meckerecke der Nation!' Briefe an das Fernsehen der DDR* (Berlin: Schwarzkopf & Schwarzkopf, 2000); Felix Mühlberg, 'Informelle Konfliktbewältigung. Zur Geschichte der Eingabe in der DDR', unpublished Ph.D. dissertation, University of Chemnitz (1999); Jonathan Zatlin, *The Currency of Socialism: Money and Political Culture in East Germany* (Cambridge: Cambridge University Press, 2007), ch. 7; Betts, *Within Walls*, ch. 6.

[45] Harsch, *Revenge of the Domestic*.

[46] See for example the chapter on gender in Mary Fulbrook, *The People's State: East German Society from Hitler to Honecker* (New Haven: Yale University Press, 2005).

of male workers and sportsmen, but the ways in which this might affect masculinity were rarely discussed.

The persistence of traditional gender roles was not unique to East Germany, of course. Across Europe, politicians, the media, and the majority of the population shared a belief in a gendered division of labour and the superior virtue of the nuclear family.[47] Inextricably linked to this was the assumption that heterosexuality was the only 'normal' way to express one's sexuality. Heteronormativity, as this complex of beliefs about gender and sexuality has become known, excluded not just gay men and lesbians, but also heterosexuals outside conventional families. In Western Europe, post-1968 social movements such as feminism and gay liberation played a crucial role in challenging these assumptions. In the East, however, men and women who felt confined by sexual or gender stereotypes had fewer fora in which to share their frustrations or develop their critique of heteronormative hegemony. Public discussion of sexuality was entirely steered by the state, and the absence of a free press or freedom of association meant that feminism and gay liberation had a limited public impact. This did not prevent sexual liberalisation altogether, but it certainly helped shape it. This book will argue that, although the right to privacy is often seen as key to sexual freedom, public discussion of sexuality is also a crucial part of this process.

The discussions which did take place, in public and in private, were influenced and even shaped by international trends and discourses. Despite the closing of the German–German border in 1961, the Berlin Wall proved remarkably permeable. West German visitors brought news, smuggled literature, and sent parcels with records, magazines, and fashionable clothes. East Germans were avid consumers of Western TV and radio, and were surprisingly well informed about developments outside the state's borders. The Western public sphere formed a crucial 'second dimension' to Eastern discourses.[48] As we shall see, young people in particular often saw themselves as part of an international cultural community, united by similar tastes in music and fashion, and by a desire to rebel against conventional norms. Those artists and activists who formulated a more systematic critique of East German

[47] See Robert Moeller, *Protecting Motherhood: Women and the Family in the Politics of Postwar West Germany* (Berkeley: University of California Press, 1996); Claire Duchen, 'Occupation Housewife: The Domestic Ideal in 1950s France', *French Cultural Studies* 2 (1991), 1–11.

[48] Simone Barck, Christoph Classen and Thomas Heinemann, 'The Fettered Media: Controlling Public Debate', in Konrad Jarausch (ed.), *Dictatorship as Experience: Towards a Socio-Cultural History of the GDR* (New York and Oxford: Berghahn, 1999), 225.

attitudes towards sex and the body often drew on Western ideas, from the ideology of gay liberation to the photography of Helmut Newton.

As I seek to explain why and where sexual liberalisation took place, the focus of this book will inevitably be on the late 1960s onwards. This is also the period of East German history about which we know least – not just in terms of sexuality, but more generally too.[49] Historians have tended to see the 1950s and 1960s as the richest period of socialist rule not just in terms of available sources, but also as the time when optimism about both economic and social change was at its peak. The 1970s and 1980s, in contrast, are often seen – with some justification – as a grey descent into disillusionment and defeatism (particularly after the Biermann affair in 1976; see pp. 106–107), culminating in the mass exodus of 1989 and subsequent collapse of the regime.[50] In terms of intimacy, however, the mid 1970s to mid 1980s was a period of growing personal freedom. Access to reliable contraception and abortion gave couples more autonomy over family planning decisions. Better housing meant that more people had comfortable homes and improved levels of privacy, and that domestic burdens such as hand washing and stoking coal stoves were somewhat lessened. Increased maternity leave gave women more time at home with young children – if they wanted it. And the growing numbers of babies born outside marriage suggest that single parenthood had lost some of its social stigma. This is not to say that East Germany experienced a 'golden age' of sexuality. As we have already seen, there are too many caveats and exclusions to endorse the 'romance' narrative. But it does not go too far to say that this was the period in which most East Germans experienced more freedom in their sexual lives than ever before.

Sources

The book aims to be a history of sexuality 'in the round', examining people's lives as well as the ways they were represented and paying attention to the experiences of minorities *and* the majority. I am interested in political, social, and cultural histories and the ways in which they overlap. 'In the round', however, should not imply that this will be an all-encompassing or comprehensive account. From secret police archives to private collections of pornography, the history of intimacy

---

[49] The best overview of the 1970s and 1980s is still Stefan Wolle, *Die heile Welt der Diktatur. Alltag und Herrschaft in der DDR 1971–1989* (Bonn: Bundeszentrale für politische Bildung, 1999).

[50] Paul Betts, 'The Twilight of the Idols: East German Memory and Material Culture', *Journal of Modern History* 72 (2000), 750–751.

can be told from an almost infinite number of perspectives. All are fragmentary, offering traces of the past rather than a transparent documentary record. Throughout this book, sources will be discussed in terms
not just of what they can tell us, but also of what they elide or omit.

Quantitative material, for example, particularly the vast swathes
of figures collected by the GDR government in its annual *Statistical
Yearbook*, can be enormously useful in plotting broader social trends
such as birth, marriage, and divorce. Many of these figures need to be
approached with caution – for example the much quoted statistic that,
by 1989, 91 per cent of women of working age were in paid employment
was significantly inflated for propaganda purposes, by including women
in education and training, on career breaks, and who were seeking
work.[51] The data on sexual behaviour also need careful consideration.
The work of East German sexologists in the 1970s and 1980s produced
some startling results, particularly with regard to the frequency of
female orgasm, leading some to conclude that East Germans were global leaders in the field of sexual satisfaction. In one study, 20 per cent
of female apprentices claimed to have had four or more orgasms the last
time they had sex.[52] Such findings need to be considered in the light
of broader methodological questions about both sex surveys and East
German opinion polling.[53] It is difficult to avoid the suspicion that at
least some of these respondents might have been telling the researchers
what they thought they wanted to hear. Even in matters sexual, the East
German imperative to overfulfil the plan may still have played a role.
Wherever they are carried out, the reliability of sex surveys – like all
surveys on personal matters – must be analysed with a close and sceptical eye.[54] Even after the collapse of communism, 16 per cent of those
who took part in a sex survey admitted that they had not answered all
the questions honestly.[55]

[51] Myra Marx Ferree, 'The Rise and Fall of "Mommy Politics": Feminism and German
Unification', *Feminist Studies* 19 (1993), 91.

[52] Walter Friedrich and Kurt Starke, *Liebe und Sexualität bis 30* (Berlin: VEB Deutscher
Verlag der Wissenschaften, 1984), p. 195.

[53] On sexology, see Chris Waters, 'Sexology', in Harry Cocks and Matthew Houlbrook
(eds.), *Palgrave Advances in the Modern History of Sexuality* (London: Palgrave
Macmillan, 2005), pp. 41–63; on the research carried out by the East German
Zentralinstitut für Jugendforschung, see Karen Henderson, 'The Search for
Ideological Conformity: Sociological Research on Youth in the GDR', *German History*
10 (1992), 318–334.

[54] Kevin A. Fenton, Anne M. Johnson, Sally McManus and Bob Erens, 'Measuring
Sexual Behaviour: Methodological Challenges in Survey Research', *Sexually
Transmitted Infections* 77 (2001), 84–92.

[55] Zentralarchiv für empirische Sozialforschung an der Universität zu Köln (henceforth
ZA) S6142: Partner III – Berufstätige 1990, 101.

This study, of course, aims to explain as well as document quantitative trends. Many of the pieces of the historical jigsaw can be found in archives. While love and sexuality were rarely discussed at the highest levels of government, state departments and organisations in areas such as youth, women, health, culture, sport, justice, and security had to grapple with the moral, legal, and political problems created by people's private lives. Sexuality was often an issue that fell between different state institutions, and it was common for complaints or petitions from the population to be bounced around from department to department. According to one senior politician, homosexuality was never discussed in the Politburo, and those responsible for health and education continually tried to palm the responsibility for this knotty topic off on each other.[56]

Throughout my research, the question of defining sexuality came up again and again. Having struggled through the snow to a particularly remote regional archive, I was disconcerted to be told, 'oh, we've got nothing on sexuality'. But luckily the absence of a 'Department of Sexuality' did not mean a dearth of material. Before long I had found a cache of correspondence about marriages between East Germans and foreign nationals, as well as abortion appeals in the period immediately preceding its legalisation. The holdings of regional archives are sometimes patchy but, precisely because of this, rich and unusual sources have often been preserved.

My experiences in the archives of the Ministry for State Security, or Stasi, the East German secret police, were less positive. It took four years from my initial application to get permission to visit these archives, and this was probably one of the instances where it is better to travel hopefully than to arrive. German legislation means that researchers do not have access to the archives' catalogues, leaving them completely dependent on the material produced by the archivist and his or her interpretation of the research topic. This presented particular problems for me, as 'sexuality' largely translated in this case as prostitution and homosexuality. Strict rules about anonymisation mean one or two pages of a much longer document are often presented out of context, and the blacking out of names makes it difficult to piece together the meaning of a document. Even when this is possible, Stasi files are often far from reliable. Agents and operatives tended to exaggerate in their reports to impress their superior officers. Vera Wollenberger, who

---

[56] Günther Schabowski quoted by Eduard Stapel in Kurt Starke, *Schwuler Osten. Homosexuelle Männer in der DDR* (Berlin: Ch. Links, 1994), p. 95.

discovered her own husband had been informing on her for almost a decade, remarked on the many inaccuracies and downright lies in her file. She warned:

If a future generation of impartial researchers were to reconstruct the face of [East German] society using these files, they would produce only a grotesque grimace, bearing no resemblance to a human countenance.[57]

There are also real ethical problems with material such as surveillance photographs of prostitutes having sex with clients. This is not to say that the Stasi material is without its uses; the material on the gay and lesbian rights movements of the 1980s is, for example, invaluable. But without the autonomy of selecting one's own material, it is impossible to leave without a feeling of dissatisfaction and anticlimax.

The printed primary sources, on the other hand, are much more lively than one might expect. *Das Magazin*, a wildly popular monthly first published in 1954, offers a uniquely East German take on sex and relationships, based around nude photographs, racy short stories, 'true life' stories of illegitimacy, and surveys on delicate topics such as 'why marriages fail'. Sex education and marriage advice manuals give an insight into changing perspectives and priorities. Thanks to the efficiencies of socialist bureaucracy, it is also possible to trace the publication histories of individual books, even those which never saw the light of day. So we can reconstruct Rudolf Klimmer's attempts to publish a book on homosexuality in the 1950s – at a time when same-sex activity was still illegal – and also see what was still unacceptable to the censor when the first books on homosexuality finally appeared in the 1980s.

Right from the start of my research, I continually came across books, films, photographs, and illustrations that seemed to say something significant about East German sexuality. Such works were also a common reference point for interviewees and those I spoke to about my work, and I was often exhorted to seek out a particular book or film for an insight into what East German intimacy was *really* like. Sexuality is, of course, inextricable from its representations, which shape and frame the way people think about and remember their own sexual experiences. It is, however, tempting for the historian to focus on representations at the expense of experiences, not least because these sources are often neater and more accessible. Mindful of my decision to explore everyday lives and experiences, I was keen to avoid straying too far into a purely cultural history. What interests me is how such sources can

[57] Wollenberger, *Virus der Heuchler*, p. 8.

help us understand the lived experience of sexuality.[58] So, for example, while nude photographs provide an important context for East German sexuality, they can also tell us something about how the state used sexuality, how people reacted to this, and how individuals appropriated, adapted, and subverted sexual imagery.

Finally, the research for this book involved a series of interviews with thirty-eight former East German citizens. Many interviewees came from southern and eastern East Germany and had spent their lives in small towns or villages. They were therefore able to provide a perspective that is underrepresented in the printed and archival sources. Some interviewees were more reticent than I had expected. This was not necessarily due to shyness or embarrassment – the interview questions deliberately avoided asking directly about sexual behaviour, but instead focused on biographical milestones such as first love, marriage, childbearing, and so on. It was nevertheless clear that many interviewees saw their life histories as entirely unrelated to the political system they had lived under. Frau J, when asked about contraception, reacted furiously: 'Who thought up these questions? They must have been a total idiot! ... That's got nothing to do with society!' Her irritation, it transpired, was due to the fact that she saw contraception as an apolitical and indeed ahistorical topic and resented the implication that East Germans had had a distinctive contraceptive experience. (Frau J was also a practising midwife, so there may have been an element of wounded professional pride at work here.)

Many interviewees were also indignant even to be asked whether living in East Germany had restricted their personal choices, and were understandably unwilling to allow themselves to be defined by a political system. Asked whether they felt they had had autonomy in their private lives, most answered 'of course'. This should not necessarily lead us to the conclusion that socialist rule had no impact on individual biographies, or that the question of autonomy is an illegitimate one for the historian. Even a cursory glance at the historical record shows that not everybody enjoyed full sovereignty over their private lives.[59] Moreover, as we shall see, the patterns of East German life could be immensely formative, particularly in one's teens and twenties when lives

[58] On the tensions between discourse and experience, see Edward R. Dickinson and Richard F. Wetzell, 'The Historiography of Sexuality in Modern Germany', *German History* 23 (2005), 291–305; Cocks and Houlbrook (eds.), *Palgrave Advances in the Modern History of Sexuality*.
[59] Betts, *Within Walls*, is an important breakthrough in our understanding of the private in East Germany. See also Paul Betts, 'Alltag und Privatheit', in Martin Sabrow (ed.), *Errinerungsorte der DDR* (Munich: C. H. Beck, 2009), pp. 314–325.

were inescapably shaped by education, training, army service, and the limited availability of housing. But there is no doubt that not everyone felt these structures to be restrictive, or that they at least chose to ignore them as far as possible. As a gay interviewee explained: 'lots of people ask, how could you be happy in East Germany? But when you're young, you feel at home everywhere. And after all we couldn't get out.'[60]

Unable to 'get out', East Germans had little choice but to try to find happiness where they could. This would prove easier for some than for others, but few could fail to notice the transformation of sexual mores that took place in their lifetimes. The context for such a metamorphosis was unpromising, particularly given the pressing legacies of the Nazi period and the traumas of the immediate postwar period. But by the 1980s, attitudes towards and discussions about sex had changed beyond recognition. This is not to say that this 'revolution' did not have its limits. As we shall see in the rest of the book, they were many.

Nevertheless, it is important to appreciate just how much change did take place. It is all too easy to imagine Cold War Eastern Europe set in aspic. But the antiquated infrastructure and outmoded fashions revealed to unforgiving Western eyes in 1989 should not lead us to believe that socialist society and its norms were static. Seen both on their own terms, and set against the West, the changes that took place in East German sexuality deserve the label revolutionary.

The chapters that follow will seek both to explain these changes and to explore their limits in six different areas: sex and the young, marriage, the relationship between sex and love, homosexuality, nudism, and erotica. These chapters will reveal the impulses behind changing mores and behaviour as well as blockages and resistances to change. In public as well as in private, individuals, groups, and representatives of the state strove to give their own meanings to sex and love. These changing meanings can, I hope, give us a glimpse into what it was like to live under socialist rule and a fresh understanding of how social norms around sexuality and intimacy adjust and evolve.

---

[60] Interview with Ingo Kölsch, 6.1.2004.

2   'A bit of freedom': sex and young people

For most East Germans, adolescence was the time when they learnt about sex and became sexually active. This was often a time of increased freedom, as one's first job, apprenticeship, or place at university offered both financial autonomy and geographical mobility. For the older generation, young people's sexuality was often a cause for concern, raising anxieties about unwanted pregnancy, loss of respectability, and uncontrolled debauchery. Indeed, as we shall see, younger generations in the GDR often displayed different values from their parents, losing their virginity younger and placing less importance on marriage. Young people were also acutely sensitive to trends in international popular culture, eagerly adopting and adapting music and fashion from the other side of the Iron Curtain. This chapter will begin by exploring the state's attitude towards young people's sexuality and particularly the shift towards a more permissive approach in the Honecker era. It will go on to ask how far young people's sexuality was shaped by state-sponsored material such as sex education books. Finally, it will explore young people's first experiences of love and sex, paying particular attention to the spaces available, even under socialism, for experimentation and discovery.

Much of the research on young people in East Germany focuses on the success or otherwise of political indoctrination: on the one hand, education and youth organisations and, on the other, non-conformist youth groups. This is understandable: the state's attempt to mould a new generation of socialists was central to East German rule, and their successes and failures tell us much about the impact of the socialist project. These topics have also left a rich paper trail in the archives: organisations such as the FDJ (Freie Deutsche Jugend, Free German Youth) documented their activities exhaustively, and the authorities were tireless in their attempts to investigate and prosecute non-conformist youthful behaviour. As a result, we know much about young people's interaction with the state, but too little about how teenagers and young adults lived their lives on a day-to-day basis, particularly those who were not members of subcultures.

The reality of teenage sexuality was inevitably rather more haphazard than the ideal types presented in books and advice columns. While experts prescribed monogamy and early marriage and childbearing, drunkenness and promiscuity also belonged to the adolescent experience. Away from the aspirations of sexologists, is it possible to reconstruct everyday teenage sexuality? Oral history can go some way here, and our interviews are complemented by other post-1989 oral history projects. There are also a number of relevant and underused contemporary sources: from the early 1970s, East German researchers carried out periodic surveys of young people's attitudes towards and experiences of sex. Inevitably, these surveys were skewed towards the preoccupations and prejudices of those who carried them out. It is also true that young people were well aware of what they were expected to say about sex. Nonetheless, these surveys contain some suggestive and illuminating material.

Also produced in East Germany, but completely different in tone and intent are a number of collections of interviews published in the 1970s and 1980s known as *Protokolle* ('transcripts' is the best translation, although as we shall see it is not an entirely accurate description).[1] The most famous and most influential was Maxie Wander's *Guten Morgen, Du Schöne*, published in 1977.[2] Wander interviewed nineteen women and girls, and allowed them to speak frankly about their lives and their struggles with work, relationships, politics, and their families. It struck a chord with East German readers, and others were inspired to apply the protocol format to other groups: Christine Müller and Christine Lambrecht published collections of 'male protocols',[3] Gabriele Eckart interviewed agricultural workers in the Havel area (although after a run-in with the cultural authorities her book was published only in West Germany),[4] and Jürgen Lemke's interviews with gay men were published in 1989.[5] All contained

---

[1] For a discussion of the *Protokoll* genre, see Albrecht Holschuh, 'Protokollsammlungen der DDR', *German Studies Review* 15 (May 1992), 267–287. The term *Protokolle* was first used in this context by the West German author Erika Runge, in her book *Bottroper Protokolle* (Frankfurt am Main: Suhrkamp, 1968).

[2] Maxie Wander, *Guten Morgen, Du Schöne* (Berlin: Aufbau Verlag, 2003).

[3] Christine Müller, *Männerprotokolle* (Berlin: Buchverlag Der Morgen, 1985); Christine Lambrecht, *Männerbekanntschaften – Freimütige Protokolle* (Halle: Mitteldeutscher Verlag, 1986).

[4] Gabriele Eckart, *So sehe ick die Sache. Protokolle aus der DDR. Leben im Havelländischen Obstanbaugebiet* (Cologne: Kiepenheuer & Witsch, 1984).

[5] Jürgen Lemke, *Ganz normal anders. Auskünfte schwuler Männer* (Berlin: Aufbau, 1989). Interestingly, Lemke had no literary background whatsoever: the *Protokolle* were a product of his interest in gay men's lives rather than literature (Archiv des Aufbau-Verlages, 2626, Thron to Müller, 25.10.1988).

interviews with teenagers, as well as with older people reflecting on their experiences of growing up.

None of these interviews should be seen as a straightforward transcription of an individual's speech. The authors omitted their own questions and interjections, presenting the interviewees' testimony as a polished monologue. As Christa Wolf explained in the foreword to *Guten Morgen, Du Schöne* (probably the most literary of the *Protokolle*): 'These texts *have* been worked at. Nobody should think that they are being given a mechanical transcription, or raw material. Maxie Wander has selected, shortened, summarised, transposed, added, set the tone, composed, and organised – but never falsified.'[6] All the *Protokolle* were shaped not only by the questions and prompts of the interviewer, and his or her subsequent editorial decisions, but also by the existence of the censor.[7] The protocols, then, are highly mediated, and it is not always easy to see where this mediation has taken place. Nevertheless, whether or not every word is 'authentic', they do transmit a strong sense of the interviewees' voices and offer a perspective on everyday East German life that is nearly impossible to find elsewhere.

Sex and the state

'He who has the younger generation has the future'[8] – the SED's approach towards young people was not dissimilar to the Jesuits' maxim: 'give me the boy of seven and I will show you the man'. If young people could be persuaded of the merits of socialism at an early age, this logic went, they would remain loyal citizens, and would be prepared to work hard and devote themselves to the future of communism. Teaching young people the right things about sex and relationships, for example, would result in sound marriages and happy family life. Both were essential if men and women were to contribute to the workforce, and children to be raised as confident 'socialist personalities'.[9]

Exactly how young people's confidence and loyalty should be won, however, was a different matter. In practice, SED approaches swung

[6] Christa Wolf, 'Berührung. Ein Vorwort', in Wander, *Guten Morgen, Du Schöne*, p. 12.
[7] See for example the extensive changes made to Christine Müller's *Männerprotokolle*: BArch DR1/2324, 224ff.
[8] Quoted in Jeannette Z. Madarász, *Conflict and Compromise in East Germany, 1971–1989: A Precarious Stability* (London: Palgrave Macmillan, 2003), p. 32. Alan McDougall points out a very similar statement by Joseph Goebbels: McDougall, *Youth Politics in East Germany: The Free German Youth Movement 1946–1968* (Oxford: Oxford University Press, 2004), p. 3.
[9] Angela Brock, 'The Making of the Socialist Personality: Education and Socialisation in the GDR, 1958–1978', unpublished Ph.D. thesis, University College London (2005).

between carrot and stick, as policy makers tried to decide whether persuasion or coercion was the better strategy. These turns in youth policy were often tied to broader political developments, but also demonstrated differences of opinion within the party leadership. The 1950s saw attempts to appeal to young people's interests in fashion, socialising, and mingling with the opposite sex.[10] But the authorities also took a heavy-handed and moralistic stance towards teenagers' interest in 'American' trends such as jazz and rock'n'roll, condemning music fans as '*Rowdies*', and playing on popular fears of sexual and gender transgression.[11] The 1960s saw a similarly split approach: on the one hand, 'Beat' music was condemned as imperialist propaganda, and its fans labelled as out-of-control enemies of the state.[12] But, on the other, politicians also tried a conciliatory tack.[13]

In the wake of the building of the Berlin Wall in 1961, Walter Ulbricht's regime was determined to prove that the GDR could compete with the West, not just economically, but also in terms of quality of life and the standard of living. The aim of a modern, forward-thinking socialism took on a particular urgency when applied to youth policy. The SED was aware that a generation was coming of age which had experienced neither capitalism nor Nazism and should, theoretically at least, be growing up as loyal socialists. The fact that many were more interested in Western rock'n'roll than the activities of the Free German Youth suggested that it might be time to try a new approach.[14] The state wanted to dispel the impression that it was against all aspects of youth culture. In an attempt to regain the initiative and convince young people that the party was on their side, the Politburo published the *Jugendkommuniqué* in 1963.

This document, authored by a specially assembled 'youth commission', was an attempt to find common ground with young people, presenting them as the 'masters of tomorrow', who held the future of East German socialism in their hands. The state needed to listen to this coming generation and heed its concerns. What is particularly interesting in this context is that the *Jugendkommuniqué* acknowledged that young

[10] Mark Fenemore, *Sex, Thugs, and Rock'n'Roll: Teenage Rebels in Cold War East Germany* (Oxford and New York: Berghahn, 2007), pp. 28–29, 107.

[11] *Ibid.*; Uta Poiger, *Jazz, Rock and Rebels: Cold War Politics and American Culture in a Divided Germany* (Berkeley: University of California Press, 2000).

[12] Michael Rauhut, *Beat in der Grauzone. DDR-Rock 1964 bis 1972 – Politik und Alltag* (Berlin: Basisdruck, 1993).

[13] Alan McDougall, 'The Liberal Interlude: SED Youth Policy and the Free German Youth (FDJ), 1963–1965', *Debatte* 9 (2001), 123–155.

[14] Dorothee Wierling, *Geboren im Jahre Eins. Der Jahrgang 1949 in der DDR. Versuch einer Kollektivbiographie* (Berlin: Ch. Links, 2002), pp. 189–190.

people had the right to fall in love and have relationships and implied that those who disapproved of this (including those within the party) were prudish and old-fashioned. 'True love belongs to young people like young people belong to socialism', wrote the *Jugendkommuniqué*'s authors, criticising those who refused to recognise the importance of love in the lives of the young. 'Unhappy love can cripple a young person's development for a long time, happy love gives him [*sic*] wings', they admonished. 'It is socialist to help young people to lead happy lives … Every true love between two young people deserves recognition. We want true, deep, clean, humane relationships, not monastic morality.'[15] The implication was that sex between young people who loved each other could not be wrong, whether or not they were married.

Despite this conciliatory tone, the SED continued to clamp down both on Beat music and on non-conformist youth cultures. By the Eleventh Plenum of the SED in 1965, the *Jugendkommuniqué* and its authors were marginalised, and SED youth policy reverted to its more traditionally paternalistic tone.[16] The *Jugendkommuniqué* did, however, represent a permanent turning point in attitudes towards youth sexuality. The cover of *Das Magazin* from May 1966 is an apt illustration of this mood (Figure 2.1). The scene is a classroom, where an extremely elderly teacher is giving a sex education lesson. Using a diagram, and reading from a book, he is attempting to show his pupils how to kiss. In the back row of the class, a boy and a girl look away from the blackboard and smile at each other. The message is clear: young people are well ahead of their teachers when it comes to matters of the heart. Love is not something that can be taught in a classroom, but will develop and blossom of its own accord. The teenagers' joie de vivre and innocent discovery are contrasted with the teacher's dusty – although certainly well-meant – instruction. Significantly, youthful sexual knowledge is not seen as unhealthy, but rather as a positive part of teenagers' lives. Young people's sexuality was no longer seen as a threat or something that could run out of control, but as an integral part of being young. Key here, of course, was the coupling of sex with love (note the teacher's didactic pointing to the heart), and the equation of sex with heterosexuality, both of which were essential parts of all mainstream discussions of sexuality.

[15] 'Der Jugend Vertrauen und Verantwortung. Kommuniqué des Politbüros des Zentralkomitees der Sozialistischen Einheitspartei Deutschlands zu Problemen der Jugend in der Deutschen Demokratischen Republik, veröffentlicht am 21. September 1963', in *Dokumente zur Jugendpolitik der SED* (Berlin: Staatsverlag der DDR, 1965), pp. 93–94.
[16] Wierling, *Geboren im Jahre Eins*, pp. 209–210.

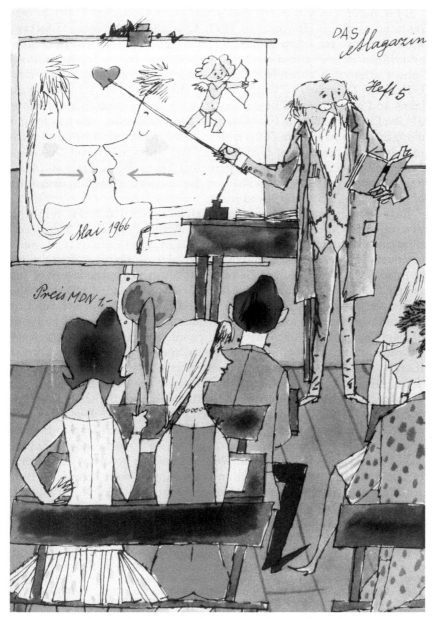

Figure 2.1: Werner Klemke: *Das Magazin*, May 1966, cover
illustration.

This superficially tolerant policy was reinforced after Ulbricht was replaced by Erich Honecker in 1971. Like all new brooms, Honecker wanted to give the impression of a fresh start. His 'Unity of Economic and Social Policy' and a new approach of 'no taboos' in the cultural sphere attempted to project the image of a prosperous, stable East Germany. To appeal to young people, the SED made its peace with jeans and long hair and began to flirt with the revolutionary glamour of Che Guevara and the East German Tamara Bunke, who had fought alongside him in Bolivia. This new cultural trend found its (anti-)hero in Edgar, the narrator of Ulrich Plenzdorf's play and novel *Die neuen Leiden des jungen W.* (*The New Sorrows of Young W.*), a dropout house painter who lives in a garden shed on the outskirts of Berlin, dreaming of girls, music, and his beloved jeans.[17]

East Germany wanted to present itself as a state which was youthful, dynamic and international. The Tenth World Festival of Youth and Students (Weltfestspiele), which took place in East Berlin in 1973, was a key part of these efforts. The World Festival was organised by the communist World Federation of Democratic Youth as a gathering of young people from all over the world. The festival was intended as a showcase for modern, progressive East German socialism and was attended by tens of thousands of visitors from outside the GDR, along with millions of East Germans.[18] For many young people the nine days of the festival were a time of dancing in the streets, staying up all night with new friends, and exciting encounters with exotic-seeming foreign visitors. The festival's visitors took over the streets of the capital, with singing and dancing taking place throughout the night (see Figure 2.2).[19] This licentiousness was even tacitly endorsed by the state: *Das Magazin*'s cover for the month of the festival adapted the official logo to include young women of European, Asian, and African appearance frolicking naked in a lily pond.[20] As Stefan Wolle points out, however, this display of tolerance and officially sanctioned merriment was accompanied by a massive programme of arrests and prosecutions. 'The World Festival of 1973 was a model for the future. A bit of freedom was now allowed, as long as it consisted only of gestures and symbols; a bit of tolerance

[17] Ulrich Plenzdorf, *Die neuen Leiden des Jungen W.* (Frankfurt am Main: Suhrkamp, 1999). The play was first performed in 1972, and the novel published in 1973.
[18] Ina Rossow, '"Rote Ohren, roter Mohn, sommerheiße Diskussion". Die X. Weltfestspiele der Jugend und Studenten 1973 als Möglichkeit für vielfältige Begegnungen', in Dokumentationszentrum Alltagskultur der DDR (ed.), *Fortschritt, Norm und Eigensinn. Erkundungen im Alltag der DDR* (Berlin: Ch. Links, 1999), pp. 257–275.
[19] See for example the interview with Ina Merkel, 'Hinterher war alles beim Alten', www.bpb.de/themen/CQPRCM,0,Hinterher_war_alles_beim_Alten.html.
[20] *Das Magazin*, July 1973.

Figure 2.2: Young people dancing at Alexanderplatz during the World Festival Games, July 1973.

was appropriate, as long as it was only applied to appearances; and a bit of revolutionary romance enjoyed benevolent toleration.'[21] And the SED's pro-natalist agenda was never too far away: as well as drinking and sleeping under the stars, the festival included a public parade of 'freshly married' couples, with brides in floor-length white dresses and veils (Figure 2.3).

Sex was a useful way of offering young people 'a bit of freedom', allowing the regime to appear to be on the side of the young while still pursuing its own agenda of a peaceful population and a healthy birth rate. An FDJ poster from 1970 (Figure 2.4) promising 'pounding hearts at no extra charge' suggested campfire singalong laced with sexual tension (as well as improbably glamorous participants). As Mark Fenemore puts it: 'Like sport, sex offered a useful potential area of overlap between young people's interests and those of the regime.'[22] The 1978 film, *Sieben Sommersprossen* (*Seven Freckles*) demonstrates the newly relaxed approach to (hetero)sexuality.[23] The teenage protagonists, Robert, 15, and Katharina, 14, meet at a summer camp in the countryside. Both come from unhappy families, which unsubtly exemplified the problems of mature socialism at either end of the social scale: Robert's parents are materialistic and obsessed with their dacha. Katharina's mother is a promiscuous drinker, and her older sister has already had a baby. Both feel neglected and uncared for. During the course of the summer, Robert and Katharina fall in love. In the film's most famous scene, they kiss, strip off their clothes, and swim in the river. They then chase each other around a field and lie naked in the grass discussing whether they should have sex. In contrast to the teenagers' thoughtful attitude towards relationships, older authority figures are portrayed as short-sighted and narrow-minded. The strict camp leader opposes the planned production of *Romeo and Juliet* on the grounds that it is not relevant to 'children'. When another girl's packet of contraceptive pills is discovered in Katharina's belongings, the camp leader decides to send her home. A young trainee teacher protests that this is unfair and that Katharina is being victimised because she comes from a poor family. In the end, Katharina remains at the camp and takes the lead opposite Robert in *Romeo and Juliet*. The camp leader is moved to tears by their performance and finally recognises the integrity of young love. The film's message was clear: even 14-year-olds are mature enough to make autonomous decisions about love and sex (the age of heterosexual

---

[21] Stefan Wolle, *Der Traum von der Revolte. Die DDR 1968* (Berlin: Ch. Links, 2008), p. 237.
[22] Fenemore, *Sex, Thugs and Rock'n'Roll*, p. 167.
[23] *Sieben Sommersprossen* (dir. Herrmann Zschoche, 1978).

Figure 2.3: Newly married couples celebrate the World Festival Games, 3 August 1973.

Figure 2.4: 'Pounding hearts at no extra charge', Freie Deutsche Jugend poster, 1970.

consent in the GDR was 14). Both Robert and Katharina were able to transcend their problematic family backgrounds and forge a relationship as two individuals. The older generation (here represented by the strict camp leader) were to understand and accommodate young love, and recognise that teenagers were not children and that their emotions were as important as any adult's.

Learning about sex

Public discussion of sex was not just a means of demonstrating empathy with young people, it was also a way of transmitting ideas about values and life choices. By the 1970s and 1980s, the state authorised the publication of quite explicit sexual advice for young people.[24] *Denkst Du schon an Liebe?* (*Thinking About Love Already?*), published in 1975, was aimed at young teenagers, 'taking their first steps on the precarious dance floor of love', as the publishers whimsically put it.[25] Illustrated with mildly psychedelic illustrations and pictures of naked teenagers, the book discussed puberty, relationships, reproduction, marriage, starting a family, and, more unusually, STDs, homosexuality, and pornography.[26] *Liebe und Sexualität bis 30* (*Love and Sexuality Until 30*), published in 1984, went even further, including – at the authors' insistence – a photograph of a couple having sex.[27]

It is worth noting, however, that such books still defined sex in relatively narrow terms, as something that should take place in long-term, loving, and monogamous relationships and that would, as a rule, result in pregnancy and childbirth. Sex advice books invariably included photographs of young parents and their babies and toddlers. Children were said to be essential to the 'full flowering of happiness' in a marriage, making the relationship between their parents 'even closer and more heartfelt'.[28] Homosexuality was mentioned, it is true, but briefly, and separated from broader discussions of love and relationships.[29]

Much effort went into sex education, resulting in part from an enduring fear that young people would learn the wrong things about sex. Rudolf Neubert had warned in the 1960s of the consequences when children learned about sex from 'uncontrolled channels' rather than 'clearly and cleanly' from their parents.[30] The aim was to make sex mutual and enjoyable, and a strong basis for relationships. But to what extent did such material shape teenagers' actual experiences? Men and women born in 1949 and interviewed by Dorothee Wierling often contrasted their prudish parents with the openness to be found in

[24] On earlier sex education material, see Fenemore, 'The Growing Pains of Sex Education'.
[25] BArch DR1/2277, 249, Verlagsgutachten, 26.8.1974.
[26] Heinrich Brückner, *Denkst Du schon an Liebe?* (Berlin: Kinderbuchverlag, 1975).
[27] Friedrich and Starke, *Liebe und Sexualität bis 30*. On the inclusion of photographs, see BArch DR1/3026, 245, Verlagsgutachen.
[28] Brückner, *Denkst Du schon an Liebe?*, p. 128.
[29] *Ibid.*, pp. 201–203; Friedrich and Starke, *Liebe und Sexualität bis 30*, pp. 290–305.
[30] Rudolf Neubert, *Wie sag ich es meinem Kinde? Ratschläge für Eltern*, 9th edn (Rudolstadt: Greifenverlag, 1968), p. 7.

East German sex advice books and in the pages of the young people's magazine *neuesleben* (*new life*). Wierling concludes: 'These texts gave matter-of-fact information and sensible advice, which was of major importance to young people confronted with bashful parents, and continued to give good service well into marriage.'[31] Interestingly, those interviewed for this project did not appear to have such strong memories of reading about sex. A number of interviewees remembered, some only when prompted, having read books such as Siegfried Schnabl's *Mann und Frau Intim* (*Man and Woman in Intimacy*) or Brückner's *Denkst Du schon an Liebe?* But they did not recall these books as having had a formative effect on their sexual development, suggesting that the influence of sexology should not be overstated.

It is also worth considering how films and books were interpreted by teenagers. Frau C offers a valuable reminder that even voracious adolescent readers did not necessarily read and digest every word. Alluding to Schnabl's *Mann und Frau Intim*, she said: 'everybody had seen Schnabl, read it, well, skimmed it. You didn't study it.' We should not assume that young people undertook a close reading of these books, nor that they applied their advice in any systematic way. Sex education and advice books can offer a useful insight into the minds of their authors, and the priorities of those in the state apparatus who authorised their publication. But they do not necessarily tell us much about the values of those who read them.

Nor does sex education in school appear to have left much of an impression. Herr S remembered the film they were shown in biology class as an anticlimax: 'We were expecting a lot more, because the older kids always said: "man, you are going to see a sex film!" In fact, it didn't teach us anything, it was too late. I had read about it, and found out about it, and I already knew what the score was.' Frau G also remembered looking forward to the sex education sessions in school, but finding them 'very biological'. They were told the facts of life, but 'not everything that goes with it [*nicht das ganze drum und dran und nebenbei*] … not even a naked man or a naked woman'. Henrike lamented the fact that sex education dealt with homosexuality in passing or not at all: 'In secondary school we had a lot of learning imparted to us, right up to the intricacies of literature and mathematics, but these things, that were really vitally important, were kept from us.'[32]

What of sex education at home? Wierling's interviews revealed an 'almost unanimous' experience of prudish parents who refused to

---

[31] Wierling, *Geboren im Jahre Eins*, p. 366.
[32] Karstädt and von Zitzewitz (eds.), *… viel zu viel verschwiegen*, p. 124.

discuss sex with their children.[33] In many cases, the sexual violence of the immediate postwar period had left a traumatic legacy. Hanna Voß described her sexual education as 'barbaric': when her mother discovered her masturbating at the age of eight or nine, she pulled her out of bed, hit her, and dragged her up to the local prison, telling her that is where she would end up if she continued with such habits. In retrospect, Voß understood her mother's anger as a result of the anxiety created by her position as a single mother in a small town and by a lingering fear of rape. At the time, however, her mother's actions had a profound impact: 'I felt dirty and unworthy and that tainted sexuality [for me] for a long time.'[34]

Some of our interviewees reinforced Wierling's findings of inadequate or even damaging sex education in the early years of the GDR. A few had their own memories of postwar violence. Herr J, who was 12 in 1945, remembered his mother disguising herself as an old lady to avoid the threat of rape. Herr L, 13 at the end of the war, remembered this period as a brutal sexual awakening:

I was there, when the Russians wanted to rape a woman, I saw how they raped her. A Russian wanted to rape me, which I didn't understand. I understood that a woman is usually there for that, but not a man! Nobody knew the term homosexuality. And I would say that my sister, who was three years younger, and I actually learnt the facts of life this way.

Frau O (b. 1949), Herr K (b. 1939), and Frau I (b. 1952) recalled little or no discussion of sex in the home. Herr H (b. 1952)'s father liked to say 'Don't come home and tell me you are going to be a father!', but offered no advice on how to prevent this turn of events. Frau N (b. 1950)'s mother made attempts to explain menstruation as part of 'becoming a woman', but only succeeded in inducing 'dreadful panic' in her daughter.

It was not, however, always the case that sex was a taboo. Frau J (b. 1951) had happy memories of learning about sex: she was able to discuss it openly with her mother, and both parents and children were often naked around the house. Herr L and Frau L (both b. 1932) remembered learning about sex as a 'completely natural process' in the family (Herr L's bad experiences at the end of the war notwithstanding). Nor was it true that those born later necessarily experienced a more liberal sex education. Questioned in 1990, 25% of young adults agreed 'fully' and 39% 'partially' with the statement 'I could discuss everything about love and sexuality with my mother.' (The figures for

---

[33] Wierling, *Geboren im Jahre Eins*, p. 366.   [34] *Ibid.*, pp. 364–365.

fathers were 10% and 24% respectively.)[35] The majority of parents, then, were not wholly comfortable talking about sex. Frau G (b. 1960) remembered her mother as very 'uncommunicative' on sexual matters, and did not even dare to ask her what to do when she got her period. Lydia, a 20-year-old tractor driver, interviewed in 1980, said: 'In our house nobody talked about sexual things. If I wanted to know something, my mother said: Ask your biology teacher! But who does that sort of thing?'[36]

It is difficult to generalise about parental attitudes. East German researchers found that those who lived in cities and towns tended to be more open with their children, as did parents who had stayed at school until 18. The study also found, however, that the more engaged parents were in political and social activities, the more open they were with their children about sex.[37] This may well have been the case, but it may also be explained by the fact that children from families which were loyal to the state were more likely to give the 'right' answers to surveys. In the end, personality may have been the only guarantee of openness. Dirk, interviewed in the 1980s, found the person he could talk to most frankly about sex was his grandfather:

Mum goes red and Dad starts to hum and haw, but Granddad doesn't have any false modesty. He explained to me: young lad, when you've got the feeling that a hundred sparrows are scooting around your balls, you've got to pull it out, or you'll end up a father.[38]

Many young people learnt about sex from friends, in the playground or in whispered conversations behind closed bedroom doors. As Herr A put it, 'We taught ourselves about sex.' Frau V, who described herself as a late developer, found out about the facts of life when a friend took pity on her after a teenage game of spin the bottle. Ute's brother explained the idea of 'safe days' for sex – but only after she had become pregnant after a one-night stand.[39] For Lydia, sexual education had taken place once she started work: 'Knowledge comes with time. When you are with men all the time, you hear a lot of things.'[40] This sort of informal sex education was, of course, exactly what the state wanted to avoid, but it was ultimately impossible to magic away parental inhibitions and ensure that every teenager read the right books in the right way.

[35] ZA S6142: Partner III – Berufstätige 1990, pp. 21–22.
[36] Eckart, *So sehe ick die Sache*, p. 41.
[37] Friedrich and Starke, *Liebe und Sexualität bis 30*, pp. 252–253.
[38] Christine Müller, *Männerprotokolle*, p. 112.
[39] Wander, *Guten Morgen, Du Schöne*, p. 99.
[40] Eckart, *So sehe ick die Sache*, p. 41.

Table 2.1: *Age at first sexual intercourse, East Germany, 1973–1990*

Age at first sexual intercourse	Students, 1972**	Young workers, 1973*	Young adults, 1979/1980***	Young adults, 1990****
% under 14		0.5	0.9	1.1
% 14	1.1	2.7	3.1	5.7
% 15	2.5	7.2	8.3	10.0
% 16	7.5	14.3	20.7	20.3
% 17	15.6	18.1	21.2	23.3
% 18	26.9	14.4	13.8	18.6
% 19	16.3	5.1	5.1	7.3
% 20	4.2	2.9	2.6	2.4
% 21 and over	2.0	2.0	0.9	3.7
% not yet lost virginity	21.1	30.0	12.5	6.4

* 67% of respondents were 19 or under.
** 92% 19 or under.
*** 44% 19 or under.
**** 18% 19 or under.

Source: ZA S6144: Partner I – Junge Arbeiter 1973, p. 55; ZA S6143: Partner I – Studenten 1972, p. 71; ZA S6145: Partner II 1979/80, p. 34; ZA S6142: Partner III – Berufstätige 1990, p. 32.

Sexual spaces

Like the rest of the population, young people's sexual behaviour moved with the times. The figures in Table 2.1, on age at first intercourse, show a strong trend towards earlier sexual experiences, with more young people in the 1970s and 1980s having sex before the age of 18. In part, this was due to changing lifestyles, particularly urbanisation. Both Frau G (born in 1960) and Herr B (born in 1951) remembered their rural childhoods as times of hardship, with little time for socialising or getting to know the opposite sex. Frau G, whose mother ran a smallholding while her father worked shifts in a factory, explained:

We went to school, did our homework, and then we had to go out into the fields. When others were playing, we had to ... either wash carrots or hoe the onions, and then there was the hay to bring in ... And we never went on holiday with father and mother, not once, our whole lives long.

Herr B, who grew up with seven siblings, remembered that money was so tight that the family sometimes lived on carrots during the winter, and his father would whittle their Christmas presents out of wood.

Clearly, there was little or no money available for the older children to spend on themselves. As family sizes grew smaller, and small farmers were absorbed into collective farms, teenagers had more time to pursue leisure activities and more money for consumer goods such as radios, bicycles, and tents, all of which allowed them to have a social life independently of their families.[41]

The data also clearly show the impact of class. From 1950, the school leaving age was 16, after which young people undertook either an industrial apprenticeship or a further two years of study to take their *Abitur* at 18.[42] Young workers tended to have sex earlier, as they entered the workforce or left home to take on an apprenticeship. Students, who remained at home while finishing school, appear to have enjoyed a flurry of sexual behaviour around the age of 18. The formal structures of education, apprenticeship, and national military service were a major influence on young people's lives. Life story accounts give a very strong sense of the way in which East German adolescence and young adulthood were shaped by these unavoidable obligations. Young people's first experiences away from home were often in a residential hostel (or *Internat*), which could be a crucial space for exploring one's sexuality. Most young people could not dream of getting a place of their own until they were married. The shared house – a ubiquitous part of West German student culture – was nearly unheard of. Life in an *Internat* did not guarantee privacy, as room-sharing was the norm, with up to four people sharing a room.[43] But it did offer an escape from the parental home and a chance to mingle with peers of both sexes. As a supervisor in one hostel put it: 'the apprentices arrive here thinking that they are finally free'.[44]

But hostel life was about more than the opportunity to have sex; it was often the first taste of social freedom, too. Frau W, who lived in a hostel in Schwerin in the late 1960s, remembered it as a 'lovely time'. She had grown up in a farming family, where she was expected to help with the farm and in the household. Her parents were strict, and her grandmother had banned her from seeing her first boyfriend, who was known as the 'bad boy' of the village. 'In a village like that, somebody had probably seen that we were standing together, and that was it – awful really, isn't it?' In contrast, the hostel gave her considerable autonomy, and life in Schwerin, with its cinema and theatre, seemed exciting. The

---

[41] See Fenemore, *Sex, Thugs and Rock'n'Roll*, p. 102, on increasing affluence and young people's leisure time.

[42] Gesetz über die Schulpflicht in der Deutschen Demokratischen Republik, 15 December 1950, www.verfassungen.de/de/ddr/schulpflichtgesetz50.htm.

[43] Eckart, *So sehe ick die Sache*, pp. 74, 151, 208.   [44] *Ibid.*, p. 199.

older girls in the hostel were given a key and were free to come and go as they liked in the evenings, so long as they were back by the 10 p.m. curfew. Frau T, who had also grown up on a farm, and lived in a hostel in Eisenhüttenstadt during the same period, recalled this time as 'my best years, the best years of my youth!' What was important to both women was not so much sexual freedom, but the freedom from domestic responsibility, the opportunity to mix with other girls of their own age and do what they liked with their spare time. As Frau T put it: 'When I was in school, and at home, I was always good and obedient and then I could finally do what I liked! And my parents weren't watching me.'

Even rural hostels could seem exciting. Christoph Dieckmann, who had experienced a strict vicarage childhood, left home at the age of 16 to start an apprenticeship as a film projectionist. His hostel in remote rural Saxony housed thirty-seven male and eight female apprentices, creating a certain degree of healthy – and unhealthy – competition for female attention. 'Dramas worthy of the movies took place. Drunkenness, intrigues, deep and unhappy love. One guy nearly threw himself in front of a train because of a girl called Elke. I stopped another one hanging himself one night in the washroom because of a girl called Marika.'[45] Dieckmann was eventually expelled for, amongst other things, 'nocturnal invasion of girls' rooms'.[46]

Clearly, discipline varied according to the nature of the hostel and the rules imposed by those in charge. Frau C described her hostel in Gera as 'very strict', with separate floors for girls and boys. 'There was a disco once a week, where you could meet them [the male apprentices]. And you could stand outside with them and chat, or have a smooch. But the possibility of spending the night together or anything like that, nobody even thought about that sort of thing.' Some hostels, however, found themselves caught up in the process of sexual liberalisation. Herr A who attended a boarding school for sports in the 1970s, recalled a very open attitude about sex. Svenja, a 35-year-old supervisor in an apprentices' hostel, interviewed in 1980, was largely sympathetic to the apprentices and their problems, and remarked on a rapid change in sexual norms:

The apprentices have completely changed in the last ten years. Sometimes I say 'I just don't get it anymore!' For example relationships between girls and boys, there are just no boundaries any more. Five years ago, if we found two people in bed together, we would have phoned their parents straight away,

---

[45] Christoph Dieckmann, *Die Liebe in den Zeiten des Landfilms. Eigens erlebte Geschichten* (Berlin: Aufbau, 2002), p. 42.
[46] *Ibid.*, p. 43.

and thrown them both out. Nowadays, we just take note of something like that. We have even talked about whether we should have 'intimate rooms' for lovers.[47]

Such tolerance was probably not experienced by everybody, even in the 1980s. Imke, a 17-year-old apprentice interviewed in the same collection, said her hostel was very strict. 'Our supervisor, Mr H, always just says: THIS IS A SOCIALIST HOSTEL. HERE YOU WILL BE EDUCATED TO BECOME SOCIALIST PERSONALITIES. It's all totally hollow – he hasn't got a clue.'[48] Nevertheless, for young people who were unlikely to get their own living space until they married – if then – hostels provided room for socialising, flirting, and sometimes sex.

Those who did manage to get a flat of their own vividly recount the sense of freedom and social opportunity it opened up: Herr D found his own flat at the age of 19 – a highly unusual state of affairs, attributable to the fact that he lived in Prenzlauer Berg in Berlin, where numerous tenement apartments became empty in the 1970s and 1980s as families moved to new housing on the outskirts of Berlin. Herr D remembered always having a 'full house' – having his space allowed him to throw parties and play as much Western rock music as he liked ('my poor neighbours!'). Ingo Kölsch was in his mid-twenties when he got his first flat (also in Prenzlauer Berg), but it is worth quoting his account here for a sense of the new and exciting possibilities opened up by a flat of one's own. 'That was the start of three wild years, which were really fantastic: young, lots of sex, my own flat, and a job which earned me enough money.'[49] As a gay man, living alone was a vital prerequisite for sexual autonomy. His flat became a hub for people visiting from out of town. As nobody had a telephone, he used to leave a note on the door saying where he was and when he would be back. He also left a key in the hall, so that friends could let themselves in. Like Herr D, his own space proved to be socially as well as sexually transformative. This experience of single life was not one shared by many East Germans, not least due to the lack of geographical mobility in the GDR: Herr D and Ingo Kölsch were lucky enough to live in Berlin, where flats were available to those in the know. About 50 per cent of our interviewees had remained in their birthplaces to the present day, and some, such as Frau I, were acutely aware of how living in rural areas and small towns had shaped their biographies. She explained: 'it's a village where I come from … it wasn't like I imagine it was like in a big city like Berlin, Halle, or Leipzig. It was, well, just a bit more isolated.'

[47] Eckart, *So sehe ick die Sache*, pp. 200–201.   [48] *Ibid.*, pp. 58–59.
[49] Interview with Ingo Kölsch, 6.1.2004.

Many teenagers, of course, remained living with their parents, often until they got married. Martin S, 20, said wistfully about his ex-girlfriend: 'If I had stayed with her, I would have had my own flat by now.' He went on to expand on some of the difficulties of continuing to live at home: 'My parents don't expect any more than I'll get up on Sunday and have breakfast with them. Sure, they'd like it if I was at home more and was part of the family. But as far as possible, I want to have my own life now.'[50] Living under the parental roof could limit one's sex life: many teenagers, like Eckart's 17-year-old interviewee, Imke, had to smuggle their partners into their bedrooms, and hope that they were not found out.[51] Some parents, however, were tolerant: only 22 per cent of young workers surveyed in 1973 felt that their parents would seriously object to them having sex with their partner.[52] René, interviewed by Christine Müller in the 1980s, spoke warmly of his parents' accepting and unembarrassed attitude: 'My sister sleeps with her boyfriend upstairs in her room, and when they come down at eleven o'clock on Sunday morning, nobody makes a snide remark, or laughs mockingly. Well, maybe me, because I'm a bit jealous of them.'[53] As Mary Fulbrook reminds us, 'the "youth" of the 1950s were the adults of the 1970s',[54] and many had a more laissez-faire approach to teenage sexuality than their parents. The easy availability of the contraceptive pill must also have allayed fears about unwanted pregnancy. Amongst Pill-users surveyed in 1990, 21% had started to take the Pill when they were 16, 20% at 17, and 16% at 18.[55]

Understandably, though, young people craved their own space. Paradoxically, for those stuck in the parental home, marriage often seemed to offer freedom, autonomy, and privacy. Chronic housing shortages meant that only married couples had any chance of getting a flat of their own. As Herr E put it: 'In those days that's the way it went: get to know each other, marry, have children, get a flat.' Frau V married in May and got a flat in October, but only because her father had good connections at the housing office. 'That was a record for the GDR!' she joked. Anke, an 18-year-old tree nursery worker, said scornfully: 'Why do most people marry at just 18? Because they think: Got to get away from the parents! Got to get a flat! And then they are divorced at 20. The state is doing something wrong there with the encouragement of young marriages.'[56]

---

[50] Lambrecht, *Männerbekanntschaften*, p. 134.
[51] Eckart, *So sehe ick die Sache*, p. 65.
[52] ZA S6144: Partner I – Junge Arbeiter 1973, p. 30.
[53] Christine Müller, *Männerprotokolle*, p. 224.
[54] Fulbrook, *People's State*, p. 116.
[55] ZA S6142: Partner III – Berufstätige 1990, p. 41.
[56] Eckart, *So sehe ick die Sache*, p. 235.

A further incentive to marry, and marry young, was introduced in 1972. Couples under the age of 26 on below-average incomes were entitled to a marriage loan, to furnish or even build a house. Up to 5,000 marks could be borrowed interest-free (for comparison, average monthly gross income was 814 marks), and used to buy furniture, fridges, washing machines, TVs, and radios. The scheme also offered powerful incentives for childbearing – the loan was reduced by 1,000 marks at the birth of the first child, 1,500 at the birth of the second and 2,500 at the birth of the third.[57] Demand for these loans far exceeded state predictions, with over 200,000 loans issued in the first three years of the scheme.[58] For young couples like Veronika and Volker V, getting married was both financially advantageous and a way of marking their adult independence. Volker explained: 'marrying is like a means of protection against your parents, to put yourself on your own feet ... you get a flat, [student] grants go up, and you get a marriage loan of 5,000 marks.'[59]

There can be no doubt that early marriage was a genuine aspiration for some. In surveys in the 1970s, 80 per cent of young workers felt it was best to be married by the age of 24.[60] But in a later survey respondents questioned about the 'right time' to marry and have children (Table 2.2) were ambiguous about marrying at a young age, with a mere 6.9 per cent agreeing without reservation that it was right to marry 'as young as possible'. (Interestingly, though, there was stronger support for embarking on childbearing immediately after marriage, implying that, for young East Germans, marriage and children went hand in hand.)

Despite such reservations, the age of marriage remained relatively low. The average age at first marriage actually dropped from 24 for men and 23 for women in 1955 to 23 for men and 21 for women in 1971, beginning to rise again only in the mid 1980s.[61] In practice, few other choices were open to those in their teens and early twenties. Travelling, living in a shared house, and experimenting with different jobs and

[57] Johannes Frerich and Martin Frey, *Handbuch der Geschichte der Sozialpolitik in Deutschland*, vol. II, *Sozialpolitik in der Deutschen Demokratischen Republik* (Munich: R. Oldenbourg Verlag, 1993), p. 415.
[58] Stiftung Archiv der Parteien und Massenorganisationen der DDR im Bundesarchiv (henceforth SAPMO-BArch) DY31/1067, 129, 'Information über Kreditgewährung an junge Eheleute', 6.5.1975.
[59] Barbara Bronnen and Franz Henny, *Liebe, Ehe, Sexualität in der DDR. Interviews und Dokumente* (Munich: R. Piper, 1975), pp. 54–55.
[60] ZA S6144: Partner I – Junge Arbeiter 1973, p. 12.
[61] *Statistisches Jahrbuch der Deutschen Demokratischen Republik 1990* (Berlin: Rudolf Haufe Verlag, 1991), p. 417.

Table 2.2: *Young people's views on marriage and childbearing, East Germany, 1979/1980*

	Agree completely (%)	Agree with reservations (%)	Hardly (%)	Absolutely not (%)
Do you think it is right to marry as young as possible?	6.9	46.1	30.0	16.9
Do you think it is right when young couples decide to have a child as soon as they are married?	23.5	49.3	19.1	8.1

Source: ZA S6145: Junge Partner II 1979/80, p. 119.

careers were not mainstream options as they were in the West. It does not seem unreasonable to speculate that, had single young people had more opportunities to live independently, they might well have delayed marriage for a few years. That is not to say that young people did not feel the urge to break away from the structures of East German life. Gudrun, 18, said wistfully, 'In a sense, we are missing out on our years of discovery [*Wanderjahre*]. There should be a period after school to catch your breath and get to know everything. It wouldn't have to be a whole year, but you need a bit of time to become freer.'[62]

Some ideas of how to 'become freer' were clearly influenced by Western post-1968 experimentation with living arrangements. Ute, a young Berlin worker interviewed in the 1970s, planned to set up a communal household (*Grossfamilie*) with her boyfriend, their child, and a couple of their friends. They had got the idea after watching a TV documentary about a similar experiment in the West. Ute rejected the conventional structures of the nuclear family: 'Man, living together like other married couples, watching TV, always the same, always just the two of you, and if you want a bit of company, you have to leave the kids alone, or the woman has to stay at home, no way!'[63] Susanne, interviewed in the same volume, shared Ute's longing for a break with convention:

Well, a commune isn't for everyone, but I think people who try something like that are great [*einwandfrei*]. Just getting to work on time – that's not enough, it's incredibly good to rethink your whole life, to do something different from

[62] Wander, *Guten Morgen, Du Schöne*, p. 140.   [63] *Ibid.*, p. 97.

the grownups. There should be more about that sort of thing on television or in the newspaper.[64]

What is interesting here is not just Susanne's critique of the East German media, but also her rejection of the values of her parents' generation. Punctuality stands here for a whole way of living, centred on work and respectability. It is not hard to see the appeal of 'rethinking' one's whole life, but in a country where even a flat was hard to come by, putting such ideas into practice was not easy. It seems probable that Susanne and Ute had no idea that such experiments were taking part in the East too. The 'Kommune I Ost' which existed in Berlin from 1969 to 1973 remained an underground phenomenon, enjoying none of the publicity attracted by its Western counterpart (see pp. 94–96).[65] In fact, the sex education book *Denkst Du schon an Liebe?* went out of its way to condemn communes as an immature and unsuccessful protest against the capitalist way of life – and therefore irrelevant to East Germans.[66] But ideas about communal living filtered through to a wider public via the Western media nonetheless.

So was early marriage merely a pragmatic choice, or does it suggest that young people agreed with the official line that sex should take place only in a long-term, loving partnership? In 1973, 92% of these surveyed agreed fully or in part that you should feel 'a deep love' for your sexual partner. However, when asked a few questions later whether sex without love could be seen as something 'natural and positive', 43% agreed fully and 33% in part, implying a much higher acceptance of casual sex.[67] The discrepancy between these two sets of answers may also be explained by respondents' tendency simply to agree with the propositions put to them in surveys. The question about casual sex was phrased in terms of 'the satisfaction of sexual needs', which may have sounded reassuringly medical. Nevertheless, a full 15% agreed that 'group sex' was acceptable, and 24% accepted infidelity in a long-term relationship (although only 13% accepted infidelity within marriage).[68]

Personal accounts of promiscuity are rarer, perhaps due to a reluctance to admit such behaviour. Nonetheless, casual sex was certainly a part of some young East Germans' lives. Of those surveyed at the end of the 1970s, 27% had lost their virginity with somebody they were not in a relationship with and, for 16%, this had been the only time they

---

[64] *Ibid.*, p. 90.
[65] Timothy S. Brown, '"1968" East and West: Divided Germany as a Case Study in Transnational History', *American Historical Review* 114 (February 2009), 69–96.
[66] Brückner, *Denkst Du schon an Liebe?*, p. 124.
[67] ZA S6144: Partner I – Junge Arbeiter 1973, pp. 52, 53.
[68] *Ibid.*, p. 59.

had sex with them.[69] Harald Hauswald's fond autobiographical account describes one such experience:

> I lost my virginity at 17 on a hitching trip to the Baltic coast. In the beer tent, a girl disappeared every evening with a different guy, and eventually it was my turn, if I'd been sober I wouldn't have dared. She had plenty of experience after all, and it went wonderfully.[70]

It is significant that Hauswald's sexual initiation took place during a hitch-hiking holiday. As Thomas Kochan's research has shown, hitching became a popular way to get around the country in the 1970s and 1980s, and added a welcome spontaneity to many young people's lives. The hitching lifestyle often went hand in hand with a love of blues music, and fans hitched from one end of the GDR to the other to attend gigs and open air concerts.[71] Music, of course, was a constant companion to twentieth-century youth identity, and East Germany was no exception. From jazz in the 1950s, through Beat and rock'n'roll in the 1960s, blues in the 1970s, and punk in the 1980s, young people's love of music inspired alarm in the hearts of the older generation. Recent research makes clear just how far Western counterculture penetrated the Eastern bloc.[72] Musical subcultures provided teenagers with space in which to experiment with appearance, behaviour, and sexuality. Hitching, concerts, discos, and hanging around on street corners were spaces largely free from adult control, where young people could develop their own sense of self. In a society where young people were expected to commit to training, education, or the army, and the age of marriage remained young, non-conformist behaviour could seem particularly transgressive, particularly when it drew on Western 'individualism'. Compared with the ideal-type young married couple with baby so prevalent in official literature, the long-haired hitchers and unsmiling punks were remarkable indeed.

---

[69] ZA S6145: Partner II 1979/80, p. 36. See also Friedrich and Starke, *Liebe und Sexualität bis 30*, pp. 133–134, for three (negative) accounts of young men losing their virginity with casual partners.

[70] Harald Hauswald, 'Sex und Saufen', in Ulrike Häußer and Marcus Merkel (eds.), *Vergnügen in der DDR* (Berlin: Panama, 2009), p. 189.

[71] Thomas Kochan, *Den Blues haben. Moment einer jugendlichen Subkultur in der DDR* (Münster: Lit Verlag, 2003).

[72] See for example Mark Allen Svede, 'All You Need Is Lovebeads: Latvia's Hippies Undress for Success', in Susan E. Reid and David Crowley (eds.), *Style and Socialism: Modernity and Material Culture in Post-War Eastern Europe* (Oxford and New York: Berg, 2000), pp. 189–208; William Jay Risch, ' "Soviet 'Flower Children' ": Hippies and the Youth Counterculture in 1970s L'viv', *Journal of Contemporary History* 40 (3) (2005), 565–584. We are soon to know much more about this important topic, thanks to Juliane Fürst's ongoing research on hippies in the Brezhnev-era Soviet Union.

Not least amongst music's anxiety-inducing effects was its sexual dimension. The authorities feared that jazz and Beat might send young people into an uncontrollable sexual frenzy.[73] Fears that young women would become promiscuous or be taken advantage of by rowdy young men were common.[74] And musical youth cultures often led young people to dress in ways that challenged gender norms: anxieties about tight trousers and stripy socks in the 1950s gave way to concern about jeans, long hair, and mini-skirts in the 1960s. By the 1970s, the authorities were worried about blues fans' adoption of hippie culture: long hair, bedraggled clothing, heavy drinking and drug abuse, and sexual 'excess'.[75] The police reported anxiously that: 'as a consequence of the Western sex wave, some girls are attending the local cultural centre in Freiberg without knickers'.[76] Even jocular discussions of such issues revealed deep-seated fears about blurring the boundaries between men and women. Werner Klemke's 1971 cover for *Das Magazin* showed a young man recoiling in surprise when the long-haired beauty he was in the process of undressing is revealed to be a man.[77]

Ideas of how young men and women should behave were remarkably persistent. In 1973, 72% of those surveyed disagreed 'absolutely' with the statement: 'Women should be faithful, it's different for men.'[78] On first glance, this seems like a decisive vote in favour of gender equality. From a different perspective, however, it is striking that 28% were prepared to admit to a sexual double standard, and it seems likely that the true figure may have been higher. Young people continued to perceive stark differences between girls and boys, the way they behaved, and how they were perceived. Petra, 16, reported scathingly: 'The teachers talk such rubbish sometimes: girls must be an example for the boys, always good, never cheeky, never untidy, never loud. Some teachers are way behind the times.'[79] The rest of her account, however, implies that her teachers were reflecting current gender norms and expectations. Boys, it seemed, quickly picked up on the message that, while girls were expected to be obedient, tidy, and unobtrusive, they had carte blanche to rule the roost. 'The boys here in the village act like they are kings.'[80]

---

[73] See the cartoon of a male singer being ravaged and stripped by female fans in Fenemore, *Sex, Thugs and Rock'n'Roll*, p. 191.

[74] Poiger, *Jazz, Rock and Rebels*, p. 199.

[75] Thomas Kochan, 'Da hilft kein Jammern. Zwischen Resignation und Aufbegehren: Die Szene lebte die Blues', in Thomas Kochan and Michael Rauhut (eds.), *Bye Bye Lübben City. Bluesfreaks, Tramps und Hippies in der DDR* (Berlin: Schwarzkopf & Schwarzkopf, 2004), p. 68.

[76] Rauhut, *Beat in der Grauzone*, p. 237.   [77] *Das Magazin*, April 1971.

[78] ZA S6144: Partner I – Junge Arbeiter 1973, p. 54.

[79] Wander, *Guten Morgen, Du Schöne*, p. 89.   [80] *Ibid.*

The metaphor of boys as young 'kings', conquering all before them, was echoed in an interview with Dirk, a 16-year-old interviewed a decade later. Dirk was part of a gang of forty boys who rode mopeds. 'We ride out to the discos in the villages. It's really cool there. When our clique rides in, we are the absolute kings. The girls are totally crazy about us boys from the city. Which isn't the case in S [his hometown].'[81]

Petra, Susanne's 18-year-old sister, struggled with these stereotypes in a passage which is worth quoting at length:

> I always wanted to be a boy. They can do whatever they like, nobody tries to talk them out of it. If a girl changes her partner often, she immediately gets a bad reputation, particularly amongst the [other] girls. They don't have any opinions of their own, they are so insanely conformist that they always put themselves down … [The boys] all think that you shouldn't take girls seriously, they are only there for sleeping with and for fun. And I have seen how well this works for them. So I wanted to be like that too … I do everything like a man – drinking, smoking, sleeping around, being lazy. But at the same time I know myself that it isn't good for me.[82]

Petra was frustrated with the other girls' collusion in their own oppression, and drawn to the autonomy and hedonism of the boys' lifestyle. Seeming to her liberated from both peer pressure and adult interference, they were free from the pressures on girls to be well behaved and unobtrusive. But Petra also implied that adopting a male lifestyle of drinking, smoking, and sleeping around had not automatically given her male self-confidence. She felt uneasy, stranded between male and female stereotypes. For young girls, the gulf between official rhetoric of gender equality and the reality could create an uncomfortable dissonance.

An interview with Martin, a 20-year-old car mechanic, suggests that young men may have felt a similar sense of conflict. Martin is, at times, openly misogynistic, criticising 'our girls in the office [*unsere Büroweiber*]' as lazy, greedy gossips and suggesting that overweight women should be sent on compulsory exercise courses.[83] Martin's description of his ideal woman makes clear how narrow his expectations of female behaviour and appearance are:

> I like girls who are natural. They shouldn't disfigure their appearance … most of them look much better when they wear their hair down, and leave their face as it is, and don't wear a thousand necklaces … Women should stay how they are seen [*wie sie gesehen werden*]. I don't like an exaggerated emancipation.[84]

---

[81] Christine Müller, *Männerprotokolle*, p. 111.
[82] Wander, *Guten Morgen, Du Schöne*, pp. 82–83.
[83] Lambrecht, *Männerbekanntschaften*, p. 138.   [84] *Ibid.*

What is interesting here is Martin's insistence on a 'natural' idea of female beauty, involving long flowing hair and minimal adornment, and particularly his conception of women as objects of a male gaze ('how they are seen'). These ideals of female beauty and passivity are strikingly similar to those prevalent in East German erotica (see Chapter 7). Later in the interview, however, there is a sense of how Martin himself may feel trapped by expectations of male behaviour. Speaking of his art student girlfriend he reflects: 'Maybe it's easier to show yourself to clever girls. They don't expect you to play the hard man, they want you to be honest and sensitive in your dealings with each other.'[85]

Young people's attitudes towards homosexuality demonstrate how deeply rooted conventional ideas about gender and sexuality were. Questioned at the end of the 1970s, 78% of respondents agreed 'fully' or 'partially' with the statement 'I instinctively disapprove of sexual contact between men.' (The figure for sex between women was 79%.)[86] Only 51% agreed unreservedly that nobody should be discriminated against because of their homosexuality.[87] Even social contact with gay men and lesbians was enough to make some young people uncomfortable. In 1990, only 41% of apprentices said that they could imagine being friends with a male homosexual, with 31% rejecting the idea outright and 28% saying that they had never considered the possibility.[88] Students surveyed in the same year were somewhat more tolerant, but nevertheless 14% freely admitted that they could not imagine being friends with a female homosexual.[89]

Coming out under such conditions was a bold step. When Winne told his class at school that he was gay, he was surprised to experience tolerance and understanding on the part of some of his close friends and even his teachers. In some ways, his sexuality gave him social status. 'There was something special about me, and I found myself interesting.' But being openly gay brought disadvantages too: even his friends expected him to clown around and simulate gay behaviour for their amusement. And once the news spread around the school, he was the subject of widespread homophobic taunting: 'Early in the morning I would step off the train and be stared at. "Oh, the gay from the second year. That's him, there he goes." With a stern look and weak knees I would march by, thinking: "Just don't look limp-wristed and effeminate."' After leaving school, Winne began to dread his looming national service. Following an unsuccessful sexual encounter, he took stock: 'I thought back over my

---

[85] *Ibid.*, p. 143.   [86] ZA S6145: Partner II 1979/80, p. 154.   [87] *Ibid.*, p. 126.
[88] ZA S6146: Partner III – Lehrlinge 1990, p. 50. Again, the figures for female homosexuality were very similar.
[89] ZA S6147: Partner III – Studenten 1990, p. 47.

life and came to the conclusion: the way my life has been will continue in the future ... The bottom line was unadulterated hopelessness.' Winne went home and attempted suicide.[90]

Not only did gay and lesbian teenagers suffer discrimination from their peers, they also grew up in a society that was at times deeply homophobic. Stefan remembered: 'Everybody I knew then despised gays and told jokes about them.'[91] A dearth of freely available information on homosexuality made it difficult for young people to imagine alternatives to heterosexuality. Even Maike, who came of age in the 1980s, and had better access to information about homosexuality than most, due to her involvement in the Protestant Church, found it difficult to identify her feelings as 'lesbian'. 'It wasn't in my field of vision. I don't know why. It never came up in school, not in biology class and not in any of the other subjects either.'[92] Not only did the lack of information in the public sphere make it difficult for teenagers to identify their own feelings, it also made coming out to their parents an often painful experience. In many cases, their families were completely uninformed about homosexuality and shared the homophobic prejudices of much of the population. Torsten asked his mother what she thought of homosexuals as they stood washing up after dinner. She immediately began telling him about a 'disgusting' gay couple she worked with, concluding that, if it was up to her, men like that would be locked up.[93] Amongst gay men surveyed in 1990, only 19% said that their mothers had tried to understand their problems; and the figure for fathers was even lower at 7%. In seven out of ten cases, their parents did not even know that they were struggling with their sexuality.[94] In some cases, coming out could have a catastrophic effect: when A's mother discovered that she was having a lesbian relationship, she stopped talking to her completely, even though they shared a flat. A found herself stuck in this unfortunate situation, as there was no possibility of finding her own place to live.[95] Even mothers and fathers who were instinctively supportive were unable to inform themselves further or to find ways in which they could support their children.[96]

---

[90] Lemke, *Gay Voices from East Germany*, pp. 102, 103, 105; Lemke, *Ganz normal anders*, pp. 188, 189, 193.

[91] Ursula Hafranke, 'Ungestraft anders', *Das Magazin*, January 1989, 44.

[92] Karstädt and von Zitzewitz (eds.), *... viel zu viel verschwiegen*, p. 216.

[93] Hafranke, 'Ungestraft anders', 45.   [94] Starke, *Schwuler Osten*, p. 149.

[95] *Psychosoziale Aspekte der Homosexualität. Gemeinschaftstagung der Sektion Ehe und Familie der Gesellschaft für Sozialhygiene der DDR und der Sektion Andrologie der Gesellschaft für Dermatologie der DDR am 28. Juni 1985* (Jena: Friedrich Schiller Universität, 1986), p. 104.

[96] For examples of tolerant parents, see Karstädt and von Zitzewitz (eds.), *... viel zu viel verschwiegen*, pp. 69, 97, 124.

Meeting like-minded people was a particular problem. It was common for people to seek out somebody they had never met, just because they had heard that they were gay or lesbian. The pursuit of love could lead to excruciating situations: Winne described how his friends would ring him up and say 'I'm at a great party where there's a gay guy who's just right for you!' He would jump out of bed and turn up at the party, only to be struck dumb with embarrassment and self-consciousness, as his friends craned to see what 'two gays were like with each other'.[97] And for those without such contacts, options were even more limited. Even when gay and lesbian groups began to appear in the 1980s, they were able to publicise their activities only through church publications, meaning that many remained unaware of such opportunities. The age of consent was also a major obstacle for gay and lesbian teenagers as it criminalised same-sex contact with under-18s. Theodor, aged 18 at the time of his interview in 1981, discussed the ambivalent attitude on the gay scene towards sex with under-18s, and hinted at the effect this had on young men exploring their sexuality:

As a young man, you're at their mercy, they are hot for you, for your fresh meat, most of them anyway. They get involved with you, but really it is just a fling and then they ditch you. Because they are afraid – statutory rape with a minor and so on. They are too shit scared to take you home with them, and they write down the wrong telephone number on purpose. Or they whisper to you, "Wait until you are eighteen, and then ... " But actually that means wait until you are human. Less than eighteen and you're a dangerous monster for them.

Yes, I was used and thus formed – for all I know, deformed.[98]

The tolerance of young people's heterosexuality evident both in the law (which placed the age of consent for mixed-sex couples at 14), and in films such as *Sieben Sommersprossen* was not extended to young gays and lesbians. Same-sex activity became legal only at 18, yet most East Germans were married by their early twenties. This left only a brief space of time for legal sexual experimentation. Some had simply not come out by this stage, even to themselves. Others, like Nicholas, were pushed into marriage by negative experiences of homophobia, unrequited love, or a feeling of alienation from the gay scene. 'To put it brutally: I used my wife all those years so I didn't have to live as a gay man.'[99] In a society where marriage and the nuclear family were held up as the most fulfilling and responsible way to live, taking another

---

[97] Lemke, *Gay Voices from East Germany*, p. 102.
[98] *Ibid.*, p. 141; Lemke, *Ganz normal anders*, p. 80.
[99] Lemke, *Gay Voices from East Germany*, p. 177; Lemke, *Ganz normal anders*, p. 257.

path was fraught with anxiety and risk. Gabriele married to 'spare' her mother, despite recognising that she loved women. She spoke of her later reluctance to leave her marriage, despite her feelings of unhappiness and conflict: 'I was frightened of that other life … I had the status of a wife, mother, and mother of a disabled child; society held me in high esteem.'[100]

Conclusion

Despite the would-be liberal tone of East German sex education, its focus on heterosexual monogamy left little room for sexual difference. Young people were subject to the same sexual norms as the rest of the population, particularly the focus on heterosexual monogamy, and were expected to conform to rather rigid sex and gender roles, particularly early marriage and young parenthood. It is hard to avoid the sense that the state co-opted teenage sexuality in an attempt both to encourage childbearing and to make itself appear more liberal and forward-thinking. This is unlikely to have been a conscious policy decision, but it is inherent in attitudes post-1963 (the year of the *Jugendkommuniqué*).

Nonetheless, there is evidence that many young people showed considerable autonomy in their sexual development. This autonomy was partially enabled by the state's hands-off approach to youthful heterosexuality in the 1970s and 1980s. Not only did this create spaces for sexual experimentation, it also encouraged parents' increasingly relaxed attitude towards teenage sex. Improved contraception, plus proximity to the opposite sex in the *Internate* (hostels), meant that young people tended to lose their virginity earlier. At the same time, differences between the experiences of young workers and students point to the formative nature of the educational experience.

Young people also provide potent evidence of the impact of Western popular culture. From Beat to punk, Western music and style provided young East Germans with a framework for experimentation and non-conformity. For a few short years, at least, young people could be part of an international 'imagined community', with shared tastes in popular culture and consumption and new ideas about sexuality and relationships.[101]

[100] Karstädt and von Zitzewitz (eds.), … *viel zu viel verschwiegen*, p. 108.
[101] On young people's 'imagined communities', see Brown, ' "1968" East and West', and Jeremi Suri, 'The Rise and Fall of an International Counterculture, 1960–1975', *American Historical Review* 114 (February 2009), 45–68.

But young people also faced significant constraints on their behaviour. These were most sharply felt by gay and lesbian teenagers, as well as girls who wished to step outside established gender roles. But housing shortages were a major restriction for almost all young people. Paradoxically, marriage – imagined in official accounts as a life of domestic and parental responsibility – seemed to some to usher in an era of greater freedom. The next two chapters will explore the extent to which this promise was fulfilled.

3   Marriage and monogamy

Wolfgang Mattheuer's painting, *Floating Lovers*, shown at the National Art Exhibition in 1972, shows a bare-legged young couple floating high above a landscape of sea and sand dunes, wrapped in each other's arms (Figure 3.1). The mood is one of romantic and sexual reverie: the couple are encapsulated in their own intimate world, isolated from the demands and travails of the outside world. It is tempting to read this picture as a direct representation of East German relationships: men and women relating as equals, freed from the oppressive demands of capitalist society. Indeed, the romantic narrative of East German sexuality tends to suggest that individuals were able to make decisions about relationships entirely based on emotion or desire. According to Wolfgang Engler, East Germans 'married or moved in together because they loved each other, and broke up because they didn't love each other any more'.[1] But as even the most idealistic of marriage guidance books admitted, such moments of escape were the exception rather than the norm, as couples grappled with the realities of work, home, and childcare. 'There will be conflicts in every marriage', advised the *Encyclopedia of Young Marriage*, 'because even under socialism life does not always go smoothly.'[2]

In fact, Mattheuer's painting was exhibited at a time of dramatic changes in East German heterosexual behaviour. The early 1970s saw the introduction of abortion on demand and the widespread distribution of the contraceptive pill. While fewer people were choosing to marry, more were getting divorced. Most strikingly, while the overall birth rate dropped, the proportion of children born outside marriage rose startlingly. Single-parent households and co-habitation became acceptable family forms. By the 1980s, these revolutionary changes resulted in a distinctively East German heterosexual culture, which sat between East and West European trends. This chapter will explore the nature of

---

[1] Engler, *Die Ostdeutschen*, p. 258.
[2] Lykke Aresin and Annelies Müller-Hegemann (eds.), *Jugendlexikon Junge Ehe* (Leipzig: VEB Bibliographisches Institut, 5th edn, 1986), p. 37.

Figure 3.1: Wolfgang Mattheuer, *Schwebendes Liebespaar* (*Floating Lovers*), 1970.

these changes, before asking what drove them and whether they provide evidence for Engler's romantic vision of East German relationships.

Heterosexual revolutions

As we saw in the previous chapter, young people often saw marriage as an escape from the parental home – a free and autonomous space where they could start their adult lives. But by the early 1970s, it was clear that marriage was far from stable. Changes were afoot in individuals' decision making about relationships and childbearing. The years immediately after 1945 had seen booms in marriage, divorce, and births, as couples sought to make up for the lost war years and absorbed the impact of prolonged separation on their relationships. By the mid 1950s, however, matters had reached a more stable footing. In 1956, there were only 15 divorces for every 100 marriages, a figure that remained stable for the next decade.[3] By 1972, however, the ratio

[3] *Statistisches Jahrbuch der Deutschen Demokratischen Republik 1970* (Berlin: Staatsverlag der Deutschen Demokratischen Republik, 1971), p. 442.

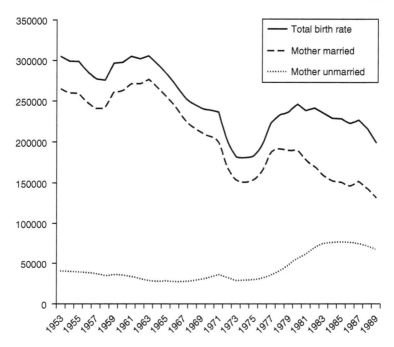

Figure 3.2: East German birth rates, 1953–1989.

of marriages to divorces had crept up to 26. It reached 30 by 1978 and peaked at 40 in 1982.[4] When marriage and divorce figures are put side by side we can see that, while the marriage rate dropped somewhat, the most powerful trend was the rise in divorce. About twice as many couples chose to divorce in the 1980s as in the 1960s.

The birth rate, which had dipped somewhat in the second half of the 1950s, rose towards the end of the decade and remained buoyant throughout the early 1960s (see Figure 3.2). Despite the building of the Berlin Wall, it seemed that East Germans remained optimistic about starting – and adding to – families. The gap between marriage and the couple's first child was often rather brief. Donna Harsch has found that, in 1962, 85% of first children born within wedlock had been conceived before their parents married.[5] In a survey of married couples in 1974, 36% had married during pregnancy.[6] Our interviewees' experiences

---

[4] *Ibid.*; *Statistisches Jahrbuch der Deutschen Demokratischen Republik 1990*, p. 403.
[5] Harsch, *Revenge of the Domestic*, p. 291.
[6] SAPMO-BArch DY30/JIV2/3A/382, 64, Information an das Sekretariat über einige Ergebnisse einer Untersuchung zur Lebensgestaltung junger Ehen, 16.4.1974.

Table 3.1: *Percentage of births outside marriage in selected European populations, 1970–1990*

	1970	1975	1980	1985	1990
East Germany	13.3	16.1	22.8	33.8	35.0
West Germany	5.5	6.1	7.6	9.4	10.5
Russian Republic (USSR)	10.6	10.7	10.8	12.0	14.6
Sweden	18.8	32.4	39.7	46.4	47.0
UK	8.0	9.0	11.5	18.9	27.9

Source: Marzio Barbagli and David I. Kertzer, 'Introduction', in Marzio Barbagli and David I. Kertzer (eds.), *The History of the European Family*, vol. III, *Family Life in the Twentieth Century* (New Haven: Yale University Press, 2003), p. xxxiii.

followed a similar pattern: of twenty-seven, nine married when a baby was on the way. Interestingly, though, these do not seem to have been 'shotgun weddings' designed to conceal the disgrace of pre-marital sex. In most cases, pre-marital sex appears to have been a given. Couples were already in a committed relationship and, while pregnancy undoubtedly nudged them towards marriage, it was by no means a disaster. 'For younger couples, it [pregnancy before marriage] means less', noted a bureaucrat from the DFD (Demokratischer Frauenbund Deutschlands, Democratic Women's League of Germany).[7] In any case, the arrival of a child made the need for a family home all the more pressing – and marriage was often the quickest remedy. The median age at childbirth was 22, six years lower than that of West Germany. Childbearing at an older age was unusual – even for second and subsequent children. In 1985, only 15% of all births were to women aged 30 or over, compared to 35% of all births in the West.[8] Frau N, who had her first child at 29, was treated like an 'elderly mother' and felt completely isolated – 'in those days, everybody had their children when they were 20'.

In a parallel trend, though, increasing numbers of babies were born outside marriage. By 1970, more than 10 per cent of births involved unmarried mothers. By the mid 1980s, this had risen to over a third. The significance of this figure becomes even clearer when it is set alongside comparable data from other European countries (Table 3.1). The divergence from West Germany is striking, with the West German rate

[7] SAPMO-BArch DY31/1067.
[8] Michaela Kreyenfeld, 'Fertility Decisions in the FRG and GDR: An Analysis with Data from the German Fertility and Family Survey', *Demographic Research*, special collection 3, article 11 (17 April 2004), 307, 309. See also Trappe, *Emanzipation oder Zwang?*, pp. 103–110.

Table 3.2: *Total fertility rate (mean number of children per woman) in selected countries, 1946–1984*

	1946–9	1950–9	1960–4	1970–4	1980–4
East Germany	1.74	2.32	2.42	1.85	1.84
West Germany	2.07	2.17	2.47	1.74	1.38
Albania	5.50	6.40	6.40	4.90	3.45
UK	2.54	2.35	2.85	2.22	1.80
USSR	3.05	2.85	2.67	2.43	2.33

Source: Marzio Barbagli and David I. Kertzer, 'Introduction', in Marzio Barbagli and David I. Kertzer (eds.), *The History of the European Family*, vol. III, *Family Life in the Twentieth Century* (New Haven: Yale University Press, 2003), p. xxii.

of births outside marriage barely doubling in the twenty years from 1970 to a conservative 10.5%. East Germany also had by far the highest percentage of births outside marriage in the Eastern bloc, with the nearest 'competitors', Estonia and Slovenia, managing only 20%. In Western Europe, only Denmark, Iceland, and Sweden had higher rates.[9] The rise in births outside marriage took place as the overall birth rate declined. Starting in the late 1960s, this downward trend took an even sharper dip after the introduction of easily available abortion in 1972.

A comparison of European fertility rates shows that East Germany was following a familiar pattern. Birth rates tended to rise until the mid 1960s (as prosperity and living conditions improved) and fall in the 1970s and 1980s, due in no small part to the wider availability of birth control. What is interesting is that the East German birth rate remained significantly higher than the West German equivalent. When we add a pan-European comparison, the East German case becomes even more interesting. If we take the rates from the early 1980s, the East German birth rate was the second lowest in the Eastern bloc (Hungary's was marginally lower at 1.80). But neither did the GDR follow a West European model: in Western Europe, only Catholic and Orthodox countries had higher birth rate – France (1.88), Greece (2.02), Ireland (2.90), Portugal (2.04), Spain (1.89).[10]

On abortion too, East Germany diverged from both the West German and Eastern bloc paths. The introduction of abortion on demand in 1972

[9] Marzio Barbagli and David I. Kertzer, 'Introduction', in Marzio Barbagli and David I. Kertzer (eds.), *The History of the European Family*, vol. III, *Family Life in the Twentieth Century* (New Haven: Yale University Press, 2003), p. xxxiii.
[10] *Ibid.*, p. xxii.

Table 3.3: *Abortions per 1,000 live births, selected European populations, 1972–1989*

	1972	1973	1980	1984	1989
East Germany	568.7	614.4	375.7	421.7	371.5
West Germany	49.9	38.3	141.3	147.7	110.6
Denmark	181.0	230.0	413.5	400.4	349.7
Russian Republic (USSR)	2365.6	2379.9	2045.7	1810.2	2049.3
UK	200.8	224.1	224.1	245.6	249.9

Source: Calculated from figures in Council of Europe (ed.), *Demographic Yearbook 2001*, www.coe.int/t/e/social_cohesion/population/demographic_year_book/2001_edition/ Germany GDR 2001.asp.

was relatively late for the Eastern bloc. Abortion had been legalised in the USSR in 1955, and countries such as Poland, Czechoslovakia, and Romania quickly followed suit. By West European standards, however, the GDR was relatively early, liberalising its abortion law four years after the UK, but earlier than France, West Germany, Sweden, and Norway.

In 1973, one year after the liberalisation of the abortion law, 38% of all pregnancies were terminated, implying both a very strong desire on the part of women to control their fertility, and that many women still lacked access to reliable contraception.[11] By 1987, 27% of pregnancies were terminated, suggesting that the take-up of the Pill had lowered, although far from eliminated, unwanted pregnancies.[12] As the figures in Table 3.3 show, East German women were significantly more likely to terminate a pregnancy than West Germans or women in the UK. (West German legislation limited abortion to 'medical' and some 'social' cases.) On the other hand, compared to the Russian Republic (and many other Eastern bloc countries), where lack of reliable birth control methods made abortion a frequent contraceptive choice, East

[11] It is interesting that the married birth rate fell more than the unmarried one upon the introduction of abortion, declining 24% from 1971 to 1973, while the unmarried birth rate fell 21%. This suggests that it was married women, most of whom already had children, who were taking advantage of the right to abortion to limit family size: *Statistisches Jahrbuch der Deutschen Demokratischen Republik 1990*, p. 420.

[12] These figures have been derived from the birth rates in the *Statistische Jahrbücher* and the reported abortion figures at Council of Europe (ed.), *Demographic Yearbook 2001*, www.coe.int/t/e/social_cohesion/population/demographic_year_book/2001_edition/Germany GDR 2001.asp. They do not include pregnancies that ended in miscarriage.

German abortion rates were moderate. In fact, the countries with the most similar abortion rates were Sweden and Denmark. As in the case of births outside marriage, East Germany resembled the Scandinavian countries rather than following Soviet-style or West German patterns.

The figures, then, tell a compelling story about changing life choices and attitudes towards the family. East Germans were keen to marry, but quick to divorce. They were also increasingly relaxed about child-bearing outside marriage, to an extent unprecedented in the Eastern bloc – and most of the Western one too. Attitudes towards abortion too were increasingly relaxed. What caused these changes? State policy is clearly part of the answer. Marriage and the family were central to the SED's plans for society. The 1949 constitution proclaimed marriage and the family to be the 'foundation of communal life'.[13] As in all indus-trialised societies, the East German family was expected to play many roles: it provided its members with accommodation and food, was a key factor in personal happiness and well-being, and supported children, both physically and economically.[14]

In the early years of socialist rule the state was still preoccupied with making families 'socialist', beginning with the wedding ceremony itself. It was a cause for concern that citizens turned to the church for significant life events such as birth, marriage, and confirmation, see-ing them as religious rather than socialist occasions. In 1958 the local party in Potsdam put together some suggestions for what a 'socialist' marriage ceremony might look like. Concerned that the marriage cere-mony itself was still tying people to the church, they suggested that civil ceremonies could be personalised by the happy couple, so long as the 'socialist content' was retained. However, the suggested speech, already in use in the small town of Pritzwalk, was somewhat forbidding, cautioning the freshly minted couple that 'a frivolous attitude towards marriage controverts the moral views of the workers'.[15] The groom was sternly informed that the women of today had important economic and political responsibilities, and he should not demand any special treatment at home. 'It is better and much quicker to do the housework together.'[16] While the apportioning of household chores was to remain

---

[13] 'Die Verfassung der Deutschen Demokratischen Republik, 7 October 1949', www. documentarchiv.de/ddr/verfddr1949.html.

[14] Göran Therborn, *Between Sex and Power: Family in the World, 1900–2000* (London and New York: Routledge, 2004); Barbagli and Kertzer (eds.), *History of the European Family*.

[15] Brandenburgisches Landeshauptarchiv (henceforth BLHA), Rep. 530, SED Bezirksleitung Potsdam, Nr 1803, p. 16.

[16] *Ibid.*, p. 19.

a live issue, such finger wagging seemed unlikely to win couples over from the traditional church ceremony. Indeed, even as late as the early 1970s, only 52% of students and 42% of young workers completely ruled out a church ceremony, with 32% of both groups declaring themselves in favour.[17] (In contrast, the socialist coming-of-age ceremony, the *Jugendweihe*, enjoyed near-universal participation.[18])

The 1965 Family Law began with the words: 'The family is the smallest cell of society.'[19] It sternly stated that: 'Socialist society expects all its citizens to act responsibly with regard to marriage and the family.'[20] The law's preamble spoke high-mindedly of 'the great personal and societal meaning of marriage and the family ... and the duty of every individual and the whole of society to contribute to the protection and the development of every family'.[21] Despite this, the years that followed saw the state and society take an increasingly pragmatic and non-interventionist approach to the details of family life. In practice, policy focused above all on maintaining and enlarging the East German workforce. The state needed to keep women in paid employment *and* maintain the birth rate – two goals which did not necessarily work well together.[22] Policy towards birth control and abortion is an excellent example of the regime's attempt to balance these two areas.

Abortion and birth control

Access to contraception was patchy in the 1950s and 1960s, leaving married couples with limited control over their fertility. Condoms were scarce, and Herr J remembered coitus interruptus as the primary means of contraception in the first postwar decades. Frau T and Frau W recalled using the rhythm method, but fully reliable contraceptives were hard to come by. This created particular problems for unmarried couples. Herr N remembered 'the panic, it's impossible to understand what that meant ... it was always bound up with risk, the whole thing'.

---

[17] ZA 6144: Partner I – Junge Arbeiter 1973, p. 19; ZA 6143: Partner I – Studenten 1972, p. 30.
[18] On the *Jugendweihe*, see Anselma Gallinat, 'Negotiating Culture and Belonging in Eastern Germany. The Case of the Jugendweihe: A Secular Coming-of-Age Ritual', unpublished Ph.D. thesis, University of Durham (2002); Anna Saunders, 'The Socialist and Post-socialist Jugendweihe: Symbol of an Evolving East(ern) German Identity', *Focus on German Studies* 9 (2002), 43–60.
[19] Familiengesetzbuch der Deutschen Demokratischen Republik, 20 December 1965, www.verfassungen.de/de/ddr/familiengesetzbuch65.htm.
[20] *Ibid.*   [21] *Ibid.*
[22] On the difficulties of combining these two goals in the early GDR, see Harsch, *Revenge of the Domestic*.

But the absence of birth control could be just as difficult for married couples. Karoline described her despair as she fell pregnant time and time again, despite trying all available contraceptive methods:

I said, Doctor, I can't go on like this, a child every year. He said: even if it's the eighteenth time, I'll still say no [to an abortion]. That's what it was like, we were animals. Not people, who have the right to decide over their own lives! When I was really at the end of my rope, they got rid of one for me in the city. In 1966 I had Andreas [her fifth child], and then the Pill arrived, that saved me.[23]

The Pill came on the East German market in 1965. East German women were initially cautious: some were concerned about its hormonal effects – particularly weight gain and loss of libido – and at first take-up was well below what had been envisaged.[24] Nevertheless, by 1970 20% of all women of childbearing age in Berlin were taking the Pill and, where the capital led, the rest of the country followed. By the end of the 1970s the Pill was well established as the default contraceptive choice.[25] Women could get contraceptive advice from their gynaecologist or from the marriage and sexual advice offices, and the price of a month's supply was kept low, at 3.50 marks.[26] Of 1,560 young women in Leipzig surveyed in 1987, 80% were using contraception: 60% the Pill, 8% an IUD or pessary, 5% rhythm method, 3% condom, and 3% coitus interruptus.[27] In 1990, 90% of young women surveyed were either on the Pill or had taken it in the past.[28]

Karoline was not alone in remembering the introduction of the Pill as a transformative and liberating moment. As another of Maxie Wander's interviewees put it, 'we all swallow this green pill for breakfast that has given us freedom'.[29] This sentiment was echoed by Frau N: 'As soon as the Pill arrived, I was a free person.' Even Frau M's mother, who was highly religious and had had nine children of her own, described the Pill as 'the greatest invention that there has ever been'.[30] It is worth

[23] Wander, *Guten Morgen, Du Schöne*, p. 243.
[24] SAPMO-BArch DY31/1078, p. 39.
[25] Gisline Schwarz, 'Von der Antibaby- zur Wunschkindpille und zurück. Kontrazeptive in der DDR', in Gisela Staupe and Lisa Vieth (eds.), *Die Pille. Von der Lust und von der Liebe* (Berlin: Rowohlt, 1996), pp. 149–163.
[26] *Ibid.*, p. 155.
[27] SAPMO-BArch DY24/13759, Hauptergebnisse einer Untersuchung 'Bedingungen und Motivationen junger Frauen in ausgewählten Kreisen des Bezirkes Leipzig zu Fragen ihres Kinderwunsches', 1987, p. 10.
[28] ZA S6142: Partner III – Berufstätige 1990, p. 40.
[29] Wander, *Guten Morgen, Du Schöne*, p. 28.
[30] See also Irene Böhme, 'Frei von dieser Angst. Über die Pille in der DDR', and the interview with 'Frau B' in Gabriele Goettle, 'Sie waren weiss, grün oder rosa … Frauen erinnern sich', both in Staupe and Vieth (eds.), *Die Pille*.

noting, however, that the Pill placed the responsibility for contraception firmly at women's feet, liberating men from worry about unwanted pregnancy. Herr D, who had led a highly promiscuous sex life, claimed to have used a condom only three times.

One factor behind the introduction of the Pill was concern about the growing demand for abortion rights in the 1960s. The restrictive abortion laws introduced by the Nazi regime had been relaxed in the immediate postwar period, as women raped by Red Army soldiers demanded the right to end unwanted pregnancies.[31] However, the law was tightened again in 1950, and permitted abortion only in cases where the mother's health was severely threatened or there were eugenic grounds for a termination.[32] These restrictive conditions resulted in a low official abortion rate, but a high number of illegal abortions – estimated to be anything between 40,000 and 100,000 a year.[33] About sixty women per year died from the results of illegal abortion.[34] Some of these abortions took place in the GDR, but other women travelled to neighbouring socialist countries. Herr N 'through incapability, bad luck, or stupidity' got two girls pregnant and had to arrange for them to travel to Poland, where abortion had been legalised in 1956.[35]

Perhaps reassured by the rise in the birth rate in the early 1960s, the regime relaxed the restrictions on abortion in 1965, allowing a very limited range of 'social' grounds for termination: for example if pregnancy was a result of rape or incest, if a woman already had five children, or if she was over 40 or under 16.[36] Women had to put their case to a commission made up of three doctors, a functionary from the Ministry of Health, and a representative of the DFD. But rather than reducing the pressure on the authorities, this measure increased it. The DFD reported in 1967 that applications for abortions had more than doubled.[37] A selection of such applications from the Potsdam area reveals that those requesting abortions were in the main married women with more than one child. Of forty-seven women, only two were childless. Nine had one child, twenty-five had

---

[31] See Poutrus, 'Von den Massenvergewaltigungen zum Mutterschutzgesetz'; Grossman, *Reforming Sex*, pp. 189–199.
[32] Poutrus, 'Von den Massenvergewaltigungen zum Mutterschultzgesetz'; Gesetz über den Mutter- und Kinderschutz und die Rechte der Frau, 27 September 1950, www.verfassungen.de/de/ddr/mutterkindgesetz50.htm.
[33] Donna Harsch, 'Society, the State, and Abortion in East Germany, 1950–1972', *American Historical Review* 102 (1997), 59, 63.
[34] *Ibid.*, 63.
[35] United Nations, *Abortion Policies: A Global Review*, vol. III (New York: United Nations, 2002), p. 38.
[36] Harsch, 'Society, the State, and Abortion in East Germany', 62.
[37] SAPMO-BArch DY31/1078, p. 58.

two children, nine had three children, and two had four children. Almost half were over 30.[38]

As Atina Grossman and Donna Harsch have shown, women's applications for permission to terminate spoke of the unbearable strain of an unwanted pregnancy.[39] Their letters give a glimpse of some of the difficulties of family life in this period, detailing inadequate and cramped living conditions, a dearth of childcare, and marriages which were often rocky. A 35-year-old mother, whose application had been turned down on the grounds that she was healthy, sent an articulate plea for the recognition of her 'social problems'. She worked full-time with children with severe special needs and lived with her husband, her mother, who was seriously ill with stomach cancer, two biological sons and a foster child, in a three-room 'glorified summerhouse', with no bathroom. Since the birth of her second child, she had suffered from a vaginal prolapse and subsequent infection. Despite all this, she had decided to continue with her current pregnancy – until her husband was ordered to undertake a period of training. His reduced salary during this period meant that it was financially impossible for her to take time off work. She wrote eloquently of the delicate balancing act between working, looking after family members, and staying healthy: 'I don't want to give up my career, which I love, but I also don't want to neglect my family members, who have had enough to put up with this past year with my poor state of health.'[40]

A 34-year-old teacher, with two children of 9 and 7, wrote that a further pregnancy would destroy her marriage. Her husband, an SED member, was a drinker and had had an affair with a woman he had met through his party work. Even the official medical report described her husband as 'weak-willed, unreliable, unsupportive, like a guest in his own home as a result of his many [party] functions'. His wife had suffered from incontinence since the birth of her first child and was depressed and tearful. After her application was turned down, she wrote to the commission:

A person is more than just his [sic] body ... Our two children mean everything to us, but this third one is the greatest misfortune that could have happened to me ... Do you really think that women are destined to take on all the burdens

[38] BLHA, Rep. 410, No. 20134.
[39] Atina Grossman, '"Sich auf ihr Kindchen freuen". Frauen und Behörden in Auseinandersetzungen um Abtreibungen, Mitte der 1960er Jahre', in Becker and Lüdtke (eds.), *Akten. Eingaben. Schaufenster*, pp. 239–257; Harsch, 'Society, the State, and Abortion in East Germany'.
[40] BLHA, Rep. 410, No. 20134.

of life? I know that my husband will never change his way of life, and that I face terrible years if this application is turned down again.[41]

An application from a 28-year-old woman, in the process of divorcing her husband, was turned down unanimously, despite the fact that she had had a nervous breakdown and both she and her children were victims of domestic violence. The social worker's report stated 'Wife and children are being beaten by the husband … I do not see any compelling reason to end the pregnancy.' The woman in question had already had one abortion, had failed to take the Pill, and had not been to a marriage guidance office or taken legal action to begin the divorce process. In this case, as in others, there is a sense that permission to terminate was withheld as a punishment for the woman's failure to comply with the state's norms and to take advantage of the resources that had been made available to her. No allowance was made for her fragile mental and physical state or the constraints of an abusive relationship.[42]

Married and unmarried mothers

While the response to individual pleas was often unsympathetic, the state eventually bowed to pressure from both the population and the medical profession and introduced abortion on demand in 1972.[43] Interestingly, Harsch points out that international pressures may also have played a role in this decision: visa-free travel to Poland was about to be introduced, which would have made it much easier for women to procure an abortion abroad. Furthermore, the party was aware of the growing abortion rights movement in the West and perhaps saw an opportunity to present the GDR as more forward-thinking and liberal in its attitudes to women.[44] Abortion was freely available up to 12 weeks of pregnancy, with the cost of the procedure and sick pay borne by the state.[45] This measure combined with the impact of the Pill to create a sharp dip in the birth rate, accelerating the gradual decline that had begun in the mid 1960s (see Figure 3.2). While in the early 1960s around 300,000 babies had been born each year, by 1971 this had dropped to 234,870. Following the legislation on abortion, which came into force in the middle of 1972, the birth rate plummeted to 180,336 in 1973.[46]

---

[41] *Ibid.*   [42] *Ibid.*
[43] Harsch, 'Society, the State, and Abortion in East Germany'.
[44] Harsch, *Revenge of the Domestic*, p. 273.
[45] Schwarz, 'Von der Antibaby- zur Wunschkindpille', p. 159.
[46] *Statistisches Jahrbuch der Deutschen Demokratischen Republik 1990*, p. 420.

Table 3.4: *Selected family policy measures, East Germany*

1950	Introduction of maternity grant and child benefit for working women with more than two children.
	Eleven weeks of paid maternity leave.
1952	Introduction of monthly housework day for married women.
1958	Maternity grant (500 marks for first child, rising to 1,000 marks for fifth and subsequent children) and child benefit extended to all families.
1965	Housework day extended to single mothers with children under 18.
1972	Maternity grant increases to 1,000 marks for all children.
	Introduction of interest-free marriage loans.
	Paid maternity leave increased to 18 weeks.
	Additional days of paid holiday for working mothers of two or more children.
	Paid leave for single parents with sick children or in the absence of childcare.
	Introduction of measures to support young mothers at university or undertaking an apprenticeship.
1976	Paid maternity leave increased to 26 weeks, with a further 26 weeks at a lower rate of pay for second and subsequent children (*Babyjahr*).
	Housework day extended to all single women over 40.
1981	Child benefit raised to 100 marks for third and subsequent children, but remains at 20 marks for first two children.
1984	Maternity leave extended to 1.5 years for third and subsequent children.
1986	*Babyjahr* extended to first child.

Source: Gunnar Winkler (ed.), *Geschichte der Sozialpolitik in der DDR, 1945–1985* (Berlin: Akademie Verlag, 1989), pp. 144–195, 384, 404; Johannes Frerich and Martin Frey, *Handbuch der Geschichte der Sozialpolitik in Deutschland*, vol. II, *Sozialpolitik in der Deutschen Demokratischen Republik* (Munich: R. Oldenbourg Verlag, 1993), pp. 391–417.

Concerned by the dip in the birth rate, the regime made concerted efforts to help women combine work and family. This represented a fundamental shift from 'negative natalism', which restricted access to contraception and abortion, to 'positive natalism', which used material incentives to encourage women to reproduce.[47] A raft of measures were introduced to coincide with the reform of the abortion law (see Table 3.4), but the policy which had the greatest impact was the *Babyjahr*, or 'baby year', introduced in 1976, which allowed working women to take a year's paid leave after the birth of second and subsequent children. Clearly aimed at tempting those who were already parents of one child or more to consider having another baby, this policy was remarkably popular. The birth rate immediately rose and, as

[47] Harsch, *Revenge of the Domestic*, p. 264.

a result, births per head of the female population remained high relative to most West European countries, and relative to West Germany in particular (see Table 3.2).

Given the East's undeniably lower living standards, pressures on housing, and high rate of female employment – all factors that might be expected to discourage reproduction – much of the credit for the buoyancy of the birth rate must go to the state's pro-natalist policies, particularly the extension of paid maternity leave in the form of the *Babyjahr* (see Table 3.4). This was not enough to stop the birth rate falling in the 1980s, but it did ensure that it fell from a higher point than would otherwise have been the case. East Germans may not have had numerous children, but they did tend to have at least one. Female childlessness was low, at 10%, and was equally distributed between income groups, in contrast to the West, which had a childlessness rate of 25–30%, rising to 40% amongst women educated to *Abitur* level or above.[48] Some women, of course, chose to remain childless. Frau F was firm in her decision not to marry or have children: 'I'm more of a freedom sort of person', she explained. But, on the whole, women without children – whether through choice or circumstance – were much rarer than in the West. The young age of marriage may have reduced cases of age-related infertility, and support for students and young workers with children played an important role too.[49]

As Harsch points out, East German social policy promoted both pronatalism and maternal employment, through a 'universal breadwinner model', which tied welfare benefits to work and prioritised young families over pensioners.[50] In this, it resembled both Sweden and Finland, providing a partial explanation for some of the statistical similarities I have already noted. As in Scandinavia, policies that made life easier for working women in general also made specific allowances for single parents (for example paid leave if children were ill or a nursery place was not available).[51] These measures both enabled and normalised lone parenthood – usually, but not exclusively lone motherhood.[52] The photographer Eva Mahn described how financial independence

[48] Kreyenfeld, 'Fertility Decisions', 287, 307.
[49] On students, see Kurt Starke, 'Kinderwagen im Seminargebäude. Die Förderung von Studentinnen mit Kind in der DDR', in Waltraud Cornelißen and Katrin Fox (eds.), *Studieren mit Kind. Die Vereinbarkeit von Studium und Elternschaft. Lebenssituationen, Maßnahmen und Handlungsperspektiven* (Wiesbaden: VS Verlag, 2007), pp. 79–91.
[50] Harsch, *Revenge of the Domestic*, pp. 308–309.
[51] Frerich and Frey, *Handbuch der Geschichte der Sozialpolitik*, p. 414.
[52] On single motherhood in the 1950s, see Elizabeth Heineman, 'Single Motherhood and Maternal Employment in Divided Germany: Ideology, Policy and Social Pressures in the 1950s', *Journal of Women's History* 12 (2000), 147–172.

and state-provided childcare combined to give women of her generation (she was born in 1947) a sense of liberation from conventional family structures:

We had a strange attitude, we women. Children yes – men only as sperm donors. Just for making babies. But marriage? No. Why would we? There were crèches, when they were little, kindergarten, after-school clubs. It was absolutely unnecessary, and we worked too. We had money too. Women worked, the children were looked after. OK, two [children] would have been too many, but one was easy. And we never thought we needed men, the poor guys were chucked out if they didn't behave the way we wanted them to. That was like an emancipation, that was our Sixties revolution, like 1968 in West Germany, but different. Nobody married any more, and the man would literally get a smack if he wasn't obedient. We are not your objects any more, you can't just own us and use us as housewives, mothers, and lovers, we'll do it alone, our own way.[53]

As Mahn warms to her theme, her tone changes from ironic and amused distance ('we had a strange attitude, we women', 'the poor guys') to impassioned engagement ('that was like an emancipation', 'you can't just own us and use us'). The shift in the balance of power since her mother's generation *was* revolutionary.[54] Not all single mothers made a conscious choice to go it alone but most benefited from financial independence and state support. Frau G, born in 1960, was entirely positive about her experiences as an unmarried mother: 'As a single woman and mother of a child, father state did everything for you.' Although nursery places were very scarce, she was given priority and was able to study as well as hold down a job that involved considerable travel outside the GDR.

Of course, the experience of single mothers was not universally positive. Women's wages remained markedly lower than men's, putting single women at a financial disadvantage.[55] Ute dropped out of university when she got pregnant and was unable to get a flat for herself and her son. As she worked shifts in a factory, she had to put her son in the weekly nursery for the first three years of his life, seeing him only at

---

[53] Interview with Eva Mahn, 14.5.2004.

[54] On women's growing sense of self-confidence, especially with regard to relationships and sexual satisfaction, see also Betts, *Within Walls*, pp. 107, 111.

[55] Annemette Sørensen and Heike Trappe, 'The Persistence of Gender Inequality in Earnings in the German Democratic Republic', *American Sociological Review* 60 (1995), 398–406; on the gender segmentation of the GDR labour market, and the differential values attributed to male and female labour, see Harsch, *Revenge of the Domestic*, pp. 246–250.

weekends. Perhaps due to the enforced separation, or to the fact that pregnancy had been unplanned and unwanted, she did not bond with her son until he began to talk.[56] But for all its stresses, motherhood outside marriage was no longer a taboo and was seen by some young women as a viable alternative to marriage. As one teenager put it: 'I can imagine having a baby without a man ... I don't know why some girls are so keen on getting married.'[57]

It is notable that the married birth rate dropped at approximately the same rate as the unmarried birth rate rose. Without further research, it is impossible to know what proportion of extra-marital babies were born to co-habiting couples and what proportion to mothers living alone. Heike Trappe's research suggests that, although many women spent periods of time living alone with their children, this was often followed by remarriage or co-habitation. Of the women in her survey born between 1959 and 1961, 36.8% spent time living along while their children were under 6 years old. But only 3.6% were single for the entire period, with 23.6% having a partner for more than half of this time, and 9.6% having a partner for less than half the time.[58] In any case, the fact that most mothers worked outside the home, and the lack of a widespread religious influence, obviated the sort of moral panics associated with unmarried mothers in West European countries.[59] Increasing numbers of single-parent families, even if such arrangements were only temporary, may have contributed to a broader acceptance of alternatives to the nuclear family.[60] Ursula Sillge, who raised her daughter with her female partner, remarked in 1986: 'My child is in a class with eighteen children, seven of them live alone with their mothers and two alone with their fathers. My daughter has certain advantages over these children, because there are two parental figures in our household. My girlfriend has gone to parents' evening in my place, and was accepted by the teachers.'[61] Granted, the relatively relaxed mores of Berlin's Prenzlauer Berg, where Sillge lived with her family, were not replicated all over the GDR, but the demise of marriage had wide-ranging consequences nonetheless.

---

[56] Wander, *Guten Morgen, Du Schöne*, p. 100.   [57] *Ibid.*, p. 113.

[58] Trappe, *Emanzipation oder Zwang*, p. 112.

[59] Elizabeth Heineman points to the importance of the discursive environment in attitudes towards single mothers. Even in the 1950s, maternal employment was encouraged and tolerance for single parenthood was much higher than in the West. See Heineman, 'Single Motherhood and Maternal Employment'.

[60] For a sympathetic cinematic depiction of single motherhood – and the search for a partner – see the 1971 film, *Her Third: Der Dritte* (dir. Egon Günther, 1971).

[61] *Psychosoziale Aspekte der Homosexualität* [1986], p. 83.

The Legend of Paul and Paula: change and continuity in gender roles

Many of the changes in East German sexual behaviour began to take effect in the early 1970s. As we have already seen in the case of young people, around this time the state began to accept that in most cases it was neither desirable nor particularly effective to interfere directly in its citizens' private lives. While in the 1950s and the 1960s party members were routinely disciplined for 'unsocialist' behaviour such as marital infidelity, by the 1970s such expectations had been quietly abandoned.[62] As Paul Betts has shown, judges and social workers in the divorce courts began to place more emphasis on individual freedom and fulfilment than on a marriage's worth for society. The private sphere was now valued more as a source of personal happiness rather than a crucible of socialist morality.[63]

Die Legende von Paul und Paula (The Legend of Paul and Paula), released in 1973, was a telling reflection of these changes in East German social expectations.[64] The film is a love story between Paula – a supermarket worker bringing up two children on her own – and Paul, a petty bourgeois functionary. Both are fleeing unhappy home lives: Paul married only because his wife was pregnant and remains with her because he loves his son and feels that respectability is important for his career. Meanwhile, Paula's life as a single mother in an unmodernised flat is one of unrelenting drudgery, with no support from those around her. In one scene, her winter's supply of coal is dumped in front of her house, and she spends hours carrying it up the stairs, one bucketload at a time. The film was radical not just in having a single mother as its heroine, but also in the way it portrayed marriage as unhappy, inhibiting, and claustrophobic, and adultery as a matter of course. Paul's wife is unfaithful during his military service, and Paula returns home from having her second baby to find her partner about to have sex with another woman. Caught *in flagrante*, all he can say is 'home already, Paula?' Paul and Paula take flight from the responsibilities of family, work, and party in love and passion. In the film's central sequence, Paula persuades Paul to skip his paramilitary meeting for a stolen evening in her bedroom, which segues into a fantastical boat ride on her flower-strewn bed. Ultimately, though, happiness eludes the couple.

[62] On the 1950s, see Andrew I. Port, 'Love, Lust, and Lies Under Communism: Family Values and Adulterous Liaisons in Early East Germany', forthcoming in *Central European History*.
[63] Betts, *Within Walls*, ch. 3.
[64] *Die Legende von Paul und Paula* (dir. Heiner Carow, 1973).

The death of one of Paula's children prompts Paul to leave his wife. He sets up home with Paula, who quickly becomes pregnant. Against medical advice, she carries the baby to term, but dies in childbirth.

Paul und Paula showed its protagonists as individuals, for whom marriage, children, work, and politics could be oppressive rather than satisfying. What is compelling about the film is Paula's insistence on her right to personal happiness and fulfilment.[65] For her, happiness is achieved through love and sexuality. Work and motherhood alone are not enough, and engagement with 'society' in the form of the party or its mass organisations barely figures. This was a film in which intimacy rather than social obligation took precedence. Director Heiner Carow and writer Ulrich Plenzdorf had set out to make a film which reflected East German life with 'unsparing honesty'.[66] The result was uncomfortable viewing for many party bureaucrats, who objected not only to its portrayal of morally bankrupt functionaries, but also its lack of an acceptable political message.[67] But after a personal intervention by Erich Honecker, the film made it to the cinema and became one of the most popular East German films ever produced. 'That's what it [life in East Germany] was like!' exclaimed Frau T. In her case, there seems little direct equivalence between Paul and Paula's tragic tale and her own story. But what the film offered was a non-ideological view of East German life, focused on relationships rather than politics, which mirrored the way viewers saw their own lives. This was indicative of a wider shift in society, where private decisions about relationships were – for the most part – no longer fraught with political significance.

Nevertheless, as *Paul und Paula* hints, the sexual revolution had its limits, not least with regard to gender roles. Both official East German accounts and the 'romantic' view of socialist sexuality suggest that heterosexual relationships were transformed by the legal and financial equality of women. In the model East German marriage, women's work outside the home gave them the increased self-esteem and financial independence to insist on partnerships based on mutuality and shared responsibility.[68] This was certainly true in theory. Advice books aimed at young couples were illustrated with photographs of children

---

[65] On this, see Irene Dölling, ' "We All Love Paula but Paul Is More Important to Us": Constructing a "Socialist Person" Using the "Femininity" of a Working Woman', *New German Critique* 82 (Winter 2001), 77–90.

[66] *Die Legende von Paul und Paula* (Icestorm DVD, 2002 (1973)), interview with Heiner Carow on DVD extras: 'Träume und Legenden – Porträt Heiner Carow'.

[67] See e.g. 'Auffassung von dem Film "Legende von Paul und Paula" ', 'Aktennotiz', and 'Einschätzung des DEFA-Spielfilms "Die Legende von Paul und Paula"', SAPMO-BArch DY30/IVB2/9.06/80, pp. 19–23, 72–75.

[68] Herzog, *Sex After Fascism*, pp. 214–215.

bonding with their fathers.[69] A section on 'equality in marriage' in the
Encyclopedia of Young Marriage was illustrated with a photograph of a
young woman studying while her husband changed the baby's nappy,
watched by a toddler.[70] The authors cautioned: 'Here [in the GDR]
love is the main reason to marry. But to sustain it, equality must be put
into practice on a daily basis.'[71] How the couple arranged this was up
to them. Household duties should be divided according to interest and
skills, without fear of being labelled a 'hen-pecked husband' or 'down-
trodden wife'.[72] In most cases, the authors admitted, men would carry
the coal up the stairs, while women would be in charge of the sewing
machine. 'But there are more than a few marriages where a handy wife
gets busy with saw, hammer, and nails, while her husband cooks or
knits elaborate jumpers for the family.'[73] This utopian vision reflected
the idea of a modern socialist marriage, based on 'equal rights', 'camaraderie', and 'respect'.[74]

Such fine words were not without some basis in fact. As Frau O
pointed out, men had to take on a certain proportion of housework and
childcare on practical grounds alone. With both parents working, often
in shifts, and without home-based childcare, labour-saving devices, or
grocery delivery, it would have been impossible for many women to
manage without some help from their husbands. Frau T returned to
work as a nurse after the 12 weeks of maternity leave that were then
statutory. Her night shift finished at 6 a.m., which meant her husband was responsible for getting their daughter up and dressed in the
mornings:

A [her husband] had to get going early, he got the bus ... to work, seven kilometres away. The bus went at ten past six, I think, and I worked until six ... so
before he went to work, to the bus, he woke B [their daughter] up early, gave
her a bottle, changed her nappy ... packed her in the pram and then he brought
the pram to me and parked it outside my workplace.

Men born in East Germany and raised by working mothers were
more likely to see such co-operation as the norm. Herr E, born in
1963, remembered his mother teaching him and his brother how to
bake cakes and wash the stairs – a fundamental redistribution of gendered work. Doris, a 30-year-old teacher, said of her son and husband,
'Stefan and Werner are much better at washing up and hoovering than
I am.'[75] This willingness to admit to domestic incompetence suggests

[69] Friedrich and Starke, *Liebe und Sexualität bis 30*, n.p.
[70] Aresin and Müller-Hegemann (eds.), *Jugendlexikon Junge Ehe*, p. 73.
[71] *Ibid.*, p. 74.   [72] *Ibid.*, p. 76.   [73] *Ibid.*, p. 18.
[74] *Ibid.*, pp. 73, 89, 10.   [75] Wander, *Guten Morgen, Du Schöne*, p. 50.

that, in her case at least, keeping a tidy house was unimportant to female self-image.

Nevertheless, it would not do to overstate the reinvention of gender roles. It is true that some interviewees saw gender relations as a way in which East Germans differed from – and were more progressive than – their Western counterparts. Even so, female interviewees were markedly more critical, particularly on the subject of equal rights in the workplace: Frau R bemoaned the poor pay of kindergarten workers: 'no man would have worked for that money'.[76] Frau C regretted the 'excessive' focus on *women's* rights, rather than an expectation that both women and men would contribute equally to household work:

When I compare it with nowadays, we were maybe a bit too fixated on women. Women had to be able to do everything ... if you had a child, you could still work full-time, then you got your housework day. And you could see there were lots of women in management, but that was just this formal equality. I think. Because they still had to do all the housework and everything at home.

This contrast between 'formal equality' and a true sense of *being* equal comes through even more strongly in the contemporary sources. Margot, married with two children, explained that she was completely equal in the workplace, but the hundreds of (domestic) 'trivialities' that she had to deal with in the course of the week made her life completely, 'grotesquely' different from a man's.[77] Another woman pointed out that supposedly inspirational role models could actually have the opposite effect:

When I used to read modern novels, or listen to the radio, I'd think: why aren't I like these fantastic women who are able to deal with everything effortlessly? Why do *I* have to be such a loser? Then I realised that reality is quite different, and the positive heroic women are just made out of paper.[78]

Expectations of women were extremely high: education, training, work, childcare, housework, shopping, not to mention voluntary work in one of the GDR's mass organisations.[79] But husbands and fathers did not always increase their contribution correspondingly. The DFD found in 1974 that only 28% of men did housework as a matter of course, and in 20% of marriages women were left to do almost all the housework. The longer a couple had been married, the less likely a man was to take on

---

[76] On the gender pay gap in the GDR, see Sørensen and Trappe, 'The Persistence of Gender Inequality in Earnings in the German Democratic Republic'.

[77] Wander, *Guten Morgen, Du Schöne*, p. 229.

[78] *Ibid.*, pp. 244–245.

[79] On the sheer quantity of housework (eight hours a day in a six-person household), see Harsch, *Revenge of the Domestic*, p. 275.

his share of the chores.[80] 'Astonishingly', the report noted acidly, 'more men than women are dissatisfied with the amount of free time available to them (34% of men as opposed to 25% of women). This certainly should not lead us to the conclusion that male respondents actually have less free time.'[81]

Family policy, such as paid maternity leave and the monthly 'housework day', tended to reinforce the already strong popular impression that domestic work was women's work. An interesting side effect of the *Babyjahr* was that it seems to have cemented childcare and the household as women's responsibility. Heidemarie Stuhler and Juliette Wedl's research found that East German women of all ages saw paid work as an integral part of women's lives, but that their attitudes towards the balance between work and home changed strikingly according to their generation. Women who married in the 1950s placed more emphasis on housework than their younger counterparts, while women who married in the 1960s tended to take a greater interest in childrearing, many choosing to work part-time.[82] Only in the 1970s did women begin to regard their jobs as a career, equal in importance to their husbands' work. As a result, many began to compartmentalise work and children to an increasing extent, some seeing the *Babyjahr* as an obstacle to their self-realisation through work. Women who married in the 1980s, however, saw work in more pragmatic terms, as a means of material satisfaction. In contrast to the more egalitarian structures of the 1970s family, where housework was shared between husband and wife, 1980s wives tended to be solely responsible for the housework: an unintended outcome of the introduction of the *Babyjahr* for the first child in 1986 (Stuhler and Wedl interviewed women who had married in the middle of the decade aud who were amongst the first beneficiaries of this policy). Patterns set in the first year of the child's life, when the woman was at home and in charge of the house, tended to persist after she had gone back to work.[83] Mothers were also far more likely than fathers to reduce their hours: in 1983, 27.6 per cent of all women worked part-time.[84] What Harsch has perceptively termed 'the revenge of the domestic'

---

[80] SAPMO-BArch DY31/1067, p. 66, Information an das Sekretariat über einige Ergebnisse einer Untersuchung zur Lebensgestaltung junger Ehen, 16.4.1974.

[81] *Ibid.*, pp. 67–68.

[82] See here also Harsch, *Revenge of the Domestic*, pp. 297–300.

[83] Heidemarie Stuhler and Juliette Wedl, 'Bleibt alles anders? Transformationen im alltag ostdeutscher Frauen', in Heiner Timmermann (ed.), *Die DDR in Deutschland. Ein Rückblick auf 50 Jahre* (Berlin: Duncker & Humblot, 2001), pp. 513–552.

[84] Harsch, *Revenge of the Domestic*, p. 314. However, part-time work was likely to be a temporary arrangement: see Trappe, *Emanzipation oder Zwang?*, pp. 150–152.

grew as time went on: in part as a result of an increasing emphasis on home life and of a growing realisation that real gender equity would be slow to come.

Between paid work, childcare, household chores, and voluntary work, East German marriages were expected to bear a significant strain. As Mary Fulbrook points out, many man also carried a 'double burden' of sorts, when their additional roles as DIYers, car mechanics, and even house builders are taken into account.[85] Voluntary work for the party or mass organisations added an extra strain to many marriages. Fritz K said regretfully in 1975, 'at home, you hardly have time for the children, no energy'. His wife, also a party member, added ruefully, 'The man comes home, is full of problems, and has to vent them first of all.'[86] Added to this was the expectation that East Germans were committed to continual professional self-improvement. Many jobs required evening courses or study away from home. Unsurprisingly, divorce rates rose sharply when either husband or wife embarked on a degree, which had to be juggled with pre-existing commitments.[87] It can come as no surprise that these practical concerns came into conflict with the official rhetoric of gender equality. The fact that 76 per cent of young workers, both male and female, felt that mothers of young children should work either part-time or not at all should therefore be seen as practical and ideological in equal measure.[88]

In some cases, the formal rhetoric of gender equality could act as an alibi for traditional male privileges. Herr J, a doctor in Berlin's main hospital, was by his own admission a serial adulterer during his first marriage. He eventually left his wife for the nurse who was to become his second wife (Frau J). He was unconcerned by the breakdown of his first marriage as 'women are independent; in the GDR they all had equal rights after all'. His second marriage saw a gendered division of labour, where he continued with his medical career while Frau J (willingly) stayed at home with their two children. 'It was completely clear, because of my role at the hospital, that I couldn't do anything like take a year off with the baby ... God forbid! That would have been out of the question for me.' The female doctors he worked with were, with one exception, childless. Like a West German man in his position, he was free to sleep around, remarry without consequences, pursue his

[85] Fulbrook, *People's State*, p. 166.
[86] Bronnen and Henny, *Liebe, Ehe, Sexualität in der DDR*, p. 14.
[87] Lothar Mertens, *Wider die sozialistische Familiennorm. Ehescheidungen in der DDR 1950–1970* (Opladen: Westdeutscher Verlag, 1998).
[88] ZA S6144: Partner I – Junge Arbeiter 1973, p. 14.

career, and leave the responsibility of contraception and childcare to the women in his life. Unlike a West German, he was also able to do so without the obligation to pay child support and without the voice of feminism in his ear. Men such as Herr J were enabled to pursue both personal and professional fulfilment, safe in the knowledge that women's rights had been assured by the state. 'There wasn't an emancipation movement or anything like that, because it was all legally regulated, that they [women] had equal rights', he concluded.

Similarly, Herr L praised the 'housework day' as a fine achievement – careless of the fact that it placed housework firmly in women's sphere of responsibilities and arguably undermined women's role in the workplace.[89] And it is clear that machismo survived even under socialism. Herr D insisted that East German women were feisty and confident, but claimed never to have done the washing up in his life. Herr A, a sports coach, commented 'of course women did more', adding that the man's role was more that of protector. Lambrecht's and Müller's interviews with men in the 1980s also show the persistence of traditional working-class masculinity in some quarters. Jörg, a 22-year-old worker, described his fellow workers with affection, but also a trace of condescension, as 'real proles, it's wonderful I tell you ... real hefty workers. They are real smart alecs, roar like lions, drink like fish, amazing! ... You shouldn't take it all too seriously though. A lot of it's machismo. No man wants to show what he really feels inside. And a man doesn't want to cry.'[90]

Müller's interview with Klaus, a groundsman and boxing trainer, gives a flavour of how these sorts of attitudes may have played out in the home. Klaus resented the impact of his wife's work on their home life and the fact that he was expected to take on some of the domestic burden: 'When her boss says "We have to work two hours extra today", my lady does it, without asking me first. Then she comes home at seven and is totally exhausted. I don't like that! ... She'd like me to come home and wash up, wash the windows, do the hoovering, go shopping and then ask humbly: "Have you got any more work for me, dear? Should I do the washing too?"'[91] As an employee of the Ministry of Culture admitted when approving publication of Müller's book: 'We are still a long way from having people straight out of communist rhetoric.'[92] Another functionary agreed that it was important to include interviews

[89] On the housework day, see Carola Sachse, *Der Hausarbeitstag. Gerechtigkeit und Gleichberechtigung in Ost und West 1939–1994* (Göttingen: Wallstein, 2002).
[90] Lambrecht, *Männerbekanntschaften*, p. 48.
[91] Müller, *Männerprotokolle*, p. 13.   [92] BArch, DR1/2324, p. 254.

with the 'bad sorts' as a cautionary example to the population. 'They belong to the present state of affairs and even in socialist society they won't "die out" that quickly, but will reproduce themselves in the children of such fathers.'[93]

Fulbrook, then, is right to point out that there were 'limits to the rethinking of men's roles'.[94] Some men, of course, rejected these roles. Jürgen explained: 'I for one don't want to play the predetermined male role. I don't want to be the strong man, the big victor and conqueror. A girlfriend once accused me of being a "softy" who wanted to cry my heart out on her "motherly bosom" – I can live with that.'[95] Marianne Motz's photograph 'Vision' offers a glimpse both of this new type of East German man and of a newly assertive female artistic voice. It pictured a naked bearded man, reclining, eyes shut and seemingly asleep, on a brass bed in the middle of a field of flowering rape.[96] Exhibited as part of the 1982 'Nude and Landscape' exhibition, this photograph playfully reversed the usual gender roles, creating an image that is both droll and provocative. The juxtaposition of a typically bearded *homo germanicus democraticus* with the tropes of the classical nude raises a smile. But it also raised questions about power, sexuality, and gender equality.[97]

However, such reshaping of masculinity could give rise to profound unease. The cover of *Das Magazin* in March 1975 featured a naked man wrapped like a snake around an inscrutably smiling woman. The man's dignity was somewhat compromised not just by his supplication but also by his blue socks. The woman, on the other hand, seemed self-possessed and to be enjoying the upper hand. While female readers expressed recognition and amusement, men wrote in to complain that 'equality had gone too far'. Tellingly, one reader was concerned chiefly with the undermining of paternal authority: 'What are our children meant to say, if their fathers are publicly caricatured like this?'[98] On the whole, equality East German style did not require or encourage a fundamental rethinking of gender roles. Rather, the emphasis of both social policy and mainstream discussion was on helping *women* to combine work and domestic duties.

---

[93] *Ibid.*, p. 246.   [94] Fulbrook, *People's State*, p. 165.

[95] Christine Müller, *Männerprotokolle*, p. 47.

[96] Marianne Motz, 'Vision', in Kulturbund der DDR, Bezirkskommission Fotografie Potsdam (eds.), *Bildmappe der Ausstellung Akt und Landschaft* (1982).

[97] See also Josie McLellan, 'Marianne Motz: "Vision"', *Rundbrief Fotografie* 16 (2) (2009), 3–4.

[98] *Das Magazin*, May 1975, 3.

Divorce

Unsurprisingly, this put marriages under significant strain. As we have seen, not only was the marriage rate in decline, but the divorce rate was also steadily increasing.[99] Much of this rise was initiated by women. Wives had always been more likely than husbands to file for divorce, accounting for 53% of all petitioners in 1958. By 1984, however, 68% of all divorces were initiated by a woman.[100] The fact that a woman could raise children on her own without social stigma, as well as women's increasing financial independence, must have played a role in their willingness to end unhappy marriages. In many cases, though, infidelity was central to relationship breakdown. In an analysis of divorces carried out in 1975, infidelity was cited as a factor in 54% of divorces (in 29% of cases on the part of the husband, in 18% on the part of the wife, and in 7% of cases both parties had begun a new relationship). Next came the catch-all 'incompatibility' with 36%, while 26% of couples frankly admitted that 'sexual reasons' lay behind their wish to divorce. Alcohol abuse – largely on the man's part – was cited by 24%, a statistic which had risen sharply since the 1950s.[101] This paralleled a sharp rise in alcohol consumption – by the end of the 1980s, the GDR had the highest per capita consumption of beer and spirits in the world, with East Germans knocking back 23 bottles of spirits per head each year.[102] It is not difficult to imagine how this drinking culture caused conflict in relationships. In Paul Betts' analysis of divorce cases in Berlin in the 1960s, three-quarters involved alcohol abuse, and between one-third and one-half involved domestic violence.[103]

A report from the marriage guidance office in Strausberg, written in 1975, concurred that alcohol abuse and infidelity were the most frequent problems they encountered. But when the counsellors discussed a couple's problems, they often found underlying problems which related to the division of labour between husband and wife. What is striking about this report is how conflict divided along traditional gender lines. Wives complained that their husbands did not do

[99] On divorce, see especially Betts, *Within Walls*, ch. 3.
[100] Mertens, *Wider die sozialistische Familiennorm*, pp. 36–37.
[101] SAPMO-BArch DY31/1067, p. 57, 'Auswertung der Ehescheidungsstatistik 1975'. Cf. Mertens, *Wider die sozialistische Familiennorm*, pp. 56–63.
[102] On alcohol abuse in the GDR, see Thomas Kochan's doctoral research, e.g. 'Rotkäppchen und der Blaue Würger – Vom Alkohol in der DDR', www.geschichts-werkstatt-jena.de/archiv_texte/vortrag_kochan_alkohol.pdf. Kochan's monograph, *Blauer Würger. So trank die DDR* (Berlin: Aufbau, 2011), was published as this book went to press. See also Fulbrook, *People's State*, pp. 103–106.
[103] Betts, *Within Walls*, p. 100.

enough around the house, preferring to work overtime and earn extra money. Husbands countered that their wives were excessively house-proud – a tendency reportedly exacerbated by competition between female workers about who kept the cleanest house – and complained that they put their energies into housework rather than sex. Unequal earning power was also a source of conflict – if a man earned more, did he deserve a greater share of the family's disposable income? And should his wife report back about how the housekeeping money had been spent? Women's desire to further themselves in their careers could create friction, as could their expectation that fathers too should take time off work if their children were ill. Alcoholism and infidelity were, the report's author argued, often a response to an unhappy marriage rather than its root cause.[104]

Heiko's account of his marriage breakdown shows how the demands of work, housing, and parenthood could combine to undermine a marriage. He met Christa when they were both students. He liked 'her opinions, her generosity, her enthusiasm, and her attitude towards sex ... I had the feeling I had met a good person.'[105] When she got pregnant, they decided to have a 'student wedding', travelling to the registry office by tram, to the disapproval of her parents. However, this early sense of partnership and camaraderie was soon eroded by the stresses of socialist life. No suitable flat became available, and when their son was born he was sent to live with Christa's parents while she finished her degree. After graduation, Christa too moved to be with her son, and it was three years before the family was able to live in the same flat. It was a difficult readjustment, exacerbated by the fact that both Christa and Heiko had stressful and tiring jobs. Heiko's work in a cement plant often required evening and weekend work, and he developed a perforated stomach as a result of conflict with his boss. Things at home also disintegrated, with arguments about money, free time, and holidays. With his hopes of a 'rich life, filled with culture', disappearing, Heiko began to drink. In retaliation, Christa spent every weekend with her parents, taking their son with her. When they finally divorced Heiko felt as if 'a piece of my life was at an end'. He moved away, and saw his son only during the holidays.[106]

Young couples were at particular risk of divorce. The supreme court reported in 1982 that marriages of less than five years made up 40% of divorces. In 1981 18% of men and 31% of women who got divorced

[104] SAPMO-BArch DY31/1066, pp. 53–54.
[105] Christine Müller, *Männerprotokolle*, pp. 101–102.
[106] *Ibid.*, p. 106.

were under 25 years old.[107] So rapid was the rise that a woman of 24 was more likely to be divorced than a woman of 28.[108] The court blamed 'premature and imprudent' decisions to marry, and regretted the fact that so few sought the help of the FDJ, state-run marriage guidance services, or members of their collective at work.[109] For its part, the FDJ reported that young people had high expectations of both marriage and their own self-development, but were ill-equipped to deal with the problems they faced in marriage.[110] One of Christine Müller's interviewees also bemoaned the younger generation's lack of moral fibre: 'Young people today are so spoilt and impatient, they split up at the first sign of friction. And think that they are so brave. No, they're cowards, otherwise they wouldn't give up so easily.'[111]

Young married couples did face particular challenges. Research carried out in 1974 indicated that only 50% of young couples were satisfied with their housing. Just 54% of couples were offered somewhere to live in their first year of marriage, and after two years of marriage only 30% had their own rental contract. A mere third of those surveyed had anything bigger than a one-bedroom flat.[112] Even after a long wait, housing was often unsatisfactory: Herr B and his wife had to wait two years to move into a tiny crumbling flat. Such housing shortages meant that couples often had to set up home with their parents. Not only did this result in a lack of privacy, but it also stood in the way of men and women developing their identity as a couple, and could result in a marriage feeling flimsy and lacking in substance. Steffi described her first marriage as 'nothing. A box room at my parents-in-law's, meeting just at the weekend, and then he was busy with his friends.'[113] Klaus also blamed inadequate housing for the breakdown of his first marriage: 'I think we would have got along quite well if her parents hadn't always stuck their noses in … [Her father] had the cheek to come into our bedroom without knocking first thing on a Sunday morning, stand next to the bed and rant at us, "It's come to this, has it, still in the sack at nine

---

[107] SAPMO-BArch DY24/13759, Oberstes Gericht der Deutschen Demokratischen Republik, 3, Zivilsenat, 7.9.1982, p. 1, Information über Probleme der Ehescheidung junger Bürger.
[108] *Ibid.*, p. 2.   [109] *Ibid.*, p. 5.
[110] SAPMO-BArch DY24/13759, Zentralrat der FDJ, Abteilung Staat und Recht, Zu Aufgaben und Möglichkeiten der Leitungen der FDJ und der Pionierorganisation, 'Ernst Thälmann' bei der Unterstützung der Kinder und Jugendlichen hinsichtlich ihrer Vorbereitung auf Liebe, Ehe und Familie, n.d. (after 1985), p. 3.
[111] Christine Müller, *Männerprotokolle*, p. 36.
[112] SAPMO-BArch DY31/1067, 60, Information an das Sekretariat über einige Ergebnisse einer Untersuchung zur Lebensgestaltung junger Ehen, 16.4.1974.
[113] Wander, *Guten Morgen, Du Schöne*, p. 178.

o'clock, when the windows need to be painted." ' The marriage broke up after two years.[114]

The effects of the lengthy separation necessitated by conscription were also profound. Young men faced a minimum 18 months of military service, and those who wished to go on to university or enter certain careers often had to agree to serve for three years. (Those who chose the non-military alternative (*Bausoldaten*) faced serious consequences for their future education and careers.) Conscripts often feared that their wives would be unfaithful in their absence – a scenario drama-tised in the film *Ete und Ali* (1985).[115] Frau N's relationship broke up during her boyfriend's military service. She reflected: 'in retrospect I think, those poor bastards [*diese armen Schweine*], 18 months, it was so important for them to have a girlfriend outside to visit, to motivate themselves and have something to look forward to. And we outside said "Hey, 18 months – I can't wait that long." ' Herr N also experienced a relationship breakup during his military service, when the mother of his child left him for another man. He remembered the army's efforts to support soldiers' relationships, even to the point of talking to wives and girlfriends if a relationship seemed in trouble. 'The problem was recognised alright, but it couldn't be prevented.'

Marriage guidance offices, like the one in Strausberg, were part of the regime's response to the rising divorce rate.[116] By 1977 there were 284 such offices, which offered a mixture of marriage counselling and advice on family life and sexual problems.[117] Their work was often highly interventionist, with counsellors involving themselves in discussions with the couple's extended family, work colleagues, and even the third party in an affair.[118] But despite these efforts, divorce continued to rise, and both couples and the state lost faith in their ability to mend broken relationships. Both Paul Betts and Donna Harsch have shown that con-cern about family stability reached its zenith in the 1960s. Faced with a petition for divorce, the courts went to great lengths to 'save' the mar-riage, often enlisting work colleagues, party comrades, and health pro-fessionals in an attempt to re-educate the couple in the ways of socialist

---

[114] Christine Müller, *Männerprotokolle*, p. 20.
[115] *Ete und Ali* (dir. Peter Kahane, 1985). Thanks to Mark Fenemore for bringing this film to my attention.
[116] For a detailed account of the development of marriage guidance, see Annette F. Timm, 'Guarding the Health of Worker Families in the GDR: Socialist Health Care, *Bevölkerungspolitik*, and Marriage Counselling, 1945–1970', in Peter Hübner and Klaus Tenfelde (eds.), *Arbeiter in der SBZ-DDR* (Essen: Klartext Verlag, 1999), pp. 463–495; Timm, *Politics of Fertility*, pp. 280–287.
[117] SAPMO-BArch DY31/1066, p. 68.   [118] *Ibid.*, pp. 11, 24, 25.

partnership.[119] Such forthright attempts at social engineering dwindled in the 1970s, as enthusiasm for state intervention – and optimism about its potential for success – waned. An emphasis on sustaining marriages for the good of society was replaced by a growing individualism, which stressed couples' rights to dissolve unhappy relationships. By the 1980s, visits to marriage guidance centres had dropped considerably, and even the courts no longer suggested that couples attempt counselling as a matter of course.[120]

Despite these problems, East Germans did not completely lose their faith in marriage, and many were happy to marry more than once. In 1989, 39% of weddings involved at least one partner who had already been married.[121] Marriage remained an important institution, but it was not necessarily seen as a lifelong commitment. Amongst young people, there was an increasing tendency towards co-habitation instead. As one man said of his children: 'They've all got a partner or a boyfriend but none of them are married. Well, that's not so important nowadays.'[122] A 1987 study found that, although 80% of young people aspired to marriage, in practice they barely differentiated between marriage and co-habitation.[123] In many cases, the priority given to married couples on the housing market may have been enough to tip the scales. Of all women born in 1960, 91% had married at least once by the time they were 50. However, a growing proportion of young people rejected the idea of marriage altogether. Of women born in 1965, 20% have never married.[124] In Anke's case at least, her aversion to marriage was in part due to the fact that she had witnessed her parents' divorce. Eighteen at the time she was interviewed, she explained: 'I never want to marry, because I've lived through all that at home. [M]aybe I'll move in with somebody. It's a lot simpler if you're not married. But I definitely want to have children, two of them.'[125] In her estimation at least, single parenthood was a less daunting prospect than an unhappy marriage.

[119] Harsch, *Revenge of the Domestic*, pp. 284, 286–297; Betts, *Within Walls*, pp. 100–108.
[120] Betts, *Within Walls*, pp. 108–115.
[121] *Statistisches Jahrbuch der Deutschen Demokratischen Republik 1990*, p. 416.
[122] Christine Müller, *Männerprotokolle*, p. 30.
[123] SAPMO-BArch DY24/13759, Standpunkt zur vergleichenden Untersuchung des Zentralinstituts für Jugendforschung Leipzig 'Junge Frauen in der Ehe und in der Lebensgemeinschaft'.
[124] Council of Europe (ed.), *Demographic Yearbook 2001*.
[125] Eckart, *So sehe ick die Sache*, p. 235.

Conclusion

By the 1980s, the East German family took many forms, including single-parent households, stepfamilies, and co-habiting couples. This reflected the increased autonomy of the private sphere and a broadening of social norms. The role played by state policy is particularly interesting. Many of the measures introduced by the state in the 1970s were designed to stabilise the birth rate and enable women to combine career and family. However, the results were not necessarily those which had been intended. Paradoxically, the economic independence enjoyed by East German women enabled couples with children to dissolve relationships that were not working. State policy did have an impact on the birth rate, but it also hastened the decline of marriage.

Equally, for all the rhetoric of equality between the sexes, evidence of real change in gender attitudes is hard to come by – while women's roles changed dramatically, men's did not. The state needed women to work, and it was prepared to put measures into place to make this possible. However, there was no political will behind a redistribution of domestic work. The romantic narrative sees gender equality as resulting in happier relationships – this may have been true for some couples, but there are also countless examples of gendered roles causing conflict in relationships. Women were not released from domestic responsibility, but they did gain some freedom to go it alone or to embark on new relationships.

However, the individual stories cited in this chapter also give a sense of the enormous diversity of experience that lay behind the statistics. For some, marriage and family life were a happy refuge from work and politics, marked by camping trips and days out on the allotment.[126] For others, the barriers to intimacy were greater than its rewards. Some women relished the independence of single parenthood – others felt isolated from the cosy domesticity of marriage. What is striking, though, is the extent to which both models of the family became acceptable ways to live. The norms of heterosexual behaviour shifted considerably over the lifetime of the GDR. But as we shall see in the next chapter, this did not result in an unrestrained sexual revolution.

---

[126] On the family as a refuge, see Betts, *Within Walls*, p. 89.

4 'The dictatorship of love': sex, love, and state hypocrisy

Tongue firmly in cheek, the historian Stefan Wolle has described the GDR as a 'dictatorship of love'.[1] For Wolle, this term encapsulates both the repressive paternalism of the SED and the infantilisation of the East German population. Emotive displays of allegiance replaced rational political debate, and citizens were able to abdicate responsibility for life's tiresome decisions to the all-powerful state. 'It was boring, but also somehow nice ... One lived in the moment, and enjoyed one's chains.'[2] Wolle's laconic description is of course deeply ironic. But others have linked love and the East German state in an entirely serious way. During the lifetime of the GDR, the connection between sex and love was central to all public discussions of sexuality. Sex advice books simply assumed that their readers were in a loving, heterosexual, monogamous relationship, and other publications continually stressed that sex without love was an empty activity, at best meaningless and at worst actively damaging. The GDR claimed to be the champion of love and intimacy, and often proclaimed its moral superiority to the West in this regard. Sex under communism was not a meaningless distraction or a commercial exchange, but an intimate and loving act between two equal partners. This link between sex and love has become a central plank of post-1989 accounts which stress the 'romantic' nature of East German sexuality and East Germans' preference for serial monogamy over promiscuity and casual sex.

How seriously should we take such claims? Was the GDR really an oasis of love and intimacy? It is certainly true that sexological writing placed enormous emphasis on the connection between love and sex. But there is also a great deal of evidence that points towards a disjuncture of public discourse and private behaviour. Firstly, it is questionable how far these values were adopted by the population. It is of course difficult to state with total authority what people actually did in bed and with whom they chose to do it. But statistical and anecdotal evidence

---

[1] Wolle, *Die heile Welt der Diktatur*, p. 126.   [2] *Ibid.*, p. 127.

certainly qualifies this particular hypothesis about East German sexual behaviour. Even official surveys showed that infidelity and casual sex were rife, and sexually transmitted diseases (STDs) a significant problem.

Secondly, and perhaps more importantly, it is clear that the East German state was happy to ignore its own rhetoric when it came to sex, love, and relationships. The authorities did not hesitate to use sex as a weapon in certain cases or to overrule emotional ties on practical or political grounds. Not only was prostitution, officially anathema to East German sexual mores, tolerated, it was also used as a vital source of information for the nation's intelligence agencies. This astonishing degree of hypocrisy is particularly apparent in the dealings of the secret police, or Stasi, who not only violated the privacy of intimate relationships, but also actively sought to destroy them. A similar level of doublethink is to be seen in the state's dealings with foreigners, who were granted neither the right to a loving relationship nor the pronatalist benefits afforded to East German citizens. The second half of this chapter examines cases in which pragmatism won out over principles and the impact of state intervention in the private sphere on the personal lives of those affected.

'Good' and 'bad' sex

Siegfried Schnabl's *Mann und Frau Intim* is probably the best-known East German publication on sex. First published in 1969, it ran to eighteen editions and is often cited as a key text in the sexual emancipation of East German women.[3] It is certainly true that Schnabl was at pains to explain female sexual function and the importance of foreplay and to encourage couples to choose positions that would best facilitate female orgasm. Schnabl also influenced books published subsequently, which prided themselves on their open-minded approach to sexual practices.[4] This focus on sexual pleasure, particularly women's sexual pleasure, appears to have borne fruit. East German sexologists were proud of the rising orgasm rate amongst women. At the start of the 1980s, 42% of young women claimed to achieve orgasm almost every time they had sex, with a further 43% achieving orgasm at least half of the time.[5]

However one chooses to interpret the statistics, it cannot be denied that the female orgasm was an important – and laudable – part of East German writing on sex. But this focus on female sexual pleasure tends

---

[3] Herzog, *Sex After Fascism*, pp. 212–213.
[4] E.g. Friedrich and Starke, *Liebe und Sexualität bis 30.*   [5] *Ibid.*, p. 186.

to conceal the fact that East German writers on sex were anything but permissive. *Mann und Frau Intim* is frequently held up as a best-selling example of positive and affirmative East German sexology. Yet, as early as the first page of the introduction, Schnabl writes:

Sexuality is by no means the most important thing in life. If it is allowed to grow uncontrollably, it will easily overwhelm the deeper content and meaning of our existence. But if it is too restricted or burdened with ideas of sinfulness, it will wither away, and we rob ourselves of many beautiful and even uplifting experiences.[6]

The metaphor is striking: like an unruly and vigorous plant, sexuality was something to be pruned, controlled, and tied back. Left to its own devices, it could and would run wild and smother other, more important aspects of life. The job of the responsible socialist citizen, guided by the paternalist sexologist, was akin to that of the assiduous gardener. Sex, and sexual feelings, had to be kept within certain boundaries, which were to be set by Schnabl and others like him. It is worth noting that *Mann und Frau Intim* had the somewhat forbidding – and revealing – subtitle: *Questions of Healthy and Disturbed Sex Life* (*Fragen des gesunden und des gestörten Geschlechtsleben*). This could not have been further from a libertarian approach: sex was about following particular guidelines and keeping within certain limits, rather than being an experimental free-for-all.

Before continuing with this discussion, it is worth saying a few words about the censorship process. All books published in the GDR had to be approved by the Ministry of Culture before they received permission to be printed. Publishers had to submit the book manuscript, plus an external report to the Department for Publishing and the Book Trade. In particularly sensitive cases, the department would commission its own reviews to make sure that a book did not contradict socialist norms. Censorship took place at all stages of this process: the ministry often demanded that certain changes were carried out before publication was allowed, but publishers had frequently insisted on an initial round of revisions before submitting the manuscript in the first place. And of course East German authors were well schooled in the art of self-censorship, using their 'inner scissors' to pre-emptively delete passages that might trouble official readers.[7]

---

[6] Siegfried Schnabl, *Mann und Frau Intim. Fragen des gesunden und des gestörten Geschlechtslebens* 5th edn (Berlin: VEB Verlag Volk und Gesundheit, 1972), p. 9.

[7] The classic work on East German censorship remains Simone Barck, Martina Langermann and Siegfried Lokatis (eds.), *'Jedes Buch ein Abenteeuer'. Zensur-System und literarische Öffentlichkeit in der DDR bis Ende der sechziger Jahre* (Berlin: Akademie Verlag, 1998).

It is tempting to blame the narrow-mindedness of some sexological texts on the state censorship. However, it would be a mistake to cast the censor(s) in an unrelentingly prohibitive and reactionary role. It is certainly true that the censorship process ensured that authors constantly related their findings and advice to the socialist project. But in some cases the censors actually expressed views that were more forward-thinking than the authors themselves. A report on Schnabl's *Mann und Frau Intim*, commissioned by his publisher, the Greifenverlag, chided Schnabl for presenting female sexuality 'as a male object'. The report's author objected to Schnabl's lascivious descriptions of 'charming' women, 'beautiful' breasts, 'delightful figures', and their effect on men. 'One look in the mirror will show many women that they do not possess such "assets", which may lead them to the conclusion that it is pointless to strive for a happy relationship', he warned.[8] Most striking is the report's criticism of Schnabl's suggestion that men naturally have a stronger sex drive, and that a 'truly loving' but less than 'hot-blooded' (*blutvoll*) woman may be happy to forgo her own sexual pleasure, and find sufficient satisfaction in surrendering (*Hingabe*) herself to her partner.[9] When the publishers eventually submitted the manuscript to the Ministry of Culture they were at pains to say that Schnabl had taken much of this criticism on board in a thorough revision of the manuscript.[10] So it seems that, rather than pioneering the importance of the female orgasm, Schnabl's reputation in this area was actually enhanced by the censorship process.

As Figures 4.1 and 4.2 demonstrate, the ways in which sex was discussed and portrayed changed markedly over time. Rudolf Neubert's *Das neue Ehebuch* (*The New Marriage Book*), published in 1957, provided a rather forbidding anatomical diagram of female erogenous zones (Figure 4.1). The *Encyclopedia of Young Marriage*, published in 1982, contained entries on 'group sex', 'love triangle', and 'sadism' (although, somewhat disappointingly, the authors did not endorse any of these activities),[11] and gave men precise instructions on how to find the clitoris and what to do when they got there.[12] An entry on sexual positions was illustrated by four photographs of a young couple having (or simulating) sex on a blanket in a field full of dandelion clocks (Figure 4.2).[13] In contrast to Neubert's diagram, this snapshot has a certain erotic charge, not least due to its slightly illicit and blurred quality. The medicalised

[8] BArch DR1/2242, pp. 499, 496–497, Prof. Dr med. habil. Misgeld, Gutachten, 20.1.1969.
[9] *Ibid.*, p. 492.   [10] *Ibid.*, p. 458, Verlagsgutachten.
[11] Aresin and Müller-Hegemann (eds.), *Jugendlexikon Junge Ehe*, pp. 75, 33, 128–129.
[12] *Ibid.*, p. 98.   [13] *Ibid.*, pp. 122–125.

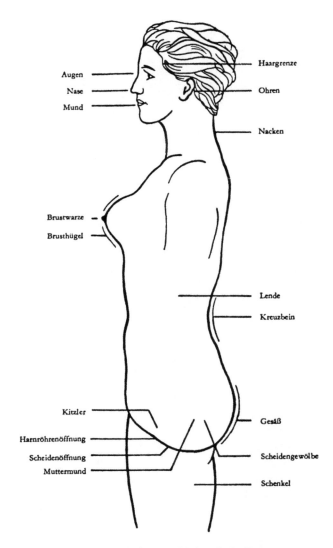

Abb. 76. *Schema der Reizbezirke der Frau*

Figure 4.1: Diagram of female erogenous zones, in Rudolf Neubert, *Das neue Ehebuch. Die Ehe als Aufgabe der Gegenwart und Zukunft* (Rudolstadt: Greifenverlag, 1957), p. 165.

Position

Position

Figure 4.2: Sexual positions pictured in Lykke Aresin and Annelies Müller-Hegemann (eds.), *Jugendlexikon Junge Ehe* (Leipzig: VEB Bibliographisches Institut, 5th edn, 1986), pp. 124–125.

prescriptive tone of the 1950s had been replaced by the suggestion of
a pastoral idyll, where marital sex is as much about pleasure as about
reproduction.

This new version of family life certainly looked quite different to
Neubert's. There was a good deal of common ground, however. Both
books saw sex as an important part of the emotional bond between husband and wife, and encouraged couples to create the right atmosphere
for love. In Neubert's case this involved an evening stroll through the
neighbourhood, rather than al fresco sex in a dandelion meadow, but
the intention was the same. There was also a shared emphasis on childbearing, with Neubert claiming 'life becomes fulfilled only with three
children. With four to six children it really starts to be varied, happy,
and fulfilled.'[14] By the 1980s, it would have been unrealistic to exhort
couples to have six children, but *Young Marriage* nevertheless implied
that bigger was better when it came to family size. While the authors
grudgingly conceded that 'each couple can decide freely when and how
many children they have', they warned that only children could be 'ego-
tistical' and missed out on interaction with siblings.[15]

The central tenet of both books, and of East German sexology more
generally, was that healthy sexuality was possible only in a loving relationship. Sex was an expression of love and intimacy, not something that
could be dabbled in for mere pleasure. The entry on 'abnormal' sex in
a 1974 sexological encyclopedia is particularly enlightening. Although
the authors began by claiming to be entirely without moral value judgement, it quickly became clear that their definition of 'abnormality' was
strongly linked to contemporary assumptions about sex and relationships. For the authors, 'abnormal' behaviour was anything which could
damage the 'inner harmony and quality of life' of those having sex.[16]
Love was seen as a vital prerequisite for 'normal' sex. 'The degree of
separation of sexuality and love is a straightforward indicator of the
perversion of sexuality ... we are therefore of the opinion that promiscuity itself can be counted as a perverse practice.'[17] It is telling that the
term for promiscuity (HwG – *Häufig wechselnder Geschlechtsverkehr* or
frequently changing partners) was widely used as a synonym for prostitution. All sex without love was seen as undesirable and perverse,
whether it was undertaken for pleasure or money.

[14] Rudolf Neubert, *Das neue Ehebuch. Die Ehe als Aufgabe der Gegenwart und Zukunft*
(Rudolstadt: Greifenverlag, 1957), pp. 270–271.
[15] Aresin and Müller-Hegemann (eds.), *Jugendlexikon Junge Ehe*, p. 42.
[16] Peter Hesse and Günter Tembrock (eds.), *Sexuologie*, vol. I (Leipzig: S. Hirzel Verlag,
1974), p. 415.
[17] *Ibid.*, pp. 427–428.

But it did not follow from this that sex with love was necessarily 'good' sex. East German sexology was preoccupied with penetrative sex. Oral sex or mutual masturbation was encouraged as a part of foreplay or as an occasional variation. Writers on sex were realistic about the fact that most women would need more than penetration alone in order to reach orgasm. Female pleasure was one of the tenets of East German sexology: but sex was still defined in terms of foreplay followed by coitus. Schnabl warned that men who preferred mutual masturbation to penetrative sex were often 'diffident' and suffered from potency problems, while women with such preferences were 'inhibited' and 'unable to surrender themselves'.[18]

Practices such as anal sex or sado-masochism were condemned whether they took place between loving and consenting partners or not. Anal sex was denounced as 'abnormal' and a 'symptom of a fixation or regression to the anal stage of libido development'.[19] Masturbation was regarded as normal during adolescence or at times when a partner was not available, as a form of physical release. It was certainly preferable, wrote Schnabl, to masturbate rather than have casual sex with somebody you did not love. Nevertheless, he added, 'it would certainly be wrong to encourage masturbation. Sexuality becomes meaningful only through the love of two people.'[20] To choose masturbation over sex with a loving partner was perverse. According to the sexological dictionary, women who chose to masturbate themselves to orgasm after sex were potentially 'neurotic', 'anorgasmic', or 'homosexual'.[21] This was not the only passage in which the authors fell back on gender stereotyping: aggression and roughness during sex were deemed acceptable, as they 'satisf[y] the needs of most women, who want to be taken or even conquered with a certain degree of vehemence'. Such gendered expectations of sex remained strictly within the parameters of masterful man and swooning woman. Sado-masochism, on the other hand, was judged to be 'psychopathological'.[22] Schnabl agreed: biting and scratching during sex was a normal part of sexual behaviour, but became unacceptable when aggressive and sadistic acts replaced coitus. Such behaviour could never lead to 'true happiness'.[23]

Even sexual fantasy came under the sexologists' lens. A man who achieved orgasm during sex by imagining exposing himself to a stranger was abnormal, because he was using his partner as a sexual substitute

[18] Schnabl, *Mann und Frau Intim*, p. 278.
[19] Hesse and Tembrock (eds.), *Sexuologie*, p. 419.
[20] Schnabl, *Mann und Frau Intim*, p. 286.
[21] Hesse and Tembrock (eds.), *Sexuologie*, p. 426.   [22] *Ibid.*, pp. 421–422.
[23] Schnabl, *Mann und Frau Intim*, pp. 302, 304.

and failing to 'create intimacy'. Confusingly, however, a woman who
fantasised about her ideal man while having sex with her husband was
not considered to be abnormal, as her fantasy centred on a 'normal
sexual object'.[24] This suggested that the real problem was not having a
sexual fantasy per se, but having a sexual fantasy that went beyond the
boundaries of the normal. Schnabl underlined this, suggesting it was
only acceptable to fantasise about a member of the opposite sex during masturbation. To think about 'a same-sex partner, a child, torture,
humiliation, a piece of underwear or any unusual practice' indicated
'beyond doubt' that one's 'sexuality found itself on a false path, which
did not lead to one's partner, but circled only around the self'.[25] Again,
there is a confusion here as to whether the true crime lies in forgetting
one's partner or in fantasising about 'abnormal' sexual objects. (Not to
mention the fact that the equation of homosexuality, paedophilia, sado-
masochism, and a lingerie fetish shows how restrictively 'normality'
was defined.) This logical slippage suggests a certain level of confusion
in the minds of the sexologists themselves: was their goal to promote
emotional intimacy or to proscribe certain kinds of 'damaging' behaviour – even if they took place only in the imagination? What is certain is
that 'good sex' was coitus in the context of a loving relationship.

It is difficult to know how far such ideals were subscribed to by the
population as a whole. Unsurprisingly, many did not allow the pro-
scriptions of sexologists to stand in the way of sexual experimentation.
Twelve per cent of students surveyed in 1990 said they had tried anal
sex, notwithstanding a complete lack of unbiased information on this
practice in even the most progressive sexual advice guides.[26] It is more
difficult to ascertain how seriously people took the link between love
and sex. Sex surveys were so skewed towards the connection between
love and sex that their findings must be treated with extreme caution.
Surveys began, as a matter of course, with questions about love. A
comprehensive study of sexual habits, carried out on students in 1972,
began by asking 'do you believe in love at first sight?', 'do you believe in
true love?', and 'have you ever written a love poem?'[27] Thus primed, 92
per cent agreed 'completely' or 'with certain reservations' when asked
whether it was necessary to feel a 'deep love' for one's sexual partner.[28]

---

[24] Hesse and Tembrock (eds.), *Sexuologie*, p. 418.
[25] Schnabl, *Mann und Frau Intim*, p. 289.
[26] ZA S6147: Partner III – Studenten 1990, p. 45.
[27] All questions in the 1972 study of students, ZA S6143: Partner I – Studenten 1972.
   Similar questions about 'true love' were asked in ZA S6145: Partner II 1979/80 and
   ZA S6142: Partner III – Berufstätige 1990.
[28] ZA S6143: Partner I – Studenten 1972, p. 69.

Small wonder that researchers were led to conclude that 'love belongs to the highest life values of young people'.[29] However, there is also evidence of widespread casual sex amongst the population.

There can be no doubt that monogamy was a widely shared social ideal, and that most people aspired to marriage or co-habitation. Inevitably, though, many East Germans enjoyed sex outside long-term monogamous relationships. Sexual experimentation was not an easy route to take, particularly given the practical barriers to privacy posed by state control of the housing market. As we have already seen, in the 1950s and 1960s the state was not afraid to exhort its citizens to live 'cleanly and decently', nor to imply that their private behaviour was not a matter for the couple or family in question alone. Private acts had public consequences, and individuals had to be aware of their societal responsibilities. A good relationship was considered not an end in itself, but a prerequisite for productive work, political engagement, and successful socialist childrearing.[30] A bad or inappropriate relationship was felt to have a negative effect not just on the couple themselves, but also on their families, colleagues, comrades, and, by extension, the future of socialism. If a worker was known to be acting in an 'immoral' way, his or her co-workers were encouraged to intervene to put him/her back on the right path.[31] Party members who were known to be unfaithful could be called before a 'party control commission' and charged with 'immoral and party-damaging' behaviour.[32]

The writer Brigitte Reimann is a compelling example of the risks of transgressing sexual and gender norms in the first two decades of East German socialism. Unlike many intellectuals who gravitated towards urban centres such as Berlin and Leipzig, Reimann's life was lived entirely in provincial small towns.[33] Married aged 20, Reimann remained near her family in the Magdeburg region for six years, until she divorced and swiftly married fellow writer Siegfried Pitschmann. In 1960, Pitschmann and Reimann moved to Hoyerswerda in Saxony, where she would live for the next eight years. At that time, Hoyerswerda

[29] Friedrich and Starke, *Liebe und Sexualität bis 30*, p. 14.
[30] Brock, 'The Making of the Socialist Personality'.
[31] See Port, 'Love, Lust, and Lies Under Communism', and Betts, *Within Walls*.
[32] Felix Mühlberg, 'Die Partei ist eifersüchtig', in Karin Rohnstock (ed.), *Erotik macht die Hässlichen schön. Sexueller Alltag im Osten* (Berlin: Elefanten Press, 1995), p. 143.
[33] On Reimann's life, see Heide Hampel, 'Reimann, Brigitte', *Neue Deutsche Biographie*, vol. XXI (Berlin: Duncker & Humblot, 2003), pp. 334–335; Ulrike Helwerth, 'Kann man in Hoyerswerda küssen? Die Schriftstellerin Brigitte Reimann (1933–1973)', in Franzisa Becker, Ina Merkel and Simone Tippach-Schneider (eds.), *Das Kollektiv bin ich. Utopie und Alltag in der DDR* (Cologne: Böhlau, 2000), pp. 26–55; Dorothea von Törne, *Brigitte Reimann. Einfach wirklich leben* (Berlin: Aufbau, 2001).

was in the process of rapid expansion from a small town into a 'socialist city', to support the giant lignite processing plant Schwarze Pumpe. As part of the 'Bitterfelder Way', which sought to break down the barriers between workers and the intelligentsia, Pitschmann and Reimann went to live in one of the new high-rise flats springing up in 'Hoy' and worked part-time in the factory as research for their writing.

Despite Reimann's initial optimism about a fresh start in Hoyerswerda, soon after her arrival she was to start an affair with the excavator driver and aspirant writer, Hans K, identified in her diaries only as 'Jon'. This extra-marital relationship was to overshadow her five-year marriage to Pitschmann and soon became the subject of factory gossip.[34] Reimann and Jon were called before party and trade union representatives to explain themselves.[35] Caught between her belief in socialism and the defence of her own emotions, Reimann at first struggled with this state interference in her private life: 'Granted, we are "people in public life", from whom society demands a clean way of life (but does this mean that love is unclean?), and despite rationality and [political] awareness, I cannot answer the question whether society really has the right to tear us apart.'[36]

Reimann proved to be more than capable of defending her choices. When party officials suggested a meeting of the local artists' collective to discuss her relationship with Jon, she agreed with alacrity, on one condition: that she be allowed to reveal the love affairs of everyone present. Her bluff worked and the functionaries backed down.[37] Cited in Jon's divorce case, Reimann found herself before a disapproving court, which contrasted her behaviour with the 'Socialist Commandments'. Not to be intimidated, she further shocked the citizen judges with her theory that socialism should abolish marriage altogether.[38] Despite this controversial stance, Reimann was in practice not averse to the institution of marriage. She went on to marry Jon after her divorce from Pitschmann in 1964. This relationship broke down in 1970 and, in 1971, she married for a fourth and final time to a local doctor.

Reimann chafed not only under the prudish strictures of provincial society, but also under the sexual double standard that existed even within the intelligentsia. As a young, striking woman, her physical appearance may have raised her profile, but it also made it difficult for her to be taken seriously as a writer and intellectual. She was furious when the head of the East German Writers' Union offered to introduce

[34] Brigitte Reimann, *Ich bedauere nichts. Tagebücher 1955–1963*, ed. Angela Drescher (Berlin: Aufbau, 2001), p. 233, Diary entry, 8.2.1962.
[35] *Ibid.*, p. 237, Diary entry 28.3.1962.   [36] *Ibid.*
[37] *Ibid.*, p. 313, Diary entry 6.4.1963.   [38] *Ibid.*, p. 242, Diary entry 1.7.1962.

her to First Secretary Walter Ulbricht, and added with a leer, 'But it's better if Lotte [Ulbricht's wife] isn't there.' 'I could have spat in his face', she wrote in her diary.[39] After an unhappy dalliance with the poet Günter Deicke, she reflected on the seeming impossibility of platonic intellectual friendships:

Why the devil was I born a woman? I am damned, just because of my sex, never to find a friend, because no man is capable of separating body and soul, because nobody understands that I want to be loved because of my intellect, my talent, or, to use that word again, my soul; because everybody expects that I will pay with sex for good conversations and the attention of an intelligent man. It makes me sick! Why is it made so hard for a woman to stay respectable![40]

Reimann's account of her first meeting with Deicke shows how sexually charged such encounters were and how Reimann herself was painfully aware of her sexual power: 'As soon as he spoke to me and looked at me, I knew that something would happen ... I can sense straight away if a man will be mine.'[41]

Reimann was the victim of restrictive gender norms that saw infidelity as a male privilege – but one which was not to be spoken of. By the 1970s and 1980s, however, such buttoned-up attitudes were becoming less prevalent. Marriage guides may still have emphasised the importance of monogamy, but glimpses of a more experimental and permissive model of sexuality were beginning to creep into even state-sponsored publications. An untitled photograph by Helga Paris, taken in 1984, was published in *Fotografie* (*Photography*) in 1989. In a scene which Reimann would hardly have recognised (and would most likely have disapproved of), two naked young women eat on an unmade double bed, duvets wrapped carelessly around them. A third naked figure leaves the room while two fully clad men join in the impromptu picnic. The books, paintings, and objets d'art scattered around the room suggest an intellectual milieu. This image hints at the sorts of bohemian subcultures that, against the odds, began to appear in the GDR in the 1970s and 1980s.[42]

As early as 1971, the GDR's chief public prosecutor (Generalstaatswalt) reported 'a rise in decadent ways of life: young people, particularly Beat fans, try to live in "extended families" or "communes"'.[43] Communes were set up in Erfurt, in Berlin, and in Kellnerstrasse in Halle, whose

[39] *Ibid.*, p. 247, Diary entry, 3.8.1962.   [40] *Ibid.*, p. 88, Diary entry 21.3.1958.
[41] *Ibid.*, p. 86, Diary entry, 4.3.1958.   [42] *Fotografie*, August 1989, p. 289.
[43] Quoted in Paul Kaiser and Claudia Petzold, *Boheme und Diktatur in der DDR. Gruppen, Konflikte, Quartiere, 1970–1989. Katalog zur Ausstellung des Deutschen Historischen Museums von 4. September bis 16. Dezember 1997* (Berlin: Fannei & Walz, 1997), p. 24.

members squatted in empty buildings to circumvent the difficulties posed by state control of the housing market.[44] Volker Petzold, a member of the Kellnerstrasse commune, remembered it as a time 'filled with work and parties, with flirtations and politics'.[45] The best-known and best-documented example of these experiments with communal living is the 'Kommune I Ost', whose name indicated their fellow feeling with those involved in setting up Kommune I and II in West Germany.[46] Erika Berthold, one of its founders, explained:

We really didn't want to play mother-father-child. We [she and her then partner Frank Havemann, who had one child] were friends with a married couple [Franziska and Gert Groszer] with two small children, who were in the throes of a marriage crisis. We often got together and thought about how we could escape this prison of marriage [*Eheknast*].[47]

Franziska Groszer concurs: 'We wanted to break out of marriage, not have to send our children to the [state-run] nurseries, and simply share everyday life.'[48] The couples and their children moved into a large flat in Samariterstrasse in Berlin-Friedrichshain. Like those involved in experiments with communal living in the West, the members of Kommune I Ost were interested in alternatives to the nuclear family, anti-authoritarian childrearing, and Eastern philosophy. 'We wanted to destroy the "bourgeois family"', remembers Frank Havemann.[49] Money was pooled, and decisions over larger purchases were made collectively. This was a practical and political community, rather than a romantic one. 'We all sought out erotic adventures, but independently from the commune', recalls Groszer.[50] But in its rejection of monogamy and the nuclear family, Kommune I Ost – and others like it – was a radical statement against the prevailing East German orthodoxy.

There can be no doubt that intellectuals, particularly in urban milieux, had more space in which to experiment. It is particularly notable that the members of Kommune I Ost were, in the main, children

---

[44] *Ibid.*, pp. 30–34.   [45] *Ibid.*, p. 236.
[46] Brown, '"1968" East and West', esp. 84ff.; Timothy S. Brown, 'East Germany', in Martin Klimke and Joachim Scharloth (eds.), *1968 in Europe: A History of Protest and Activism, 1956–1977* (London: Palgrave Macmillan, 2008), 193; Timothy S. Brown, 'A Tale of Two Communes: The Private and the Political in Divided Berlin, 1967–1973', in Martin Klimke, Jacco Pekelder and Joachim Scharloth (eds.), *Between Prague Spring and French May: Opposition and Revolt in Europe, 1960–1980* (Oxford and New York: Berghahn, 2011).
[47] Quoted Ute Kätzel, 'Kommune 1 Ost', *Der Freitag*, 20.12.2002, www.freitag.de/2002/52/02521701.php.
[48] Quoted in Christina Onnasch, 'Experiment "Kommune 1 Ost"', *Mitteldeutsche Zeitung*, 14.08.2008, www.mz-web.de/artikel?id=1217833454406.
[49] Quoted in Kaiser and Petzold, *Boheme und Diktatur*, p. 34.
[50] Quoted in Onnasch, 'Experiment "Kommune 1 Ost"'.

of the GDR's intelligentsia (Havemann's father was the dissident Robert Havemann, and Berthold's father was director of the Institute for Marxism-Leninism). It would, however, be over-hasty to conclude that only artists and writers enjoyed the freedom to step outside the boundaries of monogamy. As seen in the previous chapter, infidelity was a major factor in marriage breakdown, and statistical evidence suggests there was a growing trend towards infidelity in the 1970s and 1980s. In the early 1970s, 10% of students and 9% of young workers admitted to having had a sexual relationship with more than one person simultaneously.[51] By 1990, this had risen to 15% of apprentices, 31% of students, and 34% of young workers.[52] Infidelity was accepted by some in theory and by even more in practice. Amongst young workers, 18% said they would 'definitely' or 'probably' tolerate their partner's infidelity, and 25% said they would 'definitely' or 'probably' choose to be unfaithful themselves, were the opportunity to arise.[53] But even some of those who felt themselves unlikely to stray had succumbed in the past: 30% of those surveyed had been unfaithful during their current relationship.[54]

Kurt Starke, one of the key figures behind this study, explains these figures not in terms of sexual desire, but in terms of love and romance. He concludes that East German relationships were characterised by serial 'monogamy' accompanied by occasional infidelity. East Germans, according to Starke, had a 'romantic morality of love'. If a relationship did not meet their expectations of companionship and sexuality, they would either embark on a new one or seek fulfilment in an affair. According to Starke's interpretation, infidelity was not motivated by lust alone: 'anonymous sexual contacts were exceptional and were mostly rejected'.[55] However, the survey results themselves contest − or at least problematicise − this conclusion. Nine per cent of respondents admitted having had sex with a stranger, and 37 per cent − a significant percentage − said that they would have sex with somebody they did not know 'purely for pleasure'.[56] Amongst students, these figures rose even higher: 12 per cent had experienced sex with a stranger, and 43 per cent would be happy to.[57] These responses suggest that perhaps, in the small

---

[51] ZA S6143: Partner I − Studenten 1972, p. 73; ZA S6144: Partner I − Junge Arbeiter 1973, p. 58. In all cases, only sexually active respondents were asked this question.
[52] ZA S6146: Partner III − Lehrlinge 1990, p. 68; ZA S6147: Partner III − Studenten 1990, p. 69; ZA S6142: Partner III − Berufstätige 1990, p. 15.
[53] ZA S6142: Partner III − Berufstätige 1990, p. 55.   [54] *Ibid.*, p. 65.
[55] Kurt Starke, 'Die unzüchtige Legende vom prüden Osten', in Rohnstock (ed.), *Erotik macht die Hässlichen schön*, p. 174.
[56] ZA S6142: Partner III − Berufstätige 1990, pp. 44, 49.
[57] ZA S6147: Partner III − Studenten 1990, pp. 45, 50.

world of the GDR, people lacked not the desire for anonymous sex, but the opportunity.

The 'romantic morality of love' did not prevent some East Germans from indulging in casual sex with friends and acquaintances. A 20-year-old tractor driver interviewed by Gabriele Eckart in 1980 stated confidently: 'I'm very keen on married men. They've got experience, and let you have your freedom, I'm all for that. And the secrecy is the best bit.'[58] For others, the public nature of their infidelity may have added to its allure. Three interviewees brought up the subject of 'partner swapping' (without prompting from the interviewer): Herr L and Frau W both remembered 'swinging' taking place at work social events, while Frau T recalled that another couple had encouraged her and her husband to swap partners with them. While Herr L worked in Berlin, Frau W and Frau T lived in the provinces, suggesting that permissive sexual behaviour was not solely an urban phenomenon.[59] Nor was it necessarily more common amongst the intelligentsia. As early as 1973, 12% of sexually active young workers claimed to have experienced parties where partner swapping took place.[60] (The figure for students was 9%).[61] Herr D's interview also suggests that some working-class circles had a tolerant attitude towards promiscuity. He had vivid memories of the colourful sex lives enjoyed by his colleagues at both the state supermarket chain and a furniture factory. 'A quiet job, not much money, but lots of women, no AIDS, now and then a dose of the clap', he remembered with some satisfaction. For Herr D and his fellow workers, a trip to the sexual health clinic was a matter of routine: 'It was busy there! You met lots of your acquaintances. Sometimes half the supermarket was there.'

Statistics show that gonorrhoea infections fell in the 1960s, but doubled in the course of the 1970s, due in part to increased penicillin resistance, in part to widespread use of the Pill, and in part to liberalised sexual behaviour.[62] By 1980 approximately 50,000 cases were diagnosed each year. Only in the latter part of the 1980s did the epidemic begin to abate, due in large part to widespread condom use encouraged by anti-AIDS campaigns on West German television.[63] Sexually transmitted diseases were an everyday part of life. In 1990, 33% of those surveyed

---

[58] Eckart, *So sehe ick die Sache*, pp. 41–42.
[59] On partner-swapping parties, see also Horst's account *ibid.*, p. 96.
[60] ZA S6144: Partner I – Junge Arbeiter 1973, p. 58.
[61] ZA S6143: Partner I – Studenten 1972, p. 74.
[62] Erwin Günther, 'Geschlechtskrankheiten und AIDS in der DDR', in Joachim S. Hohmann (ed.), *Sexuologie in der DDR* (Berlin: Dietz: 1990), pp. 168–169. On STDs in the 1940s and 1950s, see Timm, *Politics of Fertility*, pp. 272–280.
[63] Günther, 'Geschlechtskrankheiten und AIDS in der DDR', p. 169.

Table 4.1: *Gonorrhoea infections per 100,000 population, East Germany, 1950–1989*

Year	Number of gonorrhoea infections per 100,000 population
1950	139
1955	211
1960	149
1967	108
1970	137
1975	233
1980	304
1985	298
1987	209
1989	135

Source: Erwin Günther, 'Geschlechtskrankheiten und AIDS in der DDR', in Joachim S. Hohmann (ed.), *Sexuologie in der DDR* (Berlin: Dietz: 1990), p. 165.

were 'somewhat' or 'very' concerned about STDs, and 5% admitted to having personally suffered from one.[64]

Sex and the state

It is not easy to know what the regime made of its citizens' behaviour. In practice, pragmatism had won out by the Honecker era, and moral interventions became a thing of the past. Official accounts tended to focus on the positives of socialist sexuality, and ignore or elide the facts that did not fit this narrative. The state's approach to sex was marked by an uneasy mixture of prudishness and pragmatism. For all their talk of building a new society, the SED leadership was profoundly socially conservative. The party leadership felt at home with the transformation of the public sphere, but the disruption of the private sphere made them deeply uncomfortable. Formal equality between men and women was as far as they were prepared to go. On the other hand, the SED and its organs were not above using sex for practical and political ends. In official discourse, healthy socialist sexuality was contrasted with West German and American sexuality, which was seen as profit-orientated and exploitative. According to this narrative, the West had replaced the link between sex and love – so important in the East – with an unhealthy and unnatural relationship between sex and money. Magazines and

[64] ZA S6142: Partner III – Berufstätige 1990, p. 91.

newspapers cited pin-ups, striptease, and prostitution as examples of the capitalist exploitation of women: contrasted, of course, with the equal rights enjoyed by women in the East. Throughout the Cold War, sexuality was seen to exemplify the chasm between capitalist brutality and socialist humanity.[65] A magazine article published in 1952 claimed that American magazines used nude photographs to distract their readers from the horrors of the war in Korea. This was 'the Strength Through Joy tradition in American portions', concluded the author, underlining not only East Germany's moral superiority to its Cold War rival, but its antifascist credentials too.[66]

A similar moral panic could be mobilised against dissenting voices within socialism too. At the infamous Eleventh Plenum of the Central Committee of the SED in 1965, delegates attacked novelists and filmmakers for their 'sex propaganda' and 'pornography', as well as for the influence of 'American amorality and decadence'.[67] Erich Honecker himself famously proclaimed from the podium: 'Our GDR is a clean state. Here there are immovable ethical and moral standards for decency and morality.' He went on: 'Our party is acting decisively against the imperialists' propaganda of immorality, which aims to damage socialism.'[68] The SED cast itself as the defender of the socialist family against a sexualised and commercialised Western offensive, which threatened to infect the East German public sphere with its unhealthy ideology.

There can be no doubt that some of the Central Committee's outrage was fuelled by genuine prudishness. Inge Lange, a former seamstress and Central Committee member, spoke of her disgust and disappointment when she realised that the TV film about land reform she had allowed her 15-year-old daughter to watch included sexual content: 'Dear comrades, if I had known the sort of disgusting bed scene that was to come, I would never have allowed her to watch it!'[69] It should be noted, however, that most of the filmmakers and writers who were the target of such virulent criticism were first and foremost political, not sexual, rebels. 'Pornography' was a useful smear, but the Eleventh Plenum was directed primarily against political criticism and artistic

---

[65] *Neue Berliner Illustrierte* 13/1952, 38.
[66] *Neue Berliner Illustrierte* 2/1952, 7. Strength Through Joy was the Third Reich's main leisure organisation.
[67] Günther Agde (ed.), *Kahlschlag. Das 11. Plenum des ZK der SED 1965. Studien und Dokumente* (Berlin: Aufbau, 2000), pp. 241, 22, 245, 242.
[68] Erich Honecker, 'Bericht des Politbüros an die 11. Tagung des Zentralkomitees der SED, 15–18.12.1965', in Agde (ed.), *Kahlschlag*, p. 241.
[69] Quoted in Wolfgang Engler, 'Strafgericht über die Moderne. Das 11. Plenum im historischen Rückblick', in Agde (ed.), *Kahlschlag*, p. 25.

autonomy. The SED's quarrel with the films banned at the plenum was not their occasional nude scenes – which were rarely sexual – but their unsparing view of life in East Germany, the autonomy and independence shown by the protagonists, and the modernist devices used to tell their stories.[70] Condemning films and books as 'pornographic' sent a clear message to the population that those who produced such material were decadent and unrepresentative of the working class.[71] The SED, like political parties everywhere, liked to place itself firmly on the side of the decent, hard-working man and woman. Invoking the spectre of pornography was a convenient way to achieve this.

The Western sexual revolution of the late 1960s and early 1970s – about which East Germans were kept well informed by the West German media – provided new ammunition for East German propagandists. They described developments in the West as a 'sex-wave' (sometimes 'sex-flood' or even 'sex-hurricane'), which commodified sex and nudity in order to sell magazines, newspapers, films, and books. 'Flooded' with sexual stimuli, the capitalist consumer became a 'slave to his urges'. The results: 'moral sell-out, brutality, loss of control and deformed emotions'.[72] Again, sex has been separated from love and intimacy, with disastrous results. In reality, comparable developments were taking place in the East too, as we shall see in the final chapter. But the perceived differences between Eastern and Western sexuality were too useful a propaganda tool to discard.

The uses of sex: prostitution

In other ways, however, the state's use of sex was both more direct and more unscrupulous. Behind closed doors, the state and its agencies were happy to use sex as a weapon. Nowhere was this clearer than in attitudes towards prostitution. Paragraph 249 of the 1968 penal code classified prostitution alongside 'unwillingness to work' (*Arbeitsscheu*) as 'asocial behaviour' which 'endangers social and public order'. It was thus

---

[70] *Ibid.*; Joshua Feinstein, *The Triumph of the Ordinary: Depictions of Daily Life in the East German Cinema, 1949–1989* (Chapel Hill: University of North Carolina Press, 2002), esp. chs. 5 and 6.

[71] See e.g. Michael Westdickenberg, '"Somit würde man die Darstellung abschwächen, daß dogmatisches Verhalten, Karrieristentum, Fehler im Justizapparat gesetzmäßig wären." Die Zensur von Prosaliteratur der DDR in den sechziger Jahren am Beispiel vom Manfred Bielers Roman *Das Kaninchen bin ich*', in Beate Müller (ed.), *Zensur im modernen deutschen Kulturraum* (Tübingen: Max Niemeyer Verlag, 2003), pp. 163–180.

[72] A. Jaritz, 'Die "Sex-Welle" oder Ausverkauf der Moral', *humanitas* 19 (1970), 6. See also Walter Hollitscher, *Der überanstrengte Sexus. Die sogenannte sexuelle Emanzipation im heutigen Kapitalismus* (Berlin: Akademie Verlag, 1975), p. 16.

punishable by up to two years in prison.[73] In practice, however, Herr L's assessment that 'prostitution was not forbidden and not allowed' nicely evokes the ambiguity surrounding this topic. In the 1950s, prostitution was perceived as first and foremost a public health problem. Prostitutes were seen as a source of venereal disease and were subject to frequent checks and controls. However, as sexually transmitted diseases became more easily treatable, attitudes towards prostitution relaxed – as long as it took place in relative discretion. Most prostitutes worked in bars, often attached to a hotel, while both Berlin and Leipzig had a well-known 'strip' for kerb crawlers. Leipzig's biannual business exhibition or *Messe* was a particular hotspot, as prostitutes congregated in the local hotels to cater for visitors to the city.[74]

The East German population were by no means unaware of the presence of prostitutes in their midst. The activities of 'easy girls' were even discussed in *Das Magazin*.[75] It is however, difficult to know just how far this knowledge went. Although several of our interviewees discussed the subject, it was hard to avoid the feeling that their memories had been coloured by retrospective revelations on television and in news magazines. Since German reunification, more or less sensationalist accounts of 'whores under Honecker' have stressed the use of prostitutes by foreign visitors to East Germany, in particular the 'bussing in' of prostitutes to the Leipzig exhibition.[76] Interviewees tended to mention these aspects of the East German prostitution scene above all else. Frau M alluded to women being 'assigned' to Leipzig to service 'people from over there' (*die von drüben*), and both Herr B and Herr E discussed a bordello in Rostock that was open to visiting sailors.[77] Herr and Frau W's exchange is an interesting example of how East Germans' own use of prostitutes could be effaced:

HERR W: Bordellos were not an issue, they were not allowed. One knew that in Leipzig, at the Leipzig exhibition, that sort of thing was necessary, and that it existed, but not for Eastern money!
INTERVIEWER: But not up here? [*In Schwerin*]
HERR W: Up here, not at all.
FRAU W: But I think there were certain addresses …
HERR W: There were probably certain ladies –

[73] Strafgesetzbuch der Deutschen Demokratischen Republik, 12 January 1968. www.verfassungen.de/de/ddr/strafgesetzbuch68.htm.
[74] Falck, *VEB Bordell*.
[75] 'Sterben die "leichten Mädchen" aus?', *Das Magazin*, April 1955, 60–63.
[76] For one particularly titillating example, see 'Stasi mit Sex und Peitschen', *Focus* 11 (2002), www.focus.de/politik/deutschland/stasi-mit-sex-und-peitschen_aid_203726.html.
[77] Cf. Falck, *VEB Bordell*, pp. 153–161.

FRAU W: – but we didn't know about them.
HERR W: – who sold themselves, but you would have had to have a bit more money in your wallet, and show a bit of a specialised interest. The normal consumer had no chance there, I think. It wasn't an issue.

At the start of this extract, prostitution is something that takes place only in Leipzig and is taken advantage of only by foreigners. Frau W intervenes to remind her husband that prostitutes did operate locally, but adds comfortingly 'but we didn't know about them'. Herr W shuts down the topic by stating that they were in any case inaccessible to the normal citizen and returns to his opening statement that prostitution was 'not an issue'. By asserting that prostitutes were used only by foreigners or the upper echelons of society, interviewees could preserve their sense of a unique East German sexual culture, free from the commercialisation and commodification of the West.

Despite these protestations, there is ample evidence that some prostitutes drew their clientele chiefly from East German men. Herr B recalled a flat in Greifswald which was widely known to be a bordello, and Herr S remembered a similar arrangement in Berlin-Lichtenberg, used by some of the soldiers in his battalion: 'It was a secret address. Somebody was making a bit of extra cash ... You went there, there was a door and a bell and a name and a code or something like that, there wasn't a sign or anything.' Herr S himself found the idea 'disgusting', but estimated that around 50 per cent of his colleagues took up the opportunity, enough for their superior officers to insist that all soldiers carried a condom while away from barracks. Such arrangements were by no means confined to large cities. One of Maxie Wander's interviewees told her matter-of-factly, 'my brothers went to the whore in the village'.[78] It is true that many prostitutes chose to specialise in clients from abroad who could pay in hard currency. But those with no access to this market could and did turn their attention to domestic consumers.

Sex and the Stasi

What Uta Falck has described as the 'marriage of convenience' between prostitution and the Stasi is perhaps the best illustration of how pragmatic the state's approach to sexuality could be. The Stasi made enthusiastic use of prostitutes as informers ('unofficial colleagues' or IMs in Stasi parlance), particularly those who had contact with Western visitors. Women were persuaded to work for the Stasi as an additional

---

[78] Wander, *Guten Morgen, Du Schöne*, p. 155.

source of income, in rarer cases out of loyalty to the state, and, in the worst-case scenario, through blackmail and intimidation.[79] The recruitment of 'IM Marlon Forster' in September 1962 was a particularly sordid affair.[80] 'Forster' was an orphan and only child, who had grown up in foster care. Since leaving school, she had worked in a series of manual jobs, most recently on the railways. Completely without family or friends, single and childless, 'Forster' lived on the margins of Leipzig society, renting a furnished room with no heating. Perhaps in a bid to escape these chilly conditions, she had taken to spending most nights in local bars. In this way, she had fallen in with a group of local prostitutes and may even have begun to work as a prostitute herself before her recruitment by the Stasi.

Despite her reduced circumstances, 'Forster''s Stasi file describes her as intelligent and 'highly talented at writing'. She was also 'lively, friendly, and co-operative' and comfortable in any social situation.[81] Where some might have seen a bright young woman down on her luck, the Stasi saw a useful source of information on Leipzig's underworld, ripe for exploitation. Branding her as promiscuous, and noticing that she had posed for nude photographs, an agent arranged to meet 'Forster' and confronted her with compromising nude photographs. She immediately agreed to co-operate, vowing that 'she would do anything to make sure that this matter was forgotten'.[82] She immediately began to tell her new masters about the workings of the Leipzig scene, explaining that most of the prostitutes' clients were 'functionaries of our state apparatus, party comrades and the like'. She added that the bar where the prostitutes assembled was also a favoured meeting place for homosexuals, mostly theology students and 'women in lespigan [sic] [*lespigen*] relationships'.[83] 'Forster' may have hoped that her openness with her Stasi handlers would extirpate the nude photographs of her past. In fact, her work as an informer served to trap her in prostitution. By 1969 she was reporting in a matter-of-fact way that she had posed for nude photographs for an illustrator of her acquaintance and then had had sex with him.[84] She continued to inform for the next thirteen years, until she was no longer able to make a living from prostitution and the Stasi let her go.[85]

The Stasi also encouraged its own operatives to use sex as a weapon in the Cold War battle.[86] At least three dozen West German women – mostly

[79] Falck, *VEB Bordell*, p. 113.
[80] The following is based on Bundesbeauftragte für die Unterlagen des Staatssicherheitsdienstes der ehemaligen Deutschen Demokratischen Republik (henceforth BStU), MfS, ASt. Leipzig, 618/75, Bd I.
[81] *Ibid.*, p. 19.   [82] *Ibid.*, p. 22.
[83] *Ibid.*   [84] *Ibid.*, Bd Ia, p. 102.   [85] *Ibid.*, Bd I, p. 54.
[86] See especially Falck, *VEB Bordell*, pp. 108–113.

secretaries in government departments – were recruited as informers, having been seduced by 'Romeo' Stasi operatives.[87] Markus Wolf, head of the Stasi's foreign intelligence, wrote jovially in his post-1989 memoirs, 'if I go down in espionage history, it may well be for perfecting the use of sex in spying'.[88] Wolf depicts female West German informers as lonely secretaries, glad of male attention, and happy to help East German intelligence for the sake of their relationships. He elides the emotional consequences: some women found their lovers vanished overnight, and others were arrested and imprisoned when the West German authorities discovered their activities. Despite their service to the East German state, these women were often deceived and lied to: in one case, Wolf arranged a 'Potemkin wedding' at the Stasi headquarters in Berlin, making sure the entry in the marriage register was destroyed afterwards. A few years later, the female agent was arrested and sentenced to four years in prison. To add insult to injury, she suffered the humiliation of discovering her marriage was invalid. Wolf shrugs off such deceptions:

As for the moral side of things, I am often asked today whether I felt guilt or shame about such machinations. On the whole, the honest answer would be no. In retrospect, some things did get out of hand, but at the time we believed that the end justified the means.[89]

Given the regime's criticism of the West, and its loudly trumpeted commitment to female equality, the Stasi's use of prostitutes and sex was hypocrisy of the highest order. It is hard to avoid the conclusion that prostitutes were seen as lesser beings, fit only for exploitation for higher ends. Equally, for all Wolf's self-exculpation, the Stasi's 'Romeos' sought to manipulate love and emotion to the state's ends.[90] The photographs of people having sex which are to be found in the archives of the secret police epitomise this absolute disregard for personal dignity.[91]

This lack of respect for the individual's private sphere also extended to critics of the regime. The Stasi was prepared not only to put relationships under surveillance, but also to interfere in them directly. As part of a policy of *Zersetzung*, or disruption, the Stasi increasingly attempted to sabotage the work of those who were critical of the SED. Sex was a useful weapon in this war of attrition. 'IM Micha', a 24-year-old

---

[87] Elizabeth Pfister, *Unternehmen Romeo. Die Liebeskommandos der Stasi* (Berlin: Aufbau Verlag, 1999), p. 131.
[88] Markus Wolf (with Anne McElvoy), *Man Without a Face: The Autobiography of Communism's Greatest Spymaster* (London: Jonathan Cape, 1997), p. 123.
[89] *Ibid.*, p. 138.   [90] *Ibid.*, p. 150.   [91] BStU, MfS, HA II/FO/143.

employee of the Protestant Church, was encouraged by the Stasi to hold 'sex parties' for senior church figures. By confronting these men with incriminating evidence, the Stasi hoped to blackmail them into informing on their colleagues.[92] Dissidents Gerd and Ulrike Poppe were the subject of sustained attempts to destroy their marriage in the late 1980s. Learning that Ulrike was thinking of leaving her husband, the Stasi instructed a male informer to invite her out to concerts and the theatre, in the hope that an extra-marital affair would seal the Poppes' fate. Simultaneously, Gerd was to be undermined at work, and the Poppes' children were to be turned against them with the help of further informers.[93]

Vera Wollenberger, an activist in the church-based opposition of the 1980s, discovered in 1991 that Knud, her husband, and father of two of her children, had been a Stasi informer throughout their marriage.[94] Known to the Stasi as 'IM Donald', Knud had reported extensively on the work of the peace group both Wollenbergers were involved with. As a result of her political activity, Wollenberger had been thrown out of the party, lost her job, and eventually forced to emigrate to England. Throughout this period, 'Knud–Donald', as she calls him in her memoir, continued to inform the Stasi about her health, discussions with her son, and spending habits, as well as intercepting her letters.[95] 'How does that work?' she asked herself after 'Knud–Donald' was exposed, 'that somebody is such a loving father and then writes reports like that? How can a person do that? I just don't understand it.'[96] As she later wrote, the experience of betrayal was 'indescribable', one that she would not wish on her 'worst enemies'. 'I would have rather sat in a Stasi jail for years than to have had to go through that.'[97]

Recruiting 'Knud–Donald' to infiltrate his own marriage was not the only tactic used to destabilise Wollenberger's peace group. As well as concerted efforts to disrupt the group's political activities, the Stasi also succeeded in destroying the friendly, family-centred atmosphere which was so important to the group's morale. Female informers were deployed in an attempt to break up marriages, and snapshots of the group swimming in the nude were used to smear Pastor Markus

---

[92] 'Sex-Partys bei Micha. Wie die Stasi die DDR-Kirchenzentrale ausforschte', *Der Spiegel* 21.9.1992, 31–32.
[93] ' "Ziel: Ein Intimverhältnis". Der Maßnahmeplan der Stasi gegen das Ehepaar Gerd und Ulrike Poppe', *Der Spiegel* 13.1.1992, 30.
[94] She has since reverted to her maiden name and is now known as Vera Lengsfeld.
[95] Wollenberger, *Virus der Heuchler*, p. 51.
[96] Jürgen Leinemann, 'Sie hat nichts merken können', *Der Spiegel*, 13.1.1992, 35.
[97] Wollenberger, *Virus der Heuchler*, p. 155.

Meckel.[98] The Stasi even planned to forge incriminating photographs in order to sow rumours about 'free love' within the group.[99] The most successful strategy was to spread rumours that one or other of the members was an informant, thereby fatally undermining the group's sense of trust. 'As everybody began to suspect everybody else', Wollenberger noted, 'it was the beginning of the end.'[100]

Wollenberger paints a vivid picture of how the secret police were able to destroy people's personal happiness as well as undermining their attempts to criticise the regime. The relationship between the singer-songwriter Wolf Biermann and the actress Eva-Marie Hagen is a case in point. When they met, Biermann was already a leading figure in oppositional and artistic circles, and a close friend of the dissident Robert Havemann. Hagen was better known as a regime sweetheart and star of musicals and romantic comedies. She and Biermann began a relationship in 1965, shortly before Biermann was publicly condemned for his criticism of the regime and banned from performing in public.[101] Over the next seven years, they pursued a passionate, tumultuous, unconventional, and at times 'open' relationship. Hagen and Biermann were in many ways emblematic of East German artistic bohemia and its attempts to escape conventional patterns of life and work. As Hagen reflected in her diary in 1971: 'At least one is spared standing at the assembly line, a bourgeois marriage, or – at the other extreme – going on the game.'[102] Even when they were no longer lovers, they remained intimately involved in each other's lives: when Biermann was permanently banished to West Germany in 1976, Hagen took it upon herself to look after his new girlfriend and baby until they were all able to move to the West.

In 1998, Hagen published a collection of their letters, her diary entries, and extracts from her Stasi file. It is a fascinating glimpse into the personal impact of state persecution. As a result of her association with Biermann, Hagen lost her role as one of the GDR's leading actresses, and was reduced to long runs in provincial theatres. This enforced separation, as well as their professional frustrations, put all their personal relationships under severe strain. Hagen's ex-husband sent comprehensive reports to the Stasi, and passed on letters between his daughter Nina and Biermann. Worst of all was the sense of being

---

[98] *Ibid.*, pp. 36, 34. Meckel was later to become a Social Democratic parliamentarian in reunified Germany.
[99] *Ibid.*, p. 33.   [100] *Ibid.*, p. 58.
[101] Biermann's work was condemned for, among other things, having 'strongly pornographic characteristics': Honecker, 'Bericht des Politbüros', p. 245.
[102] Eva-Marie Hagen, *Eva und der Wolf* (Düsseldorf: Econ, 1998), p. 389.

constantly under surveillance and their awareness that all their letters and phone calls were being monitored. At times, they attempted to make fun of their watchers. Hagen broke off a letter to Biermann to address the Stasi directly:

Nose-sticker-inner must be a boring career. Whoever is in charge of overseeing Wolf Biermann's letters and contacts from all over the world must have steam coming out of his ears ... And my declarations of love – what brazenness. Where is the line between public order and pornography? You dung beetle! I hope a bolt of lightning strikes your optic nerve, that you get a truncheon in the base of your spine while you are peeping under our bedcovers, you enslaved soul.[103]

The abrupt transition from jokiness to anger in Hagen's intervention makes clear the psychological strain they were under. As Biermann put it in March 1970: 'Spying causes the most damage in an area where it originally had no interest at all: love.'[104] He was only half-right: the damage caused by deliberate state interference in relationships became clear only after the collapse of the East German state.

Falling in love with a foreigner

Dissidents were not the only people whose relationships could be damaged or even terminated by the state, as bi-national couples discovered to their cost. East Germany liked to present itself as a beacon of socialist internationalism and, by 1989, a total of 190,000 foreigners made up 1.2% of the East German population. While some had lived in the GDR for many years, over 50% were contract workers or foreign students, visiting on a temporary basis, either to gain a qualification or work experience or as contract labour in East German industry.[105] Most of these students and workers were young and single. Many – although not all – were young men. (A significant proportion of Vietnamese workers, for example, were female.) They may have come to East Germany to work or study, but their contact with the East German population went well beyond the workplace or lecture hall. Despite the fact that foreigners often lived in separate accommodation, experienced linguistic and cultural difficulties, and faced considerable racism from sections of the East German population, relationships between foreigners and East Germans were common.[106] Surveyed in the early 1970s, 17% of students and 19% of young workers said they had had a relationship

---

[103] *Ibid.*, p. 133.   [104] *Ibid.*, p. 225.
[105] Damian Mac Con Uladh, 'Guests of the Socialist Nation? Foreign Students and Workers in the GDR, 1949–1990', unpublished Ph.D. thesis, University College London (2005), p. 8.
[106] Mac Con Uladh, 'Guests of the Socialist Nation?', ch. 6.

or relationships with foreign citizens. Most of these relationships were with Europeans, but 5% of students had had relationships with non-Europeans. (The figure for workers was only 2%, presumably because at this point in time they had had fewer opportunities to meet non-Europeans. Foreign labour was used in significant amounts only in the 1970s and 1980s.)[107]

There were many reasons for East Germans and foreigners to fall in love, most of them nothing to do with nationality. Nevertheless, the fact that East Germans had limited travel opportunities gave even the closest of neighbours an exotic allure. Frau F, who had several relationships with West German men, explained: 'There was a lot of curiosity at work. And the chance to have a fancy night out and be treated for once. The chance to look over the fence for a bit.' Of course, students and contract workers had nothing like the spending power of West German business travellers. But a similar sense of novelty and excitement may have played a role.

Despite the fact that these relationships were often as committed as any between East Germans, human emotions were frequently trumped by economic and political concerns. Unlike their contemporaries, couples in which one partner was foreign had to apply to the state authorities for permission to marry.[108] In some cases, these applications were motivated by the classic East German pattern of early marriage and family formation. In others, marriage was a means of making a relationship permanent and keeping both partners in the same country. Such permission was difficult to obtain. Foreign workers and students were seen as temporary guests of the GDR. Marriage would have meant either that the foreign worker would have had to remain in East Germany or that his wife would have had to leave the GDR for good. (In most cases, the foreign worker was male.) The state authorities saw both solutions as undesirable. In fact, East German law made it extremely difficult for a woman to take her husband's nationality upon marriage.[109] The fact that many couples applied for permission to marry at the point when the foreign partner's visa was about to expire made it easy for the authorities to dismiss such cases as 'sham marriages', designed to keep the foreign partner in the country or to give the East German partner an escape route from the GDR.

No doubt such marriages of convenience did exist. But the correspondence relating to appeals against the refusal to grant permission

[107] ZA S6143: Partner I – Studenten 1972, p. 72; S6144: Partner I – Junge Arbeiter 1973, p. 58.
[108] *Familiengesetzbuch der Deutschen Demokratischen Republik.*
[109] Mac Con Uladh, 'Guests of the Socialist Nation?', p. 158.

to marry certainly gives the impression that the majority were genuine and that the consequences of enforced separation were dreadful. Cases in Brandenburg in the mid 1970s involved men from Algeria, Austria, Belgium, Colombia, Costa Rica, Denmark, Greece, Italy, Iran, Mali, Syria, West Germany, and Yugoslavia.[110] In many cases, the East German applicant already had a child with her intended husband. In several instances, female medical students had fallen in love with a foreign colleague: a particular problem because of the training costs that would be wasted were newly qualified East German doctors to move abroad. Socialist internationalism had its limits, and they were often financial. The GDR was not unique in this regard: Vietnamese contract workers who wished to marry and remain in East Germany were expected to repay the cost of their stay to the Vietnamese state – at least 8,000 marks.[111]

Despite the many obstacles, it was not unknown for permission to marry to be granted. Ingrid K was 20 when she met James G, a 20-year-old forestry student from New Jersey, at the World Festival Games in Berlin in 1973. Unlike many of the fleeting relationships of the festival, Ingrid and James remained in touch, and in the summer of 1974 he visited her for four weeks. During this visit, they got engaged, and Ingrid applied for permission to marry and leave the country.[112] She wrote: 'It is very hard for me to want to leave here [East Germany]. I've been living here for 21 years, and was brought up here. My father is in the party, and my mother is a trade union steward ... Therefore the reasons that I want to leave the country are exclusively personal ones.'[113] Ingrid's strategy of stressing her family's loyalty to the East German state, and her persistence in applying for permission to leave the country five times in 18 months, paid off. The authorities eventually recommended that she be allowed to marry and move to the USA.[114]

Other families were not so lucky. Pierre P came to East Germany from Upper Volta (known today as Burkina Faso) as a 26-year-old apprentice mechanic in 1968. The photograph in his file shows a handsome, frowning man with a receding hairline and a moustache.[115] Within a few months he had settled in well, barring a few problems adjusting to the

---

[110] BLHA, Rep 401, Nr 14486, Eheschliessungen mit Ausländern, 1975–1978.
[111] Mike Dennis, 'Die vietnamesischen Vertragsarbeiter und Vertragsarbeiterinnen in der DDR', in Karin Weiss and Mike Dennis (eds.), *Erfolg in der Nische? Die Vietnamesen in der DDR und in Ostdeutschland* (Münster: Lit Verlag, 2005), p. 38.
[112] BLHA, Rep. 401, Nr 14486, letter from Ingrid K to Abteilung Inneres Potsdam, 21.1.1975.
[113] *Ibid.*
[114] BLHA, Rep. 401, Nr 14486, Schachtschneider to Wenzel, 14.1.1975.
[115] His case is documented in SAPMO-BArch DY34/10550.

cold of the East German winter, and was already speaking good German. Having qualified, he began an evening course to become a master mechanic. Pierre seems in many ways to have been a model 'guest worker', keen to better himself and to integrate into East German society. He was to discover, however, that the desire for such integration would not be reciprocated. In 1973 he wrote to the national trade union:

> Since I got to know and fell in love with an East German citizen, and she became pregnant, I have been determined to fulfil my moral obligations to the child – who has since been born – and her mother ... It is unthinkable for me to have to return to my homeland without marrying and bringing my wife and child with me. I can't avoid the impression that there is considerable variation in decisions about marriages between East German citizens and citizens from developing countries, which I cannot find any explanation for ... I am a human being and have feelings ... if I have to leave behind what is dear and precious to me, my heart would break.[116]

His pleas fell on deaf ears, and he was forced to return to Upper Volta. Five months later, after a bout of yellow fever, he wrote from Ouagadougou that he had found work and was building a house, but that the separation from his 'wife' and daughter would 'destroy his life'. 'I would fight to the death for them', he wrote. 'You are a father too, what father is separated from his child?? ... I beg of you, it is not political, only humane. I am sure that you will do something.'[117] This impassioned appeal also went unacknowledged. The trade union replied in the most impersonal of terms, congratulating Pierre on his new job and admonishing him for turning down a promotion. No mention was made of his daughter, her mother, or a possible return to the GDR.[118]

As Pierre had deduced, there was little consistency of decision making in such cases. Much was left to the whim of local functionaries, who were as prone as the rest of the population to the sort of racism that associated foreignness (and especially blackness) with sexual threat.[119] Frau N, growing up near Dresden in the 1960s, was told repeatedly by her mother: 'For God's sake, don't bring any Negroes home!' ' "Negro"

[116] *Ibid.*, Pierre P to Freier Deutscher Gewerkschaftsbund (Free German Trade Union Federation, FDGB), 17.12.1973.
[117] *Ibid.*, Pierre P to Peuker, 9.5.1974.   [118] *Ibid.*, Selbmann to Pierre P, 1.6.1974.
[119] On perceptions of African contract workers as sexually forward, see Annegret Schüle, ' "Die ham se sozusagen aus dem Busch geholt". Die Wahrnehmung der Vertragsarbeitskräfte aus Schwarzafrika und Vietnam durch Deutsche im VEB Leipziger Baumwollspinnerei', in Jan Behrends, Thomas Lindenberger and Patrice Poutrus (eds.), *Fremde und Fremdsein in der DDR. Zu historischen Ursachen der Fremdenfeindlichkeit in Ostdeutschland* (Berlin: Metropol Verlag, 2003), pp. 309–324, esp. pp. 313–314. On xenophobia, see Jonathan Zatlin, 'Scarcity and Resentment: Economic Sources of Xenophobia in the GDR, 1971–1989', *Central European History* 40 (2007), 683–720.

was the worst thing that could happen in this little village, an absolute catastrophe', she remembered, reflecting that her mother's warnings had instilled in her a 'primal fear' of black people which persisted to the present day. As Damian Mac Con Uladh points out, there was also a sexist aspect to many people's attitudes towards bi-national relationships, which cast the East German woman as a hapless victim of foreign sexuality.[120]

This was not the only way in which racism and sexism intersected to undermine women's autonomy and independence. The fertility of female contract workers was also placed under state control. From 1980, all non-European workers who became pregnant were to be deported to their home countries.[121] Each year, around 1% of Vietnamese women workers returned home because of pregnancy.[122] Those who did not wish to leave East Germany, or who feared the consequences if they returned home pregnant and unmarried, were left with few options. Many tried to conceal their pregnancies as long as possible, to obtain a legal abortion, or to end the pregnancy themselves. Doctors found themselves in a difficult position, as the abortion law allowed abortions to be carried out on foreigners only in life-threatening cases. The medical officer for Brandenburg reported in 1983 that foreign women, particularly Vietnamese contract workers, were requesting abortions in increasing numbers, and threatening suicide 'as a matter of routine' if they were refused.[123] As a result of such pressures, an agreement was reached in 1987 that all Vietnamese women who became pregnant were to be offered a choice between abortion and deportation.[124] This was a shocking contrast to the GDR's usual pro-natalism: the maternal urge and the right to combine work and family life considered so fundamental for East German women was utterly disregarded when it came to their Vietnamese colleagues. But even this unappealing choice was not extended to all national groups.

In 1988 doctors in Rathenow in the Havelland informed the local authorities of two cases involving workers from Mozambique, both in their very early twenties. Both women were more than three months' pregnant and had tried to end their pregnancies using a refill for a ball-point pen, suggesting that this method was well known in their circles.[125]

[120] Mac Con Uladh, 'Guests of the Socialist Nation?', p. 172.   [121] *Ibid.*, p. 179.
[122] Dennis, 'Die vietnamesischen Vertragsarbeiter und Vertragsarbeiterinnen in der DDR', p. 39.
[123] BLHA, Rep. 401, Nr 31571, Müller, Bezirksarzt, Abt. Gesundheits- und Sozialwesen, an Min.f. Gesundheit, HA Med. Betreuung, Sektor Mutter und Kind, Genn. Dr Rayner, 3.8.1983.
[124] Mac Con Uladh, 'Guests of the Socialist Nation?', p. 179.
[125] BLHA, Rep. 410, Nr 31571, Wolf an Machan, 8.8.1988.

The medical officer for the area reported that a further four women from Mozambique were pregnant and expressed concerns that further attempts at abortion might follow.[126] The state authorities responded that legal abortions were available only with permission in writing from the Mozambique embassy.[127] They reported that experience in Magdeburg showed that persuading women to go on the Pill, and ensuring that they received ample social support, was the only way to reduce the number of pregnancies. It was also suggested that abortions could be justified on medical grounds if need be.[128] What is particularly striking is that the support extended to East German single mothers was not even considered for foreign workers. This racial aspect of East German sexual and family policy is too consistent to be ignored.

The discrimination that foreigners and those who loved them faced could take a profound personal toll. Mac Con Uladh reports the case of a 23-year-old contract worker from Mozambique who, facing the end of his contract and separation from his pregnant girlfriend, committed suicide. His girlfriend wrote to the representative of the Mozambique workers:

Both governments, ours and yours, must think hard in the future about the fact that if young people come to work here, there will also be love between people. Whether they are black or white. Why can't we just live together? X [her boyfriend] is a victim of these government measures. I will do everything to make sure that his mother finds out the truth, so that she knows who murdered her son.[129]

Conclusion

As with many other areas of life in the GDR, representatives of the socialist state were happy to hand down advice on sexuality and relationships. Some of this advice came with the best of motives and a concern for people's quality of life. Nevertheless, it also had the effect of setting strict notional limits on heterosexual behaviour. The East German sexual revolution was based on the premise that sex and love were inextricably linked, and that this was the distinguishing feature of socialist sexuality. However, there is ample evidence that this was not the case for all. Sex outside marriage had always taken place, of course, and by the 1970s and 1980s relaxed social norms meant that

[126] *Ibid.*, Machan an Wittig, 9.8.1988.
[127] *Ibid.*, handwritten notes, dated 11.8.1988.
[128] *Ibid.*, handwritten notes, dated 24.8.1988.
[129] Cited in Damian Mac Con Uladh, 'Alltagserfahrungen ausländischer Vertragsarbeiter in der DDR', in Weiss and Dennis (eds.), *Erfolg in der Nische*, p. 65.

more people were free to experiment. Their appetite for sex outside loving relationships, and their willingness to experiment with non-reproductive sex, complicates the frequently expressed view that, when it came to East German relationships, love really did conquer all.

Even more damaging for the 'romantic' view of East German sexuality, however, is the willingness of the regime to ignore the hallowed link between sex and love for pragmatic ends. Sexual autonomy was only for favoured citizens: an unfortunate minority faced severe state intervention in their private lives. In these cases, the state did not respect love at all and sometimes actively encouraged sex without love. The circumstances of such cases were often very different. Foreigners and their lovers deliberately called upon the archetypes of socialist family life, while some dissidents, such as Wollenberger, stressed the happiness and stability of relationships within church circles. Reimann, Hagen, and Biermann, on the other hand, consciously challenged monogamy. Prostitutes were sometimes motivated by money; in other cases circumstance played a big role. What united them all was their placement outside the sexual norm by the hypocrisy of the state. Party leaders were happy to prescribe moral standards and to claim that East Germany was a world leader in matters of the heart and the bedroom. But there was also a widespread willingness to compromise these principles if political necessity or expediency willed it. Intimate relationships could be used as a selling point for socialism, but they could also be used to exclude, to intrude, and to divide and rule in the 'dictatorship of love'.

5   Gay men, lesbians, and the struggle for the public sphere

If the heterosexual attitudes discussed in the previous chapter under-mine the narrative of East German sexual tolerance, the experiences of gay men and lesbians go still further, questioning commonly held assumptions about the solidarity and friendliness of life in the GDR. Writing in the year 2000, Olaf Brühl, a gay man who had grown up in East Germany, stated bitterly:

> my friends and i felt precious little of the much-heralded cosiness and neigh-bourliness of our *village*, the GDR. gays were gutless and their families were intolerant. the first duty of the citizen was to be *inconspicuous*.[1]

The story of East German homosexuality is one of failed liberalisa-tion at the level of both state and society. Although same-sex activ-ity between adults over the age of 18 was decriminalised in 1968, this purely legal measure proved to be sorely inadequate. Gay men (lesbian activity had been invisible in the eyes of the law) had won the right to have sex in private, but faced sometimes insurmountable difficulties in meeting potential partners, finding suitable living space, building a social life, and coming out to family and friends. East German society, with its stress on long-term heterosexual relationships and family life, was profoundly heteronormative. In this, of course, it was not unique. For centuries, gay men and lesbians across Europe had been invisible at best, subjects of lethal persecution at worst. The 1950s emphasis on work and family tended to reinforce the visibility of heterosexuality, particularly marriage, at the expense of other sexualities.

The Western gay liberation movement that emerged in the early 1970s, however, challenged this invisibility of homosexuality in the public sphere and gave gay men and lesbians a public identity and campaigning movement. But the nature of the socialist state forbade a

---

[1] Olaf Brühl, 'Schwulsein 2000: Arschficker oder Arschkriecher? Kleines schwules Glossar eines Außenseiters', in *Schwulsein 2000. Perspektiven im vereinigten Deutschland* (Hamburg: MännerschwarmSkript Verlag, 2001), p. 176.

similar movement in the East. This chapter describes attempts to bring homosexuality into the public eye, and the impact this had on gay and lesbian lives. In the absence of freedom of expression, this was a difficult task. But the successes enjoyed by gay rights activists, as well as the limitations created by state control of the press and the right to assemble, demonstrate a crucial wider point: sexuality goes well beyond what takes place in the bedroom. Liberalisation requires not only the decriminalisation of private actions, but public activism too.

Homosexuality before decriminalisation, 1945–1968

Homosexuality and 'socialist morality' were to prove difficult bedfellows throughout the lifespan of the East German state.[2] For all the increasing liberality surrounding heterosexuality, attitudes towards same-sex contact were much slower to change. In the 1950s, the prosecution of male homosexuality was accompanied by widespread homophobia within the state and throughout the population.[3] The East German government had adopted paragraph 175 of the 1871 legal code, while carrying over paragraph 175a of the Nazi legal code. This legislation forbade 'unnatural desire' between men, with particular provision for the 'seduction' of men and boys under the age of 21.[4] It remained on the statue books until 1968, despite attempts at decriminalisation in 1952 and 1958.[5] Illegality and the fear of arrest were a heavy burden for gay men who had lived through the Nazi period. Invisibility was a problem for gay men and lesbians alike. East German books and newspapers were all but silent on the issue of homosexuality until the late 1960s, and the few references that did creep in were invariably derogatory.[6]

Rudolf Klimmer, head of the psychiatric clinic at a Dresden hospital, was one of only a few advocates of homosexual rights. Klimmer had been arrested and imprisoned twice under the Nazi regime and, although he kept his past a secret, he made strenuous public attempts

---

[2] See particularly Jennifer Evans' important article, 'Decriminalization, Seduction, and "Unnatural Desire" in the German Democratic Republic', *Feminist Studies* 36 (3) (2010), 553–577.
[3] Jennifer Evans, 'The Moral State: Men, Mining and Masculinity in the Early GDR', *German History* 23 (2005), 355–370; Jennifer Evans, '*Bahnhof* Boys: Policing Male Prostitution in Post-Nazi Berlin', *Journal of the History of Sexuality* 12 (2003), 605–636.
[4] Grau, 'Liberalisierung und Repression'; Grau, 'Return of the Past'.
[5] Grau, 'Liberalisierung und Repression'.
[6] Jennifer Evans, 'Decriminalization, Seduction, and "Unnatural Desire" ', 555–560.

to have homosexuals officially recognised as 'victims of Nazism'.[7] He also petitioned the authorities tirelessly for the decriminalisation of homosexuality and gave numerous talks on the subject. A glimpse into Klimmer's correspondence shows the hostile environment he faced. A letter from the Union of the Victims of Fascism ruled that homosexuals could become members only if they could prove that they had *resisted* the Nazi regime – merely being persecuted was insufficient. There was no recognition of the impossibility of resistance for isolated gay men – as with other social groups such as Jews and Jehovah's Witnesses, they were measured against the yardstick of communist resistance. The letter went on:

Nobody denies that Nazi law, insofar as that is not a contradiction in terms, cracked down on homosexuals in a brutal way. But these brutal methods were used against many groups: this does not mean that they were political opponents of National Socialism. For example, criminals were sentenced to death and executed for crimes which other regimes would have punished with a more lenient sentence.[8]

This comparison and association of homosexuality and criminality left no doubt that gay men could expect to find few friends in the GDR. Even Karl-Heinz Mehlan, professor of social medicine and a progressive advocate of birth control, wrote to Klimmer: 'Opening the floodgates to same-sex activity is not compatible with the principles of socialist morality.'[9] Given this chilly climate, it can come as no surprise that Klimmer never publicly revealed his sexuality, referring to his long-term partner as his 'stepson'.[10]

Nonetheless, Klimmer doggedly continued with his attempts to educate the East German authorities about homosexuality singlehandedly. Chief amongst these efforts was a book manuscript that argued that homosexuality was a biological condition which in no way undermined public morality. Homosexuals were valid members of society, and their sexual proclivities should not be criminalised. The manuscript was taken on by the Greifenverlag, which had a record of left-wing sexual education literature dating back to the Weimar era.

[7] On Klimmer's experiences under Nazism, see Günter Grau, 'Ein Leben im Kampf gegen den Paragraphen 175. Zum Wirken des Dresdener Arztes Rudolf Klimmer 1905–1977', in Manfred Herzer (ed.), *100 Jahre Schwulenbewegung* (Berlin: Verlag Rosa Winkel, 1998), pp. 47–64.
[8] Schwules Museum Berlin, Klimmer Nachlass, VVN, Generalsekretariat Berlin to Klimmer 23.6.1949.
[9] Schwules Museum Berlin, Klimmer Nachlass, K.-H. Mehlan to Klimmer, 17.12.1959.
[10] Grau, 'Ein Leben im Kampf', p. 60.

The Greifenverlag's proprietor, Karl Dietz, had a reputation with the state authorities as 'a publisher who defends the most outlandish manuscripts the most stubbornly'.[11] His tenacity was tested to the limit in this particular case: the manuscript was rejected by the censors in 1950 and again the following year.[12] Klimmer and the publishers revised the manuscript and submitted it for approval once more in July 1956.[13] Nine months later, after consultation with the Ministry of Health and the Ministry of Justice, permission to print was refused once again.[14] This was on the grounds that a discussion of decriminalisation would be 'out of place' at the present time, as the East German state faced more important questions.[15] This may have been a coded reference to the fact that decriminalisation had been discussed behind closed doors, but dropped in the wake of the 1953 Workers' Uprising (see p. 177), after which the party focused its efforts on meeting the population's material needs, leaving other 'less pressing' concerns to one side.[16] Klimmer published the manuscript in West Germany in 1957, but Dietz continued his efforts for East German publication. In 1962, he was advised by the Ministry of Culture that the topic was suitable only for publications aimed at doctors.[17] Homosexuality, this implied, was a medical problem, about which the general population had no need to inform itself.

Why, then, was homosexuality decriminalised in 1968, when earlier attempts to remove paragraph 175 from the statute books had failed? As Günter Grau has shown, when decriminalisation eventually took place it was not with a bang, but with a whimper. The commission set up to guide the legal reform ruled that homosexuality was a 'biological problem' rather than an 'illness'. Homosexuals could not help their nature, 'even if they really wanted to'.[18] Nevertheless, a new paragraph 151 criminalised same-sex relations between an adult and a young person under the age of 18. This introduced a new inequality between hetero- and homosexuals – the age of consent for heterosexual relations was 14 – and criminalised some lesbian relationships for the first time. Oddly, the commission had dismissed the idea of homosexual 'seduction' as 'absurd', on the grounds that one's nature was either homo- or heterosexual. But they still felt the need to 'protect' those between 14 and 18.

---

[11] BArch DR1/5015, 28, Böhm to Ostmann, 29.5.1957.
[12] Schwules Museum Berlin, Klimmer Nachlass, 'Greifenverlag zu Rudolstadt', undated.
[13] BArch DR1/5015, p. 20.   [14] BArch DR1/5010, p. 38.
[15] *Ibid.*   [16] Grau, 'Return of the Past', 10–14.
[17] BArch DR1/5010, p. 25.   [18] Grau, 'Liberalisierung und Repression', 336.

Decriminalisation brought East German legislation into line with more progressive (in this matter) socialist states such as Poland and Czechoslovakia, and also pre-empted West German decriminalisation by one year. All this was good for the modern, progressive image the GDR strove for. In fact, decriminalisation did not require a major change of practice. Prosecutions for consensual same-sex relations in the 1960s were probably not that numerous, albeit extremely painful for those unlucky enough to be accused.[19] The most profound problem facing gay men and lesbians was not one of illegality but invisibility. While homosexuality was now grudgingly permitted in private, tolerance of homosexuality in public was to remain extremely rare.

Sex in public: attempts to create a public sphere in the 1970s

Officials often argued that gay men and lesbians should be content that homosexuality was no longer a crime. But for many, the issue of their presence in public was vital. Most had experienced complete isolation in their teenage years and beyond. Christiane was thirty before she had her first same-sex relationship: 'I had imagined that I was the only lesbian in this town – not even lesbian, I didn't understand that then – the only woman who felt that way.'[20] All knew the difficulties of making contact with other gay and lesbian people, and the shortcomings of contact ads, bars, and – for gay men – cottaging sites.[21] Even those who lived in cities found it hard to meet others and were painfully aware that their counterparts in rural areas had it even worse. One of the founders of the lesbian publication *frau anders* recalled:

I come from a provincial town myself, from Suhl. At lesbian get-togethers I met other lesbians, who had hunkered down on their own somewhere and were very lonely. Then they would travel for hundreds of kilometres just to meet a pen friend, only to find that it wasn't worth it. They were in hiding, they spent their whole lives in hiding.[22]

[19] Klaus Berdl/Vera Kruber 'Zur Statistik der Strafverfolgung homosexueller Männer in der SBZ und DDR bis 1959', *Investito-Jahrbuch für die Geschichte der Homosexualitäten* 12 (2010), pp. 58–124, gives figures for the period up until 1959. There are as yet no figures for the 1960s.
[20] Kerstin Gutschke, *Ich ahnungsloser Engel. Lesbenprotokolle* (Berlin: Reiher Verlag, 1991), p. 19.
[21] See my unpublished article 'Sex, Sociability and Surveillance: Gay and Lesbian Spaces in East Berlin, 1968–1989'.
[22] Karstädt and von Zitzewitz (eds.), ... *viel zuviel verschwiegen*, p. 195.

Even when people had found a way to accommodate their sexuality in private – by finding a partner or a sympathetic group of friends – they craved opportunities to discuss their lifestyle openly in public. Those who plucked up their courage to come out to family, friends, and colleagues often experienced incomprehension or rejection. If and when these initial reactions gave way to acceptance, gay men and women felt that a huge weight of secrecy and subterfuge had been lifted off their shoulders. Individual coming out was frequently a first step towards broader activism, with the aim of a visible homosexual presence in society. Many were haunted by the knowledge of others' unhappiness. Eduard Stapel, a vicar who became one of the leading lights of the gay rights movement, estimated that he had buried between fifteen and twenty gay suicide victims.[23]

The term *Öffentlichkeit* comes up again and again in memoirs, interviews, and contemporary accounts. This is often translated as 'the public sphere', but depending on context can also be rendered as 'in public', 'publicity', or 'the general public'. In fact, many gay men and lesbians felt strongly that the problems of homosexuality in the public sphere encompassed all three of these areas. Their personal experiences of coming out had underlined their wish to be as open about their relationships as any heterosexual.[24] They were also sharply aware that public life was completely dominated by heterosexuality, to the extent that there was not a single openly gay person in East German public life. As Eduard Stapel put it: 'As a gay man, I have been stuffed full of heteropropaganda from the minute I was born: books, films, my environment, it was all the same.'[25] Public discussion of homosexuality was seen as an antidote to the isolation and helplessness felt by many and as a step towards making homosexuality a normal, accepted part of everyday life. Finally, the need to educate the general public was undeniable. Nobody was able to escape some degree of homophobia, from casual remarks to systematic bullying and persecution. Only when the general public – and its representatives in the state apparatus – accepted homosexuality as on a par with heterosexuality would such problems begin to disappear.[26]

---

[23] 'Schwulenbewegung in der DDR. Interview von Kurt Starke mit Eduard Stapel (SVD)', in Starke, *Schwuler Osten*, p. 100.

[24] See Gabriele S's account in Karstädt and von Zitzewitz (eds.), ... *viel zuviel verschwiegen*, p. 116.

[25] 'Schwulenbewegung in der DDR', p. 105.

[26] See Marinka Körzendörfer's remarks in Karstädt and von Zitzewitz (eds.), ... *viel zuviel verschwiegen*, p. 160.

Older men and women had experienced an alternative public sphere in the bars and clubs of West Berlin. 'Tommy' was a regular visitor to Rudi's Bar in Kreuzberg, which held all-female dances. She was actually in West Berlin when the Wall was built in August 1961 and had to talk her way through the border to get back to the East.[27] Whilst the West was no longer physically accessible post-1961, it remained a key influence. Rosa von Praunheim's film *Nicht der Homosexuelle ist pervers, sondern die Situation, in der er lebt* (*It Is Not The Homosexual Who Is Perverse, but the Society in Which He Lives*), a key moment in the emergence of the West German gay liberation movement, was shown on West German television in 1973. Its insistence on a public, politicised homosexuality was electrifying. Eduard Stapel saw it at the age of 19, and realised that he was not alone in his homosexuality.[28] 'Anna' and her partner were inspired to seek out similar people through a contact ad.[29] As West German popular and academic interest in homosexuality grew, more publications began to make their way over the border. Ursula Sillge persuaded Deputy Minister for Culture Klaus Höpcke (colloquially known as the 'book minister') to allow her to import a substantial library on homosexuality on academic grounds.[30] Other material made its way through illicit channels. The Stasi discovered that the West Berlin magazine *Siegessäule* (*Victory Column*, a reference to a well-known cottaging area around the famous West Berlin landmark) was being smuggled in, possibly with the help of an employee of the West German embassy.[31] Not only did such literature provide an insight into the West German gay scene and political developments, it could also inform East Germans about what was going on in their own country. Mirjam found her way to the gay-friendly Café Prenzlau only thanks to a tip from a West German friend, who had read about it in a gay city guide.[32] And of course all such literature was eagerly passed from hand to hand. Sillge used her hoard of Western literature to run a private library.[33] According to one Stasi informer, plans were afoot to catalogue all literature available on homosexuality in the GDR, along with coded information on where it could be found.[34]

[27] Karstädt and von Zitzewitz (eds.), … *viel zuviel verschwiegen*, pp. 56–57. See also Gutschke, *Ich ahnungsloser Engel*, p. 137, on the lesbian scene in 1950s West Berlin.
[28] 'Schwulenbewegung in der DDR', p. 100.
[29] Karstädt and Zitzewitz (eds.), … *viel zuviel verschwiegen*, p. 94.
[30] Interview with Ursula Sillge and Inge Buck, 26.6.2010.
[31] BStU, MfS, HA XX/9 Nr 1976, p. 1.
[32] Gutsche, *Ich ahnungsloser Engel*, p. 40.
[33] Karstädt and Zitzewitz (eds.), … *viel zuviel verschwiegen*, p. 146.
[34] BstU, MfS, HA XX/9, Nr 1972, p. 11.

East Germans may have been forbidden to visit the West, but curious West Germans often frequented East Berlin cafés and bars, bringing information and literature with them. In one isolated but influential instance, a representative of the West European gay liberation movement was actually able to speak directly to an East German audience. British-based activist Peter Tatchell was invited to give a talk at the 1973 World Festival Games (*Weltfestspiele*) in East Berlin, as part of a delegation from the British National Union of Students. Tatchell was one of a number of leftist celebrities – including Angela Davis – who had been invited to give the event a sense of international flair. The events inspired by his visit, however, showed that the authorities' tolerance of youthful high jinks during the festival was not extended to the homosexual population. Tatchell had been able to smuggle hundreds of gay liberation flyers into the country, some of which circulated throughout East Germany for years to come.[35] Members of the Homosexuelle Interessengemeinschaft Berlin (HIB), a nascent gay rights group, circulated the flyers during Tatchell's talk, and Tatchell and other international visitors carried out an impromptu demonstration a little later in the festival, which was photographed and documented by the Berlin police force.[36]

The HIB actually predated the World Festival by six months.[37] It had been officially founded on 15 January 1973, to mark the screening on West German television of von Praunheim's *Nicht der Homosexuelle ist pervers*.[38] The members of the HIB were convinced that 'homosexual emancipation is part of the success of socialism, it's just that the people in charge don't realise it yet. So we want to educate them.'[39] The HIB saw itself as both a self-help group and a campaigning organisation, providing support and a social network, but also demanding that homosexuality be discussed in public. Their attempts to 'educate' the authorities fell on stony ground, but the group found two sympathetic mentors

---

[35] Olaf Brühl, 'Sozialistisch und schwul. Eine subjektive Chronologie', in Wolfram Setz (ed.), *Homosexualität in der DDR. Materialien und Meinungen* (Hamburg: Männerschwarm Verlag, 2006), p. 109.

[36] Interview with Peter Rausch, 28.6.2010; interview with Michael E, 24.6.2010. Photographs of the demonstration can be found in Landesarchiv Berlin (henceforth LAB), C Rep. 303, Nr 642. I am very grateful to Mark Fenemore for bringing this file to my attention.

[37] See also my unpublished article on the HIB, 'The Transnational History of East German Gay Liberation'.

[38] Peter Rausch, 'Seinerzeit, in den 70ern', in Setz (ed.), *Homosexualität in der DDR*, p. 154. The film had been shown by the regional broadcaster WDR in 1972, but the 15.1.1973 screening on ARD, the premier West German channel, was the first accessible to East German viewers.

[39] *Ibid.*

in Rudolf Klimmer and Charlotte von Mahlsdorf. Von Mahlsdorf, East Germany's best-known transvestite, had inherited a large house on the outskirts of Berlin, where she was able to found a private museum of nineteenth-century furniture.[40] Von Mahlsdorf had hosted parties at her house since the 1960s, and offered the group the use of her basement, which she had furnished with the interior of a legendary Weimar bar, the Mulackritze. This got around the difficulties of finding a meeting place. The group began to meet twice a month, combining discussions on coming out, STDs, and other topical issues with drinking and dancing.[41] Von Mahlsdorf remembered in typically lyrical style: 'lesbian mothers, gay fathers, ordinary workers, actors, engineers, doctors: they all met in the Mulackritze'.[42]

But the HIB still experienced severe difficulties, not least in informing people about their work. The only way to publicise events was to make carbon copies on a typewriter, seven at a time.[43] (It was also heavily scrutinised by the authorities: indeed, it later transpired that von Mahlsdorf herself had acted as a secret police informant in the 1970s, although there is no evidence that she gave the Stasi any information on the HIB.)[44] Ursula Sillge heard about the group 'from the friend of a friend of a friend', and resolved to organise a women-only event. The invitation welcomed all 'appropriately interested girl friends' and was distributed by a chain of women, each passing invitations on to the lesbians that they knew. On the day in question (8 April 1978), 100 women arrived – but were turned away by the police.[45] As a result, all meetings at von Mahlsdorf's were forbidden, and the work of the HIB fizzled out.

Growing visibility in the 1980s

The East German gay rights movement gained momentum again only in the early 1980s, when it was given the opportunity to organise under

---

[40] See Charlotte von Mahlsdorf, *Ich bin meine eigene Frau. Ein Leben*, ed. Peter Süß (Munich: Deutscher Taschenbuch Verlag, 1995); see also the interview under the name 'Lothar' in Lemke, *Ganz normal anders*, pp. 54–75. On Mahlsdorf and her representation after 1989, see Jens Richard Giersdorf, 'Why Does Charlotte von Mahlsdorf Curtsy? Representations of National Queerness in a Transvestite Hero', *GLQ: A Journal of Lesbian and Gay Studies* 12 (2006), 171–196.
[41] Rausch, 'Seinerzeit, in den 70ern', p. 157.
[42] Von Mahlsdorf, *Ich bin meine eigene Frau*, p. 174.
[43] Rausch, 'Seinerzeit, in den 70ern', p. 155.
[44] The Stasi's final report on von Mahlsdorf's stint as 'IM Park' suggests that she provided them with very little useful information: BStU, MfS, XV 3269/71, pp. 103–104.
[45] Karstädt and von Zitzewitz (eds.), *... viel zuviel verschwiegen*, pp. 137–138.

the umbrella of the Protestant Church. This may seem an unlikely alliance and certainly disrupts the usual narrative of modern sexuality in which religion is the enemy of liberalisation. Indeed, the relationship between activists and the church authorities was far from easy at times. But in the 1980s the church offered a whole range of groups, from pacifists through to environmentalists, feminists, and punks, rooms to meet in and access to vital equipment such as duplication machines. This partial public sphere, enabled by the Church–State Agreement of 1978, was seized upon by gay men and lesbians who were eager to meet like-minded people, support each other, and lobby for change. Like their predecessors in the HIB, the church groups had an important social function, but also a campaigning one too. They were determined to bring these issues to a wider audience. Usually called 'working groups' (*Arbeitskreisen*), the groups organised a very wide range of activities, from 'coming out groups' to parents' evenings, talks by experts, literature readings, and of course social events.[46]

The process of starting a group was not always easy: would-be activists in Berlin had to go from parish to parish to find one that was willing to accommodate them.[47] Making contact with potential members could also be a challenge: Eduard Stapel's recruiting grounds included both church congresses and cottaging sites.[48] Once word spread, however, the first groups began to draw large crowds and soon inspired groups in other cities. According to Stasi reports, the Leipzig group initiated by Stapel was drawing crowds of 70–100 people on a fortnightly basis, and up to 300 people for particularly interesting events, only a year after its formation in spring 1982.[49] By 1984 the Stasi were aware of further groups in Magdeburg, Dresden, and Erfurt, and at least four groups in Berlin (three of them under the mantle of the church).[50] By the mid 1980s, gay activism had reached even provincial towns. In January 1986 a nationwide meeting of working groups was attended by representatives from Berlin (four groups), Dresden, Karl-Marx-Stadt, Erfurt, Halle, Leipzig, Magdeburg, Jena, Rostock, and Brandenburg.[51]

The working groups were embraced by many as a social space. But their semi-public nature was also vitally important. In their early

---

[46] See for example the programme of 'Schwule in der Kirche' for 1984: BStU, MfS, BV Berlin AIM 1121/87, p. 186.

[47] Karstädt and von Zitzewitz (eds.), … *viel zuviel verschwiegen*, p. 159.

[48] 'Schwulenbewegung in der DDR', p. 96.

[49] BStU, MfS, HA XX/4/1884, p. 3.

[50] *Ibid.*, HA XX/AKG Nr 78, pp. 7–44, Ankunft und Übersicht über Anzeichen des Mißbrauchs homosexueller Personen in der DDR und deren bisherige operative Bearbeitung.

[51] *Ibid.*, HA XX/AKG Nr 853, pp. 236–237.

stages, many groups were preoccupied with 'coming out', and meeting and talking together in public were often a potentially liberating experience. It is worth quoting Gabriele S at length, not least for her repeated return to the idea of *Öffentlichkeit*:

It was like opening a sluice ... You could experience your own identity, I felt that I was in public [*in der Öffentlichkeit*]. The church was a piece of the public sphere [*ein Stück Öffentlichkeit*], although their rooms weren't the wider public sphere [*die grosse Öffentlichkeit*], but for me it was public [*Öffentlichkeit*]. To be able to gather up the courage to stand up in meetings and say 'I am a lesbian woman and live with my girlfriend', to do that in public [*öffentlich*] was very important for me and for building my self-confidence.[52]

The groups were remarkably quick to move beyond the semi-public space of church halls and meeting rooms. Significantly, their first actions in the broader public sphere attempted to commemorate the gay and lesbian victims of the Nazi regime. A wreath was laid at Buchenwald in July 1983, and in March 1984 eighteen members of the Berlin group 'Lesbians in the Church' laid a wreath in Ravensbrück.[53] Building on these events, groups from all over East Germany planned co-ordinated wreath laying ceremonies at Buchenwald and Sachsenhausen on 30 June 1984: Christopher Street Day, the German equivalent of Gay Pride Day (the name is a reference to the site of the Stonewall riots). The activists involved had been entirely up front about their plans, even going so far as to ask for contact details of homosexual veterans of the concentration camps, and offering material for use in the redesign of the Buchenwald museum.[54] The official response was co-ordinated by the Stasi, who agreed the following line with the veterans' organisation and the management of the concentration camp sites: homosexuality could not be recognised as a 'separate problem' in the history of the concentration camps. 'Many homosexual concentration camp inmates were criminals, and the number of homosexuals murdered in concentration camps was a very small part of those killed by the fascists.' The choice of Christopher Street Day was also seen as inappropriate, as this was not a national day of commemoration and 'did not lie in the interest of the state'.[55] Although the groups were initially given permission for a

---

[52] Karstädt and von Zitzewitz (eds.), ... *viel zuviel verschwiegen*, p. 112.
[53] On Ravensbrück, see BStU, MfS, HA XX/AKG, Nr 520, pp. 357–358. On lesbian struggles with the authorities over this issue, see Dara Bryant, 'Queering the Antifascist State: Ravensbrück as a Site of Lesbian Resistance', *Edinburgh German Yearbook 3. Contested Legacies: Constructions of Cultural Heritage in the GDR* (New York: Camden House, 2009), pp. 76–89.
[54] BStU, MfS, HA XX/AKG, Nr 524, pp. 189, 190.
[55] *Ibid.*, p. 191.

guided tour around the site, they were subsequently told that they were allowed to visit the camp only in an individual capacity. Anything that suggested an organised group event was to be avoided, included the planned laying of wreaths that commemorated the homosexual victims of Nazism in the groups' names.[56]

The day itself was marked by a heavy secret police operation. A set of photographs from the Stasi photo archives show that those assembling at Weimar train station were observed, and then followed to the Buchenwald site, where even purchases from the gift shop were covertly photographed.[57] In all, fifty-nine people attended, many fewer than the organisers had originally hoped for. The group was allowed to lay two wreaths, but ribbons bearing inscriptions mentioning homosexuality were removed.[58] Lesbian singer-songwriter Maike Nowak recalled:

> There were seventy of us all stood in a throng
> When the order arrived that *that* wording was wrong.
> Once the ribbons were off, and the wreaths stood quite plain,
> The Stasi took us all the way to the train.[59]

In Berlin, the organisers tried to cancel the trip to Sachsenhausen altogether, but fifteen people travelled there anyway.[60] Following the authorities' warnings, they did not attempt to lay their wreath. A surviving photograph shows that its inscription included a quote from Brecht which pointedly alluded to the gay community's subordinate position in East German society: 'If the lowly do not think about the lowly, they will not survive.'[61] In the evening, a church service to commemorate gay and lesbian victims of Nazism, led by Stapel, was attended by 150 people. A Stasi report noted that the restrictions placed on the day's events seemed to have made activists even more determined to pursue future activities.[62]

With these actions, the groups placed themselves in a continuity of gay history which encompassed not only the persecution of the Nazi

---

[56] *Ibid.*, pp. 201–202.
[57] *Ibid.*, HA XX/Fo/236 Bild 27, Bild 28, Bild 29, Bild 30, Bild 47, Bild 48. Unfortunately these photographs are not dated, but their position in the file and the fact they were taken in summer make it extremely likely that they relate to the 1984 event.
[58] According to the Stasi, the ribbons bore inscriptions along the lines of 'We remember the gay victims of concentration camps.' However a photograph of what seems likely to be one of the wreaths reveals that the ribbon in fact reads 'We remember the thousands of murdered homosexuals': BStU, MfS, HA XX/Fo/236, Bild 16.
[59] Karstädt and von Zitzewitz (eds.), *… viel zuviel verschwiegen*, p. 187.
[60] BStU, MfS, HA XX/AKG, Nr 524, p. 225.
[61] *Ibid.*, HA VIII/Fo/439, Bild 41.
[62] *Ibid.*, HA XX/AKG, Nr 524, p. 226. The reference to Eduard Stapel as the leader of the service is on p. 191 of the same file.

period, but also Klimmer's attempts to gain recognition for homosexual victims of fascism in the 1950s. But the wreath laying also represented the collision of two political traditions: the antifascism of the East German state and the gay liberation activism of the West. Those behind the commemorations were trying to bring homosexuality into the wider context of East German life, and where better to start than with the antifascism that lay at the heart of the regime's rhetoric and self-understanding.[63] Asserting that homosexuals too had been victims of fascism was a way of re-establishing homosexuality as part of the progressive tradition of German history. The decision to do so on Christopher Street Day located these actions firmly in the broader context of gay liberation, and its insistence that society must accept and adapt to the reality of homosexuality.

The state's refusal to countenance such commemoration demonstrates the inflexibility of the SED's ideas about the past. Those who had been persecuted on the basis of their race, religion, or sexuality did not fit easily into the dominant paradigm of political victimhood, i.e. that only communists had been true victims of Nazism. And, in the case of homosexuality, it is hard to avoid the conclusion that the guardians of antifascism felt it would trivialise or demean the sacrifices of communist resistance fighters. One can also speculate on the motives of the communist veterans who had survived the camps. To take the survivors of Buchenwald as an example: according to Eugen Kogon, '[same-sex] sexual activity among heterosexual inmates was widespread'.[64] They would surely have witnessed, and some would have participated in, same-sex activity during their incarceration. Added to this was the fact that prisoners who had been sent to Buchenwald for homosexual activity were automatically assigned to the punishment company, frequently experimented upon, and often sent to the notoriously dangerous *Aussenlager* or satellite camp.[65] Communists, in contrast, were much higher up the prisoner hierarchy, and their involvement in the administration of the camp meant that they were often protected from the most gruelling aspects of camp life.[66] This, of course, was a part of the camp

[63] See Josie McLellan, *Antifascism and Memory in East Germany: Remembering the International Brigades 1945–1989* (Oxford: Clarendon Press, 2004).
[64] Kogon quoted in Wolfgang Röll, 'Homosexual Inmates in the Buchenwald Concentration Camp', *Journal of Homosexuality* 31 (4) (1996), 18.
[65] Günter Grau, *Homosexualität in der NS-Zeit* (Frankfurt am Main: Fischer, 1993), pp. 327–339. See also David A. Hackett (ed.), *The Buchenwald Report* (Boulder: Westview Press, 1995), pp. 172ff.
[66] On communist involvement in the running of Buchenwald, see Lutz Niethammer, *Der 'gesäuberte' Antifaschismus. Die SED und die roten Kapos von Buchenwald* (Berlin:

experience never alluded to in East German accounts. Their focus on a heroic narrative of resistance barely mentioned everyday activities, let alone potentially sensitive areas such as the communists' involvement in the running of the camps or the inevitable sexual contact between men who, in some cases, were imprisoned for the entire twelve years of Nazi rule. Those who took part in same-sex activity under such conditions probably never thought of themselves as 'homosexual', and to see 'homosexuals' officially remembered on a wreath must have been an strange experience, touching on memories not just about sex, but about power relations within the camps, and the privations and accommodations of survival.

Despite such difficulties, the church gay rights movement grew quickly, and inevitably underwent a degree of fragmentation. On the whole, church groups did not try to present a united front: an annual nationwide meeting was intended to swap experiences rather than co-ordinate activities. As in the Western gay liberation movement, the groups tended to be dominated by gay men, and lesbians began to feel the need for a forum to discuss issues specific to them. In Berlin, they quite rapidly formed their own, very active group, 'Lesbians in the Church' (mentioned earlier), which offered an all-female space for women to meet and talk about their experiences, and concerned itself with a feminist as well as a gay rights political agenda.[67] Lesbians in Jena founded an illegal magazine called *frau anders*, which literally translates as 'woman different' – with the implication not only that lesbians had different problems to gay men, but also that they had specific concerns within the women's movement.[68] Nevertheless, lesbians continued to meet with and to co-operate with gay men to a much greater extent than in the West. The Berlin group 'Gays in the Church' had many regular female attendees and frequent female speakers/performers: for example, in the second half of 1984, three out of eight invited guests were female.[69]

Akademie, 1994), and Jorge Semprun, *Was für ein schöner Sonntag!* (Frankfurt: Suhrkamp Taschenbuch, 1984).

[67] For example, they produced a leaflet demanding better support for victims of rape and domestic violence, women-only meeting spaces, and a women's taxi service. A copy of this leaflet can be found in BStU, MfS, HA XX/9, Nr 1951, p. 57. It was probably authored by Marinka Körzendörfer in July 1986. On 'Lesbians in the Church', see especially the interview with Ramona Dreßler, Bettina Dziggel, and Marinka Körzendörfer in Karstädt and Zitzewitz (eds.), ... *viel zuviel verschwiegen*, pp. 155–186.

[68] Karstädt and Zitzewitz (eds.), ... *viel zuviel verschwiegen*, p. 189.

[69] 'Schwule in der Kirche. Programm für das 2. Halbjahr 1984', private archive, Ingo Kölsch.

Also at the start of the 1980s, a Berlin-based group led by Ursula Sillge emerged which operated independently of the church. A veteran of the HIB of the 1970s, Sillge had continued to campaign on gay rights issues and began to form the nucleus of a group of activists. Sillge's group, which became known as the 'Sunday Club', included both lesbians and gay men. The Sunday Club was more consciously assimilationist than some of the church groups and aimed to integrate gay men and lesbians into socialist society.[70] This, it was felt, was a matter of practical accommodations and changes in legislation. Principal among their demands was space in which to meet, but they also continued to lobby the authorities on issues such as contact ads, housing rights, and public depictions of homosexuality.[71]

Church groups tended to advance a more overarching critique of society, rather closer to Western gay liberation. Instead of co-operating with the regime, much of their activity aimed to build up an autonomous public sphere. Many activists felt that a complete rethinking of gender and society would be necessary in order for homosexuality to be fully accepted.[72] 'Church' groups also tended to take a broader view of homosexual behaviour, attempting to eradicate prejudices in the broader gay community, for example against *Tunten* – 'queens' or effeminate gay men.[73] Ingo Kölsch remembered travelling all over East Germany to give a talk entitled 'The Queen in Us', and in January 1989 the Berlin group 'Gays in the Church' organised an event called 'I'm a Queen – What Can I Do, What Do I Want, What Am I Allowed to Do?'[74]

It would not, however, do to overplay the differences between the groups' approaches. Sillge and her associates took part in the nationwide meetings of the church groups, and there was inevitably a degree of overlap in the membership. Where possible, people simply gravitated to the group where they felt most comfortable. Henrike, who was in her early forties when she got involved with 'Lesbians in the Church', remembered her involvement with the group as an 'amazingly liberating' time, which opened her eyes to all sorts of sexism in society. For all her affection for the revolutionary zeal of the (younger) church

---

[70] Ursula Sillge, *Un-Sichtbare Frauen. Lesben und ihre Emanzipation in der DDR* (Berlin: Ch. Links, 1991), p. 99.
[71] For examples of Sillge's contacts with the authorities, see Karstädt and Zitzewitz (eds.), ... *viel zuviel verschwiegen*, pp. 253ff.
[72] See Sillge's description of 'Lesbians in the Church' in Sillge, *Un-Sichtbare Frauen*, pp. 105–106.
[73] Clayton Whisnant suggests 'pansy', 'fairy', and 'queen' as possible translations of *Tunte*: Clayton J. Whisnant, 'Styles of Masculinity in the West German Gay Scene, 1950–1965', *Central European History* 39 (3) (2006), 367.
[74] Interview with Ingo Kölsch, 6.1.2004; BStU, MfS, HA XIS, Nr 707, p. 47.

activists, she eventually moved to more assimilationist activities, parting ways from the 'very militant women's libbers' and their critique of the GDR. 'Although I was in no sense a friend of the East German state, I preferred the idea of changing things through small reforms.'[75]

State responses to activism

The official response to this flowering of activity was far from uniform. Rank-and-file officials who encountered petitioners or lobbyists tended to be dismissive of their demands. Homosexuality, they argued, had been decriminalised, and that should be the end of the matter. Activists' arguments about the need for homosexuality to exist in the public sphere, and their demands that the state enable this, were met with incomprehension. When Ursula Sillge asked whether gay men and lesbians might be allowed to organise their own social events, the response from the Ministry of the Interior could have passed for a sublime parody of heartless bureaucratic misapprehension:

All citizens are offered the opportunity to take part in events which serve the evolution of a culturally rich socialist communal life and the further development of the socialist way of life ... As you yourself write in your petition, you have the same right as any other citizen to take part in such public events, in order to fulfil your needs for company, dance, and entertainment. Societal experience shows us that the special regulation over and above these principles requested by you is not required. Your petition is hereby considered to have been dealt with.[76]

Decriminalisation had, it was felt, discharged the state's responsibilities, by allowing homosexual behaviour in private. Further discussion in public was both unnecessary and, functionaries implied, unbecoming. As Politburo member Kurt Hager was reported to have said, 'anyone who sees homosexuality in political terms is a fool'.[77] The regime's one-size-fits-all approach to social policy refused to acknowledge that gay men and lesbians had particular needs which could not be met within the somewhat narrow confines of East German life, with its stress on marriage and childbearing.

Such intransigence, however, coexisted with a liberal tendency within the state, particularly amongst academics and doctors and in the cultural sphere. An early example of this was Volker Koepp's documentary

[75] Karstädt and Zitzewitz (eds.), ... *viel zuviel verschwiegen*, p. 129.
[76] *Ibid.*, p. 265; Facsimile of Hauptabteilung Schutzpolizei, Ministerium des Inneren to Ursula Sillge, 28.3.1984.
[77] BStU, MfS, HA XX, Nr 7214, p. 185.

short, *Tag für Tag* (*Day by Day*), released in 1979. The film centred
on Karin, a female welder from Swann in Mecklenberg. Karin, in her
mid-thirties, is portrayed as a model worker, who acts as a trade union
representative and helps out younger colleagues. Far from conventionally feminine, she is funny, charismatic, and good-looking. The film
describes her as 'ledig' (single or unmarried) but the voice over men-
tions in passing her 'girlfriend Jutta', and she is seen wearing what
looks like a wedding ring. Although her sexuality is never spelled out,
the signs were clear for those who wished to see them.[78] Also in 1979,
psychologists in Berlin had begun to work with a group of lesbians to
set up a discussion group. This collaboration broke down when the
women involved felt their autonomy was compromised by the psychologists' wish to steer their discussions for research purposes.[79] The 1980s
were marked by both a growing academic interest and a more equal
collaboration with gay men and lesbians. Emblematic of this trend were
two conferences on 'Psychosocial Aspects of Homosexuality' held in
Leipzig and Karl-Marx-Stadt in 1985 and 1988 under the auspices
of the Society of Dermatology and the Society for Social Hygiene.
Activists such as Stapel, Sillge, Hubert Thinius, and Günter Grau
shared a platform with sexologists, dermatologists (on account of their
professional interest in STDs), representatives from the Marriage and
Sexual Counselling Service, and specialists in sex education.[80]

The academic sphere was of course not uniformly progressive. Many
professionals began with an attitude of tolerance and pity, and some
were able to move towards unconditional acceptance more quickly than
others. The first East German book devoted to homosexuality, Reiner
Werner's *Homosexualität* (*Homosexuality*), had an unfortunate tendency
to medicalise and judge. Werner was a professor of forensic psychology,
who led a research group on homosexuality, but instead of the 'knowledge and tolerance' promised in the book's subtitle, he delivered only
clichés and homophobic prejudice. Gay men, Werner suggested, made
excellent hairdressers and waiters, perhaps because 'they want to compensate for their [homosexual] nature'. 'Their engagement, their sen-
sitivity, their ability to conform', he went on, also made them ideally
suited to work in the theatre or opera.[81] Werner's supposed tolerance

[78] *Tag für Tag* (dir. Volker Koepp, 1979).
[79] Sillge, *Un-Sichtbare Frauen*, pp. 91–92.
[80] See the published proceedings: *Psychosoziale Aspekte der Homosexualität.* [1986];
*Psychosoziale Aspekte der Homosexualität. II. Workshop der Sektion Andrologie der
Gesellschaft für Dermatologie der DDR und der Sektion Ehe und Familie der Gesellschaft für
Sozialhygiene der DDR am 23. April 1988* (Jena: Friedrich Schiller Universität, 1989).
[81] Reiner Werner, *Homosexualität. Herausforderung an Wissen und Toleranz* (Berlin:
Verlag Volk und Gesundheit, 1987), pp. 162–163.

failed him entirely when it came to queens (*Tunten*) who had, he wrote, 'failed to sufficiently control and regulate their own behaviour in relation to gender roles'. 'If you are not accepted and even found repellent by those around you, it is never a mistake to look for the cause in your own behaviour. Queens do not do this.' Werner followed this stern judgement with a staggeringly homophobic pen portrait of limp-wristed, loose-hipped, lisping, and bitchy queens, concluding that 'behavioural training' was perhaps their only hope.[82]

Werner was not alone in his essentialist view of sexuality. The endocrinologist Günter Dörner argued that homosexuality was caused by stress during pregnancy, leading to increased levels of oestrogen.[83] Dörner's research was heavily criticised by activists, both for its methodological weakness and for its attempt to find a 'cause' for homosexuality (and by implication a way to prevent it).[84] Their refutations, however, reached only a small audience, while Dörner's research remained influential amongst a much wider medical audience and beyond. (Herr L, for example, referred in his interview to 'hormonal changes during the development of the foetus', adding, 'he [the homosexual] can't help it'.) The SED were in fact more comfortable with the idea of homosexuality as biologically determined. As a 1985 position paper put it, in reference to Dörner's research, 'the better the natural biological causes of homo- and heterosexuality are recognised, the stronger the moral obligation to recognise each other as completely equal'.[85] If homosexuals had not chosen their sexual preferences (the paper compared homosexuality to left-handedness and hair colour), then society needed to make allowances for their particular needs.

The state's approach to transsexuality is a striking example of this. As early as 1976, the Ministry of Health agreed procedures for carrying out sex changes.[86] The number and success of these operations are unclear. Peter Rausch remembered a couple active in the HIB: Bärbel,

[82] *Ibid.*, pp. 106, 108.
[83] See Florian Mildenberger's excellent discussion of Dörner's work in 'Günter Dörner – Metamorphosen eines Wissenschaftlers', in Setz (ed.), *Homosexualität in der DDR*, pp. 237–272.
[84] See for example Harald Stumpe and Frank Böttger's contribution to the second conference on homosexuality and the discussion that followed: 'Methodenkritische Bermerkungen zu Dörner's Untersuchungen "Pränataler Streß als möglicher ätiologischer Faktor der männlichen Homosexualität"', in *Psychosoziale Aspekte der Homosexualität II*, pp. 201–211.
[85] SAPMO-BArch DY30/IV2/2.039/4 (Büro Krenz), Zur Situation homophiler Bürger in der DDR (Analyse des Phänomens und Lösungsvorschläge), April 1985, p. 69.
[86] Ministerium für Gesundheitswesen, 'Verfügung zur Geschlechtsumwandlung von Transsexualisten [*sic*]', 27.2.1976, Archiv Sonntags-Club, exhibited in 'Verzaubert im Nordost', Museumsverbund Pankow, 10.6–12.12.2010.

a nurse, had met Barbara, a male-to-female transsexual, during her hospital treatment. They fell in love, got married, and Bärbel later had a child by artificial insemination.[87] In other cases, the outcome appears to have been less successful.[88] What is particularly interesting is the state's willingness to deal with transsexuality, in no small part due to the fact that it could be seen as a medical condition that could be 'cured' by professional intervention. It is clear that many doctors and academics would have preferred to see homosexuality in this light too, as something which was, if not treatable, at least diagnosable and quantifiable.

The shortcomings of academic work on homosexuality were, however, overshadowed by a far more intrusive and repressive state presence: that of the secret police. In common with all the groups under the church's umbrella, gay rights groups found themselves the object of intense Stasi surveillance (Figure 5.1). The archives contain hundreds of reports on activists, including exhaustive documentation of their meeting places, right down to the content of church notice boards.[89] Informers reported regularly on both planned activities, and the conduct of meetings. 'IM Max Schneider', a church representative based in Leipzig, gave accounts of working group meetings, conferences, discussions between church and state officials, and a concert in Jena where, he noted, the audience's appearance 'ranged from decadent to solidly middle class'.[90] Activists were well aware that the Stasi were listening in. Stapel operated on the assumption that every letter could be opened and that every group had an informer. Naturally this led to a degree of self-censorship, and he remembered stepping in if radical political opinions were voiced in the groups, 'so that nobody walked into a trap'. Even romantic or sexual encounters needed to be approached with caution: the Stasi sent a boy to seduce Stapel, but the honey trap was apparently botched when the informant fell for him and spilled the beans.[91]

The Stasi were, by and large, not concerned about same-sex activity per se, but more about its perceived political and security implications. In short, they were worried about the possibility that gay rights groups

[87] Interview with Peter Rausch, 28.6.2010.
[88] See the interview with Amanda Z in Thomas Karsten and Holde-Barbara Ulrich, *Messer im Traum. Transsexuelle in Deutschland* (Tübingen: Konkursbuch, 1994), esp. p. 155, which describes the suicide of her friend Melanie after an unsuccessful operation.
[89] See for example BStU, MfS, HA XX/9, Nr 1680, which contains 150 pages of maps and photographs, but ultimately does little more than document where groups met. The church notice board (which bore no mention of homosexuality) is on p. 16.
[90] *Ibid.*, Nr 1972, p. 15.
[91] 'Schwulenbewegung in der DDR', p. 101.

Figure 5.1: Stasi surveillance photograph, 1986.

would destabilise the regime.[92] In this sense, they were classed along-side groups concerned with peace or the environment. Nevertheless, Stasi reports do reflect a deep-seated homophobia, not least in their frequent references to 'homos'. Stasi officers also tended to give operations against gay men and lesbians suggestive titles, such as 'Operation Brother' (gay men are sometimes referred to in German as 'warm brothers'), 'Operation After Shave', and, in the case of one man whose partner had died, 'Operation Widow'.[93]

It is also worth noting that Stasi surveillance was not limited to activists, but extended to gay men in politically sensitive occupations. 'Operation Lover' was launched when a major in the border troops was rumoured to be displaying 'homosexual behaviour'. Despite the fact that his military record was exemplary, both his (rumoured) lover and his secretary were recruited as informers, and his phone and flat were tapped. This frantic activity bore little fruit: the major returned home at 6 p.m. each and every night, watched TV 'without interest', and took only work calls. The Stasi agents changed tack, bugging the informer's flat and telephone instead (to check that he was trustworthy), and simply confronting the major with the rumours. He immediately admitted to a single, long-term homosexual relationship, which had since come to an end. Despite this, and the fact that the concluding report judged him to be a 'politically and ideologically reliable and technically highly qualified person', he was discharged from the army. The Stasi, how-ever, were so impressed by him that they planned to recruit him as an informer once he took up a new position.[94]

Stasi surveillance and disruption were one side of the state's response to demands for gay rights. The other was to make limited concessions.[95]

---

[92] See in particular an interview with a former Stasi officer: Eike Stedefeldt, 'Zur wei-teren Veranlassung. Ein Interview mit dem MfS-Offizier Wolfgang Schmidt' in Setz (ed.), *Homosexualität in der DDR*, pp. 185–202.

[93] On Operation After Shave, see Eduard Stapel, *Warme Brüder gegen Kalte Krieger. Schwulenbewegung in der DDR im Visier der Staatssicherheit* (Magdeburg: Landesbeauftragte für die Unterlagen des Staatssicherheitsdienstes der ehemaligen DDR Sachsen-Anhalt, 1999); for Operation Widow, see interview with Ingo Kölsch, 6.1.2004.

[94] BStU, MfS, HA I, Nr 13148, pp. 769–782.

[95] Former Stasi officer Wolfgang Schmidt claims that many liberalising measures were suggested by the Stasi themselves, in particular by a position paper written by him in 1983 which suggested permitting contact ads, commemorating the vic-tims of fascism, allowing gay couples to apply for a joint residence, and equalising the age of consent. No documentary evidence has emerged to support this claim: Stedefelt, 'Zur weiteren Veranlassung', p. 191; Günter Grau, 'Sozialistische Moral und Homosexualität. Die Politik der SED und das Homosexuellenstrafrecht 1945 bis 1989 – ein Rückblick', in Detlef Grumbach (ed.), *Die Linke und das Laster. Schwule Emanzipation und linke Voruteile* (Hamburg: MännerschwarmSkript Verlag, 1995),

This tendency manifested itself in a 35-page position paper written in 1985 and circulated to Politburo members including Kurt Hager and Egon Krenz.[96] The paper, which originated in the 'interdisciplinary working group on homosexuality' that had been set up at Berlin's Humboldt University the previous year, concluded that 'it is time to effect a public transformation in normative opinion formation, [and] by the means of the media to cautiously, but single-mindedly overcome historically originating "blemishes" and to solve practical questions, which until now have prevented the full integration of homophile citizens due to a false assessment of the situation'.[97] The paper was highly critical of some aspects of gay life, particularly anonymous sex between gay men, but saw such 'problems' as a result of their marginalisation in East German society. It recommended that steps be taken to educate the general population and to integrate gay men and lesbians into socialist life, particularly discussion in the media, further academic research and education, specialised advice for homosexuals, equalisation of the age of consent, relaxation of the rules on contact ads, and recognition of homosexual partnerships when allocating housing.[98] (Interestingly, a discussion paper written by Klaus Laabs a year previously had made very similar suggestions, albeit in more radical and uncompromising language. Laabs was expelled from the SED for his efforts.)[99]

As yet, no record of the SED's discussion of this position paper has come to light. But, over the course of the next few years, many of its suggestions were put into practice. Same-sex contact ads were now allowed, albeit on the condition that they did not include the words 'gay', 'lesbian', or 'homosexual'. The Sunday Club eventually received official recognition, and was able to produce a newsletter and answer letters from all over the GDR.[100] Late in the decade, discussions of what it was actually like to live as a homosexual started to reach a mass, mixed audience. The production of both a documentary (*Die andere*

p. 135. A dissertation written by a Stasi captain in 1986 recommends that the state take measures to integrate homosexuals into socialist society but, as this post-dates the 1985 position paper, it should be seen as following rather than leading such trends. See Rainer Wetzel, 'Einige Probleme der weiteren Einbeziehung staatlicher und geselleschaftlicher Kräfte zur vorbeugenden Verhinderung des politischen Missbrauchs homosexuell veranlagter Personen in antisozialistischen Zusammenschlüssen und zu feindlichen Aktivitäten', 5.12.1986, BStU, MfS, JHS 20633.

[96] SAPMO-BArch DY30/IV2/2.039/4 (Büro Krenz), Zur Situation homophiler Bürger in der DDR (Analyse des Phänomens und Lösungsvorschläge), April 1985, pp. 43–77.

[97] *Ibid.*, p. 60.   [98] *Ibid.*, pp. 61–67.

[99] Starke, *Schwuler Osten*, pp. 44–47.

[100] Sillge, *Un-Sichtbare Frauen*, p. 101. For an example of one of the letters, see Karstädt and Zitzewitz (eds.), *... viel zuviel verschwiegen*, p. 131.

Liebe (*The Other Love*)) and a feature film (*Coming Out*) about male homosexuality was authorised. East German radio broadcast a series of programmes called 'Mensch Du! Ich bin homosexuell' ('Hey You, I'm Homosexual') and 'Mensch Du! Ich bin lesbisch' ('Hey You, I'm Lesbian'), which were made with the co-operation of groups such as Lesbians in the Church.[101] And in 1989 *Das Magazin* carried a series of articles on being gay which went beyond the usual platitudes about difference and tolerance. The author started from the assumption that 'the lives of gays and heterosexuals are not so cleanly divided as many think. The gay East German citizen starts life as a baby, not a 30-year-old hairdresser.'[102] What was particularly striking about the series was its acknowledgement of popular homophobia and intolerance and their effects on gay men. 'The first of our many cruelties against gays takes place when they are not even grown up. Five out of a hundred boys, "educated" about homosexuality with a nudge and a wink, as Uncle Kurt and Aunt Amanda slap their thighs over the latest gay joke, see their future before their eyes: a future as a dirty faggot.'[103]

The premiere of *Coming Out*, on 9 November 1989, the very night the border between East and West Berlin was opened, marked the pinnacle of this liberalisation. *Coming Out* (the title was in English, not German) told the story of Philipp, a teacher in his late twenties. Despite a warm relationship with his pregnant girlfriend, Tanja, Philipp is unable to deny his sexual feelings towards men, suppressed since a homophobic incident in his teens. He falls in love with Matthias, a younger man, but is torn between his two lovers. Only when he meets an older gay man, whose experiences in a Nazi concentration camp made him a lifelong communist is Philipp able to come to terms with his sexuality and face the future with new optimism. *Coming Out* was daring not only in its choice of Philipp's profession – he is portrayed as a dedicated, inspirational teacher – but also its frank depiction of Philipp and Matthias' love-making. Much of the film was shot on location in East Berlin gay bars and cottaging sites, and many of the extras were regulars on the 'scene'.

Coming Out went into production only after it had been personally approved by Kurt Hager, the Politburo member responsible for culture. An important factor here was that it was to be directed by Heiner Carow, one of East Germany's most successful film directors, responsible for

---

[101] Günter Grau (ed.), *Lesben und Schwule – was nun? Chronik – Dokument – Analysen – Interviews* (Berlin: Dietz, 1990), pp. 88–90.
[102] Ursula Hafranke, 'Ungestraft anders', *Das Magazin*, January 1989, 43. The series continued in *Das Magazin*, February 1989, 24–29, and May 1989, 44–49.
[103] Hafranke, 'Ungestraft anders', 46.

box office hits such as *Die Legende von Paul und Paula* and *Bis dass der Tod euch scheidet* (*Until Death Do You Part*), which tackled delicate issues such as infidelity, domestic violence, alcoholism, and abortion.[104] If anybody could be trusted to produce a politically, aesthetically, and commercially successful film about homosexuality, it was Carow. But there was also a sense that the party felt this was a politically necessary film. Hager conceded that it would be very controversial, 'as homosexuality has been a taboo for many people until now', but nevertheless wished Carow 'every success' with the project.[105] A report from one of Hager's underlings suggested that the film might 'counteract prejudice and discrimination against homosexuals' and indeed encourage its viewers to think about broader issues of tolerance and respect.[106] Interestingly, this report on the film contains a complete reversal of the sort of attitudes Rudolf Klimmer faced in his efforts to gain recognition for homosexual concentration camp survivors:

What is particularly politically significant in this film is the episode where Philipp meets an old comrade, who was terribly tortured by the fascists and thrown into a concentration camp because of his sexuality. There he experienced the solidarity of communists and found his way into the party. This connects the film's central problematic with the legacy of antifascism as well as with the goals and ideals of the revolutionary workers' movement. This scenario reminds the viewer of the historical fact that communists and homosexuals were victims of fascism and fought together against their tormentors.[107]

To imply that communists had unreservedly supported homosexual concentration camp inmates was mendacious, particularly given the ongoing controversy about the commemoration of gay and lesbian victims of Nazism. Note too that Philipp's inspirational mentor is a party member, creating the misleading impression that the SED were in the vanguard of gay rights. In fact, only four years earlier, homosexual concentration camp inmates had been described as criminals. In this context, the author's willingness to associate antifascism – the holy ideology of the East German state – with homosexuality was something very new, which, like *Coming Out*, represented a real sea change in attitudes towards homosexuality.

[104] *Die Legende von Paul und Paula* (dir. Heiner Carow, 1973); *Bis daß der Tod euch scheidet* (dir. Heiner Carow, 1979).
[105] SAPMO BArch DY30/vorl.SED 42314, Kurt Hager to Hans Dieter Mäde, DEFA-Studio für Spielfilme, 21.7.1988.
[106] *Ibid.*, Abt. Kultur, Information und Stellungnahme zum DEFA-Filmszenarium 'Coming Out', Berlin 8.6.1988.
[107] *Ibid.*

The limits of liberalisation

Nonetheless, this liberalisation should not be overstated. It is true that people in positions of power were gradually coming to terms with the fact that gay men lived in their midst. Lesbians, on the other hand, were rather less visible and were ignored in most publicly available information, including the *Das Magazin* series. But liberalisation was at its heart a pragmatic attempt to quell the feared radicalisation of the homosexual population. Ludwig Mecklinger, the minister for health, reported to the Stasi in early 1985 that Willi Stoph, the chairman of the Council of Ministers, regarded a 'more vigorous inclusion of homosexuals into our society as an important political problem'. While Stoph made reference to the support of the Weimar-era KPD for homosexual rights, he was quick to say that the issue needed to be approved by the party leadership first.[108] As Jennifer Evans has pointed out, the 1985 position paper was 'not a celebration of difference … but a call for greater institutionalisation and mediated desire'.[109] In truth, communists were still deeply ambivalent about homosexuality, as their unwillingness to allow a genuinely open public discussion of the issue showed.

That is not to say that liberalisation did not have an effect on people's lives. The semi-tolerance of the church groups seems to have had the most radical impact, bringing people together and giving them opportunities to discuss their experiences. For Ingo Kölsch, getting involved with a church group in Berlin allowed him to live a normal life as a gay man and to forge friendships which last until the present day.[110] Informal circles of friends could have a similar function, of course. As one lesbian remembered: 'Of course, we had lots of friends. We often met here at mine or in other flats, had a fun get-together and talked about anything and everything. You couldn't just sit at home, that was out of the question … We were a very mixed bunch, a real mix of artists and ordinary people.'[111] But many needed help finding like-minded companions. A West German lesbian writer described a visit to a well-known weekly disco in Weissensee, estimating that it had been attended by 400–600 people in the course of the night, many of them visiting from outside Berlin.[112] Such opportunities to mingle were few and far between, and many publications were simply too limited in their circulation to reach much of the gay community. Ulrich Berkes'

---

[108] BStU, MfS, HA XX, Nr 7214, p. 185.
[109] Jennifer Evans, 'Decriminalization, Seduction, and "Unnatural Desire"', 567.
[110] Interview with Ingo Kölsch, 6.1.2004.
[111] Karstädt and Zitzewitz (eds.), … *viel zuviel verschwiegen*, p. 58.
[112] Grau (ed.), *Lesben und Schwule*, p. 78.

Eine schlimme Liebe (*A Bad Love*), a diary that openly described his life with his partner Martin, was published in 1987 in an edition of only 7,500 copies.[113] Not until the very last year of the GDR did books on homosexuality start to appear in larger editions: 60,000 copies of Jürgen Lemke's collection of interviews with gay men were published in 1989.[114] Limited liberalisation could not reach everyone, particularly those outside large towns and cities. In a city as large as Dresden, there was only one bar where gays and lesbians could meet, and even there an entirely innocuous show of affection, such as an arm around a shoulder, could be enough to have you shown the door.[115] For those in rural areas, the situation was much worse. A samizdat invited readers to imagine the isolation of provincial lesbians:

Perhaps you've just been left by your girlfriend, because in the end she plumped for husband, children, pets, garden, the works do at the side of her respectable spouse ... You have to protect your parents. My God, what would the neighbours think, not to mention Hilde and Heinz in Wuppertal, the friends on the allotment, the guys at the workshop, the church choir ... The terrible loneliness starts when your workmates say goodbye each afternoon and overwhelms you on Fridays with the last 'have a nice weekend'.[116]

Here, the East German sense of community, which was experienced by so many heterosexuals as one of the best things about life under communism, actually heightened the isolation of gays and lesbians. Those who did not fit societal norms were not necessarily included in the camaraderie of the workplace, the family, or shared leisure activities. The 'niches' of private life could exclude gay men and lesbians, many of whom craved private and public acceptance. 'I have to keep it a secret from my work collective', said one lesbian. 'They all think "Ugh, homos!"'[117] Even the influence of the West (Hilde and Heinz in Wuppertal) could be experienced as conservative and repressive. The fact that this article was written in 1989 speaks volumes about how little attitudes had changed.

Despite the claims of sexologists that the norms of socialist society were 'irreconcilable with a rejection of the homosexual',[118] homophobia was clearly widespread amongst the East German population. Even in 2006/7, many heterosexual interviewees were unenlightened about

---

[113] BArch DR1/2136, p. 192.   [114] BArch DR1/2143a, p. 574.
[115] Karstädt and Zitzewitz (eds.), ... *viel zuviel verschwiegen*, p. 78.
[116] *Ibid.*, p. 289.
[117] *Psychosoziale Aspekte der Homosexualität* [1986], p. 107.
[118] Kurt Starke, 'Zur Erforschung der Homosexualität', in *Psychosoziale Aspekte der Homosexualität* [1986], p. 173.

homosexuality. 'I don't think anything of lesbians, and I don't think anything of homos', said Herr K. 'It's an illness, these people are ill.' Frau M referred to gay men as 'hermaphrodites' (*Zwitter*), adding 'they walk funny, don't they?' She then went on to dismiss the existence of lesbianism completely. Herr H justified homophobic bullying in the army as a product of its time: 'It may well be that they were victimised. I mean, today it's all seen a bit differently, they are the way they are. I don't have anything against it, but they should leave me alone, let's put it like that.' Those who had had social or professional contact with 'out' gay men and lesbians, such as Herr B, Herr D, Herr J, Herr S, and Frau V were much more likely to take a tolerant view. For many interviewees, however, homosexuals remained shadowy, impersonal figures. Frau F never knowingly met anybody homosexual, even when she was studying for a Ph.D. in Berlin. Frau I was also unaware of any gay men or lesbians of her acquaintance. When asked whether homosexuality was a taboo in East Germany, she replied, 'I don't think it existed in that way.'

Public homosexuality may have been rare, but public homophobia certainly was not. Frau W and Frau R both remembered gay men being called '175ers', a reference to paragraph 175.[119] Interviewed in the early 1980s, one lesbian spoke of her colleagues' 'comments that in Hitler's time I would have been shot or gassed'. She went on: 'such comments were especially strong when I was troublesome or critical, for instance about men cheating on their wives, when the wife is expected to sit quietly at home'.[120] The mere fact of homosexuality was threatening enough, but what seemed particularly unsettling was the way homosexuality's questioning of gender roles undermined a widely shared denial of the remaining inequalities between men and women, and the impact this had on marriage and family life.

Had the events of autumn 1989 not prevented the regime from heading into its fifth decade, the increasing visibility of homosexuality would probably have continued. *Coming Out* alone would have had a big impact on both gays and lesbians and the general public. It is unlikely, however, that gay groups and subcultures would have been allowed to develop further. East German political identity was too inflexible to allow for different identities and allegiances. There was no reason why there should have been a conflict between socialism and homosexuality,

---

[119] Herr B, on the other hand, remembered this term being used as a jokey means of (self-) identification. In his theatrical milieu, asking somebody 'is your birthday on the seventeenth of May' was a way of asking 'are you gay'?

[120] Jeffrey Davis and Karl-Ludwig Stenger, 'Lesbians in the GDR: Two Women', *New German Critique* 23 (1981), 91.

any more than there was a preprogrammed conflict between socialism
and heterosexuality. The difference was twofold: firstly, heterosexuality
was the norm, and every aspect of public life reflected this and, secondly, the regime had a vested interest in heterosexuality as a means to
population growth.

Throughout this story, the West remains a crucial influence – but
there is also a strong divergence of East and West German experiences.
East Germany lacked both an unfettered gay liberation movement
and a full-fledged 'scene'. One result was the relatively unfragmented
nature of the gay community. Even though in some cities lesbians and
gay men formed separate groups, they still met and co-operated. The
dearth of gay meeting places also meant that the gay community was far
less differentiated by sexual preference than in the West. Indeed, once
the Wall was opened, some East Germans were somewhat alienated
by the sexually oriented nature of the West German gay scene.[121] (It is
also worth mentioning that the lack of freedom of movement into and
out of East Germany, along with the dearth of injectible drugs, meant
that AIDS was a more minor problem than in the West.)[122] On the
other hand, gay men and women were necessarily more integrated into
heterosexual society in some respects: for example, 'Lesbians in the
Church' co-operated with heterosexual women's groups, and many circles of friends were a mixture of gay men, lesbians, and heterosexuals.

Conclusion

What do the experiences of gay men and lesbians tell us about the
broader picture of East German sexuality? First of all, they make clear
that there was little that was romantic about many homosexual lives.
It could be extremely difficult for gay men and lesbians to meet each
other, to come out to their immediate friends and family, and to discuss
their circumstances openly. Even many champions of the homosexual
cause within the state took a restricted view of what sorts of homosexual
behaviour were acceptable. Erwin Günther's concluding remarks at the
1985 Leipzig conference condemned queens, cottaging, and promiscuity as 'immoral behaviour' which 'damaged the process of rethinking,

[121] Til Streu, 'Eins zu Eins für Ostler', *magnus* 3 (December 1989), 37; reprinted in
Grau (ed.), *Lesben und Schwule*, pp. 96–102.
[122] By the end of 1989, only 84 East Germans had been diagnosed as HIV positive, compared with 37,052 in the Federal Republic. See Rainer Herrn, *Schwule Lebenswelten
im Osten. Andere Orte, andere Biographien. Kommunikationsstrukturen, Gesellungsstile
und Lebensweisen schwuler Männer in den neuen Bundesländern* (Berlin: Deutsche
AIDS-Hilfe, 1999), p. 20.

tolerance, and acceptance of equal rights on the part of the heterosexual majority of the population'.[123] Part of the problem was that both the regime and many of the general public imagined sexuality in very narrow terms. It was assumed that every heterosexual was in a stable, monogamous, happy, lifelong, fruitful marriage, when of course this was often far from the case. But this assumption made it easier to condemn or judge gay and lesbian behaviour. Ultimately, the focus on monogamy and childbearing did not just affect attitudes towards homosexuality: it also undermines the claim that East German sexual mores were more liberal and progressive than those in the West.

There were also pragmatic reasons for the state's refusal to engage with activists' demands. Public policy that enabled heterosexual relationships had an immediate pay-off in terms of the birth rate and the economic function served by the nuclear family. Homosexual relationships were not seen in these terms, and gay rights crept up the political agenda only in the 1980s when it became a political problem. Nevertheless, functionaries' reactions cannot be explained by indifference alone. In many cases, they appeared to go out of their way to impede homosexual relationships, for example the ban on same-sex contact ads.

Homophobia, both latent and overt, was rife in East German society and indeed has persisted to the present day. It is both interesting and regrettable that this fact has been largely ignored outside the literature specifically about homosexuality. Accounts of East Germany as a sexually liberal society, not to mention sexual *Ostalgie* ('ostalgia', or 'nostalgia for the East') rest on either ignorance or distortion of the gay and lesbian experience of socialism. Thomas Brussig, for example, celebrates the lack of a gay 'scene' and criticises the (Western) kind of gay man who 'thinks he is great, just because he shows everybody he is gay'.[124] The implication is that gay men and women were unproblematically accepted and integrated into East German life, without any need to draw attention to themselves. This refusal to think about the difficulties of homosexual invisibility is typical of the sort of heteronormativity that pervades writing on this subject.[125]

Finally, the incomplete liberalisation demonstrates the importance of the public sphere.[126] This was painfully clear to activists, whose work from the World Festival Games onwards centred on bringing

[123] *Psychosoziale Aspekte der Homosexualität* [1986], p. 92.
[124] Brussig, 'Aber der Sex war schöner', 99.
[125] See also Engler, *Die Ostdeutschen*, pp. 257–273.
[126] See also Bryant, 'Queering the Antifascist State'.

homosexuality into the public eye, often at considerable personal risk. Impulses from abroad played a crucial role here, borne over the border on TV channels or in the luggage of sympathetic Western visitors. State concessions came only when gay rights groups found a measure of publicity under the wing of the church. But the church groups, as well as the academic activities of the 1980s, also demonstrate the limits of the socialist public sphere. Stasi surveillance was the most obvious sign of state control, but the absence of freedom of expression meant that activists also lacked the means of controlling their own political agenda. The resultant reliance on the goodwill and judgement of others – be they church officials, local functionaries, or academic collaborators – inevitably limited their demands. Publicity was needed not just to impel liberalisation, but also to push the limits of discussion further. The limited nature of the public sphere meant that a sexual revolution for gay men and lesbians remained nothing more than a dream.

6   The naked republic: nudism

Nudism was an important and highly visible part of the East German sexual revolution. There can be no doubt that East Germans were unusually at ease with nudity. In a survey carried out in 1990, 68% of apprentices between the ages of 16 and 18 had swum in the nude. Amongst young workers in their twenties and thirties the figure went up to 81%, and amongst students it was as high as 87%.[1] As one joke put it: 'What do you call a gathering of two or more GDR citizens? An illegal meeting. Or a nudist beach.'[2] Such widespread nudity was unparalleled across Europe. In France, Britain, and Spain, where nudism was tolerated, segregation was the norm. In Soviet resorts in Crimea and the Baltic states, nudism was kept cordoned off behind tall fences, a practice also common in other Eastern bloc states such as Hungary and Bulgaria. The only other socialist state with substantial levels of nudist activity was Yugoslavia, where Croatian nudist beaches attracted an international following.

Indeed, since the fall of the Berlin Wall, nudity has been seized upon as one of the most visible markers of East German difference. While nudism was well established in certain West German beaches and parks (the English Garden in Munich being the best-known), it was by no means accepted as a matter of course. Nudists tended to be confined to assigned areas: it was acceptable to be naked on particular beaches or when visiting the sauna, but not elsewhere. Camps run by nudist organisations allowed keen nudists to swim, socialise, play sport, and eat and drink in the nude, but these tended to be members-only. What was striking about East Germany was not that people bathed in the nude, but that nude and clothed swimmers mingled freely. In comparison to many societies, both East and West Germans had a relatively relaxed attitude towards nudity, but Westerners were used to much

---

[1] ZA S6146: Partner III – Lehrlinge 1990, p. 47; ZA S6142: Partner III – Berufstätige 1990, p. 42; ZA S6147: Partner III – Studenten 1990, p. 43.
[2] Bürgerinitiative Wald-FKK, www.waldfkk.de/messages/4450.htm.

clearer boundaries. For them, nudity was a legitimate choice, but one that should be exercised only within designated spaces. After reunification, newspapers avidly reported on the 'underpants wars' of the Baltic coast, in which West German tourists demanded lines of demarcation between nudist and non-nudist beaches, as was the norm in the West.[3]

As the 1990s wore on, the ubiquity of nudism became an indelible part of the mythification of the defunct GDR, and a highly visible site of difference between East and West. For West Germans it was a symbol of the simple, almost pre-modern, life on the other side of the Wall. In this interpretation, it was often presented as a form of resistance or at least 'inner emigration' from communist rule.[4] For East Germans, as West German economic and political power established itself, ease with nudity became a feature of East German identity which consciously challenged Western norms. West Germans' insistence that nude and clothed bathers should be strictly segregated served as a metaphor both for East German insouciance and for West German encroachment on East German territory – in this case the beloved site of fondly remembered holidays. In this interpretation, nudism was often glossed as a sign of the liberal nature of East German sexual culture. Herr S said, 'I have the feeling that the Wessis [West Germans] are rather prudish. People then [in the GDR] just all lay down beside each other ... Nowadays you get a funny look if you lie in the wrong place.' In the West, it is implied, the naked body could be seen only in a sexual way, and attitudes towards nudism were prudish and repressed.

These debates point to the sometimes troubled relationship between nudism and sexuality. Nudism is not strictly speaking a sexual activity, as its practitioners have always been at pains to point out. Some would argue that the history of nudism has little to do with a history of sexuality. However, as we shall see, it is difficult to break the psychological link between sex and the naked body. Particularly in the first decade of communist rule, nudism was seen by the state to have sexual overtones. And there is also evidence that some visitors to the

---

[3] See for example Alexander Ferguson, 'Germany's Divide Exposed in Underpants War', *Independent*, 25.8.1992.

[4] Ina Merkel, 'Die Nackten und die Roten. Zum Verhältnis von Nacktheit und Öffentlichkeit in der DDR', *Mitteilungen aus der kulturwissenschaftlichen Forschung* 18 (36) (1995), 80, 82. One Easterner, interviewed about the screen representations of East Germany after 1989 pointed out scathingly: 'this nudist-beach story, it is really shown a lot ... Perhaps they try to find something exotic in that: "well, they didn't have anything, the poor things. Had to claim some territory for themselves after all"' (quoted in Kathrin Hörschelmann, 'Audience Interpretations of (Former) East Germany's Representation in the German Media', *European Urban and Regional Studies* 8 (3) (2001), 195).

nudist beach experienced it as an erotic place. This chapter will ask how nudism's popularity should be interpreted. Was it an expression of East German's easy approach to sexual matters, a means of resistance against the regime, or simply a relatively cheap leisure pursuit?[5] But before tackling these questions, it is important to establish just why nudism became so popular, despite attempts on the part of the authorities to control it and even to ban it outright.

Nudism and the state

By 1949, German nudism already had a long and varied history. It first emerged at the turn of the century, in the *völkisch* nationalism of Richard Ungewitter and the health-centred middle-class reform movement.[6] After the First World War, however, nudism became a mass phenomenon, with both left- and right-wing nudist movements flourishing during the Weimar Republic.[7] When the Nazis came to power, they initially tried to stamp out nudist culture. Soon, however, a compromise was struck, allowing not only organised nudist groups but also a degree of spontaneous naked bathing at lakes and at the seaside, particularly during the war years.[8]

---

[5] On these issues, see also McLellan, 'State Socialist Bodies'.

[6] Chad Ross, *Naked Germany: Health, Race and the Nation* (Oxford and New York: Berg, 2005); Judith Baumgartner, 'Freikörperkultur', in Diethardt Kerbs and Jürgen Renlecke (eds.), *Handbuch der deutschen Reformbewegung 1880–1933* (Wuppertal: Hammer, 1998), pp. 103–114; Arno Klönne, 'Das "Ja zum Leibe" – mehrdeutig. Zur politischen Geschichte der Freikörperkulturbewegung', *Vorgänge* 33 (3) (1994), 27–32.

[7] Michael Andritzky, 'Berlin – Urheimat der Nackten. Die FKK-Bewegung in den 20er Jahren', in M. Andritzky and Thomas Rautenberg (eds.), *'Wir sind nackt und nennen Uns Du'. Von Lichtfreunden und Sonnenkämpfern. Eine Geschichte der Freikörperkultur* (Giessen: Anabas, 1989), pp. 50–105; Baumgartner, 'Freikörperkultur'; Ulf Erdmann Ziegler, *Nackt unter Nackten. Utopien der Nacktkultur 1906–1942* (Berlin: Nishen, 1990); Klaus Toepfer, *Empire of Ecstasy: Nudity and Movement in German Body Culture, 1910–1935* (Berkeley: University of California Press, 1997).

[8] Matthew Jefferies, 'For a Genuine and Noble Nakedness? German Naturism in the Third Reich', *German History* 24 (1) (2006), 62–84; Ulrich Linse, 'Sonnenmenschen unter der Swastika. Die FKK-Bewegung im Dritten Reich', in Michael Grisko (ed.), *Freikörperkultur und Lebenswelt. Studien zur Vor- und Frühgeschichte der Freikörperkultur in Deutschland* (Kassel: Kassel University Press, 1999), pp. 239–296; Dietger Pforte, 'Zur Freikörperkultur–Bewegung im nationalsozialistischen Deutschland', in Andritzky and Rautenberg (eds.), *'Wir sind nackt und nennen Uns Du'*, pp. 136–145; Arnd Krüger, Fabian Krüger and Sybille Treptau, 'Nudism in Nazi Germany: Indecent Behavior or Physical Culture for the Well-Being of the Nation' *International Journal of the History of Sport* 19 (4) (2002), 33–54; Michael Hau, *The Cult of Health and Beauty in Germany: A Social History, 1890–1930* (Chicago and London: University of Chicago Press, 2003), ch. 8.

In the chaos that followed German defeat in 1945, nudists found it relatively easy to re-establish old organisations and bathing spots,[9] and by the early 1950s there were a host of groups active throughout the GDR, many of them with formalised membership and sites dedicated to nude bathing.[10] But, despite their early successes, the legal position of these groups was increasingly precarious. A law passed in 1949 ordered the integration of all independent leisure groups into either the newly formed national trade union (FDGB), the FDJ, or the new national cultural organisation, the Kulturbund. This piece of legislation was not specifically aimed at nudist groups: rather, it was part of a general campaign to bring all leisure activity under the control of the state. Other hobby groups, such as those for dog breeders and allotment holders, were invited to join the relevant section of the FDGB or Kulturbund. But nudists were not accommodated within any of the newly formed socialist organisations. This spelt the end of legally organised nudism in East Germany.

Initially, it was membership of a nudist group that was considered illegal, not the act of nude bathing itself. Indeed, the police authorised nude bathing at traditional spots in places such as Ahrenshoop, Hiddensee, and Zinnowitz on the Baltic coast.[11] The 1953 season saw a total of nineteen official nudist beaches,[12] and the authorities in Thuringia also allowed nude swimming at a number of inland lakes.[13] Press photographs indicate a fairly relaxed attitude towards nudity, with captions describing the nudist beaches as 'paradise on earth'.[14] However, those who strayed off the authorised stretches of coast could expect police questioning and possible fines (Figure 6.1).[15]

---

[9] See for example the approval process for the Freikörper-Kultur-Bund Gross-Berlin in LAB, C Rep 101, Nr 153, p. 197. In 1948, the Interior Administration of the Soviet Zone noted that nudism was not banned, so long as it was morally sound and did not cause a public disturbance: BArch DO1/11.0/HVDVP (Hauptverwaltung der Deutschen Volkspolizei) Nr 898, p. 1, untitled document, Deutsche Verwaltung des Innern in der sowjetischen Besatzungszone, 30.8.1948.

[10] Many of these were based in traditional nude bathing spots to the south-east of Berlin around Königs-Wusterhausen, but there was also nudist activity in Erfurt, Gera, Weimar, Dresden, Köthen (near Halle), and Rudolstadt. See the police records in BArch DO1/11.0/HVDVP, Nr 898.

[11] *Ibid.*, p. 33, DVP (Deutsche Volkspolizei) Mecklenburg to HVDVP, 11.10.1951.

[12] *Ibid.*, p. 52, DVP Rostock to HVDVP, 28.8.1953.

[13] *Ibid.*, p. 17, Chief Inspector Lust, HVDVP, to Secretary of State Warnke, MdI (Ministerium des Innern), 15.11.1950.

[14] Bundesarchiv Bild 183-20742-0001, Freikörperkultur an der Ostsee, 12.8.1953; Bundesarchiv Bild 183-20742-0005, Freikörperkultur an der Ostsee, 12.8.1953.

[15] SAPMO-BArch DY27/1306. 'Zur Diskussion', June 1953, signed by Mr B 'on behalf of 9 workers', BArch DO1/11.0/HVDVP Nr 898, p. 11; 'Betr. Nachtkulturverbände', DVP Sachsen to HVDVP, 20.9.1950.

Figure 6.1: Sign forbidding nudism, Warnemünde, 1953.

Soon even the 'paradise' of the authorised beaches came under threat. In 1954, the minister for the interior, Willi Stoph, demanded a total ban, arguing that 'there is no legal foundation for nude bathing'.[16] This was untrue: Nazi legislation of 1942 was still on the books and allowed nude bathing in places where it could not be seen by third parties.[17] Stoph's ban also represented something of a U-turn: in 1953,

---

[16] BArch DO1/11.0/HVDVP Nr 898, p. 56, Hausmitteilung, Minister for the Interior Willi Stoph to General Inspector Seifert, HVDVP, 5.6.1954.
[17] 'Polizeiverordnung zur Regelung des Badewesens', *Reichsgesetzblatt I* (Berlin: Reichsverlagsamt, 1942), p. 130.

the State Secretariat for Internal Affairs had concluded that individual nude bathing should be allowed to continue and that the authorities should approach the issue with a light touch. There was, for example, no objection to nude bathing at inland lakes, so long as the location was sufficiently remote.[18] Why, then, did Stoph call for a ban only a year later? Regional officials on the Baltic coast, at the sharp end of policing nudism, had begun to press for nudism to be outlawed altogether.[19] They claimed that a hard core of serious nudists was attracting large crowds of curious onlookers, many of whom were themselves inspired to take off their bathing costumes. Apart from the public order implications, officials feared that this would lead to the formation of nudist organisations.[20] Stoph bowed to this pressure, and abandoned the ruling of the year before. Nude bathing could henceforth take place only where there was no access for third parties. Significantly, though, it was forbidden to fence off areas for nude bathing, as this was felt to be the first step towards the setting-up of nudist camps. The result was a de facto ban on nudism.

Clearly, though, there was more to this than the regional tail wagging the national dog. Berlin officials were not prone to letting the provinces dictate policy unless there were sound grounds for action. In this case, nudism stirred up a whole host of anxieties, not just about sex, but also about politics, ideology, and the recent German past.

Right from the start, the authorities portrayed nudists as immoral and motivated by sexual desire. There were claims that nudists had stripped innocent passers-by of their clothes, talk of 'obscene behaviour in public, even in front of children',[21] and allegations that the vast majority of those taking part in nude bathing were 'not people who are interested in keeping their bodies healthy, but people who are looking for sexual satisfaction'.[22] Local authorities were ordered to work closely with the police in order to end the 'mischief being carried out beneath the cloak of nudism on the beaches of the Baltic sea'.[23] The police on the island of Rügen had reported in 1952 that groups of 150 to 200 nudists were 'stopping citizens of the GDR who wish to rest near this

---

[18] BArch DO1/11.0/HVDVP Nr 898, p. 50, State Secretariat for Internal Affairs to the HVDVP, 18.6.1953.

[19] *Ibid.*, p. 56, Hausmitteilung, Minister for the Interior Willi Stoph to General Inspector Seifert, HVDVP, 5.6.1954.

[20] *Ibid.*, p. 58, General Inspector Seifert, HVDVP, to Minister for the Interior Willi Stoph n.d. [June 1954], p. 62, Seifert to regional DVP, 25.6.1954.

[21] *Ibid.*, p. 62, Seifert to all regional DVP chiefs, 25.6.1954 (draft).

[22] *Ibid.*, p. 58, General Inspector Seifert, HVDVP, to Minister for the Interior Willi Stoph n.d. [June 1954].

[23] BArch DO1/10.0/174/4, p. 90, MdI to regional authorities, 31.7.1954.

area or walk through it, undressing them and throwing them in the sea. Boats near the coast, some of them carrying women and children, are being capsized and their occupants thrown in the water too. Citizens' watches and cameras have been rendered unusable by this.'[24] The contrast between law-abiding, clothed 'citizens' and delinquent nudists was underlined by the fact that female nudists had begun to 'paint their breasts with toothpaste and wear particularly flamboyant make-up'.[25]

This moral panic was often expressed in class terms, as a conflict between decadent, bourgeois intellectuals and morally 'clean' proletarians. Local police reports stressed that the ban had been greeted approvingly by the workers,[26] and the Ministry of the Interior described nudity as a threat to the 'natural and healthy feelings of our working people',[27] echoing Nazi legislation on nude bathing that banned behaviour which might 'injure the healthy and natural sensitivities of the people [*Volksempfinden*]'.[28] One way of underlining this, and of marginalising nudists, was to mobilise the FDJ: groups of young people from an FDJ holiday camp were used to patrol the beach at Ahrenshoop in August 1954, declaring, witnesses claimed, 'today we're allowed to give [you] a good thrashing'.[29] This emphasis on class conflict demonstrates both the SED's ideological approach to rule in the 1950s and the extent to which sex and politics were intertwined.

For communists, organised nudism had particularly unsavoury political connotations. The Weimar proletarian nudist movement had been predominantly Social Democrat-aligned, most notably in the form of the 'Body Culture Schools' set up by Adolf Koch to promote nude gymnastics. Koch was a utopian socialist who felt that physical exercise and fresh air could help the working class overcome the effects of poverty, malnutrition, and hard work on their bodies. He was anti-drinking, anti-smoking, and liberal on sexual matters, arguing for the legalisation of homosexuality and abortion, and the acceptance of sex and child-bearing outside marriage. He was also a committed pacifist.[30] None

[24] Landesarchiv Greifswald (henceforth LAG), Rep 202/1, 12/008, p. 6, 'Bericht', DVP Bergen, 22.8.1952.
[25] *Ibid.*
[26] BArch, DO1/11.0/HVDVP Nr 898, p. 75, DVP Rostock to HVDVP, 4.11.1954.
[27] BArch DO1/10.0/174/4, p, 55, Otto, MdI, to Dr B, 18.6.1953.
[28] 'Polizeiverordnung zur Regelung des Badewesens', p. 130.
[29] SAPMO-BArch DY27/1306, Prof. Dr-Ing. H. Kirchberg, an den Vorsitzenden des Förderungsausschusses für die Deutsche Intellingenz, Herrn Prof. Dr Kastner, 29.10.1954. Cf. LAG, Rep. 200, 8.3.2., Nr 28, p. 45, Rechenschafts-Bericht über den Verlauf der Badesaison 1955 in den Seebädern des Kreises Wolgast.
[30] Cf. Spitzer, ' "Nackt und frei" '; Spitzer, 'Die "Adolf-Koch-Bewegung" '; Andritzky, 'Berlin – Urheimat der Nackten'.

of these principles fitted in well with the altogether more militaristic and sexually straight-laced communism of the early Cold War. The anti-Social Democratic purges that had taken place in the late 1940s and early 1950s proved an even more fundamental stumbling block. In this context, nudism was automatically suspect. As the state sport organisation put it, in no uncertain terms: 'The "nudist unions" were a by-product of the disintegration of imperialism in the area of body culture and sport ... as an expression of imperialist decadence, "nudist unions" cannot be tolerated.'[31]

The fact that Koch was active in the re-emerging nudist movement in West Germany led to a third grounds for suspicion: that many of those indulging in nude bathing in and around East Berlin were petty-bourgeois West Berliners. The Motzener Lake south of Berlin had been the spiritual home of German nudists during the 1920s, and many returned there after the war. The *Märchenwiese*, or Fairy-Tale Meadow nudist area, was shut down when a police investigation discovered that its users were 'business people, intellectuals, and white-collar workers', the majority of whom lived in West Berlin and were not sympathetic to the GDR. 'It is obvious', the report concluded, 'that this is not a case of simple naked swimming, but of a West Berlin nudist group.'[32] The Ministry of the Interior decreed that this cross-border tourism would have to come to an end: 'The GDR has no interest in tolerating enemy elements in the most beautiful regions of Brandenburg. The grounds would surely be a wonderful holiday camp for our FDJ and thereby offer a greater number of our working young people rest and relaxation.'[33]

Worst of all, however, were the associations with Nazism, particularly the spectacular visibility of the nude or semi-nude body in certain areas of Nazi culture. From Leni Riefenstahl's *Olympia* to the public sculptures of Arno Breker and Josef Thorak, such images of the body contributed to the postwar belief that the public display of nudity sprang from suspect motives. The East German authorities concluded that those wishing to rebuild nudist traditions were Nazi sympathisers. This view gained credence when it was discovered that a former Nazi Party member was running a commercial nudist operation out of a trade union-registered allotment group in Erfurt.[34] Concerns about the racial connotations of the nude body were further inflamed by the so-called Cameroon parties which took place on the Baltic beaches

[31] BArch DO1/11.0/HVDVP Nr 898, p. 30, Weißig, Deutscher Sportausschuss, to HVDVP, 28.8.1951.
[32] *Ibid.*, p. 17, Chief Inspector Lust to Secretary of State Warnke, MdI, 15.11.1950.
[33] *Ibid.*, p. 25, Malz, MdI to Brandenburg MdI, 4.12.1950.
[34] *Ibid.*, p. 9, Kolb, HVDVP, to DVP Weimar, 19.8.1950.

every summer. Nudists gathered on the beach at night, with painted bodies and elaborate headgear, to elect a 'tribal leader' who formed the centre of the night's celebrations. As Karl Maron, chief of police and deputy minister of the interior, put it, not only were such events 'an insult to the ethics and customs of the Negro peoples', they 'in no way contributed to securing friendship between nations'.[35] If the regime was understandably uncomfortable with the racial subtext of the Cameroon parties, it was equally ill at ease with their hedonistic nature. Bodies were for work, not pleasure, and those lucky enough to have a seaside holiday should spend their time resting and recuperating, not living it up at potentially racist festivities.

Nudists resist the ban

Nudists, then, were seen variously as sexual miscreants, Social Democratic revivalists, Nazi sympathisers, West German day-trippers, and morally dubious party-goers. In each case, their hobby was interpreted as politically dangerous and ethically suspect. Nudists – not surprisingly – portrayed themselves in quite a different light. Accused of public order offences, they claimed that their actions were simply self-protection against peeping toms. Members of the intelligentsia stressed their need for quiet and relaxation during their holidays and emphasised that the problem was not nudism, but the behaviour of those narrow-minded enough to try to disrupt it. As the 56-year-old Rudolf S put it in 1955: 'The prudish aunts who even in this day and age think that they have to get worked up about these progressively minded people [i.e. nudists] will always find reasons to oppose it [nudism]. People who see something dirty in their naked neighbour should put their own house in order first. They only seek out these particular bits of the beach to gratify their own desires.'[36]

Nudists were also quick to point to the hypocrisies in the regime's position. One man wrote to the Ministry of the Interior claiming that its own employees were driving nudists to act in self-defence: 'Would you let yourself be called a "dirty pig" by a 17-year-old boy ... ? Or let yourself be photographed against your will from boats five metres away from the shore (which were only rented to employees of the Ministry of the Interior)?'[37] A common tactic amongst petitioners was to criticise

[35] *Ibid.*, p. 78, Chief of Police Karl Maron to Karl F, 10.12.1954.
[36] LAG, Rep. 200, 8.2.3., Nr 9, p. 77, Rudolf S to RdB (Rat des Bezirkes) Rostock, 17.9.1955.
[37] BArch, DO1/11.0/HVDVP Nr 898, p. 80, Karl F to Karl Maron, 9.2.1955.

the regime for not being progressive enough, while stressing their own socialist credentials. One concentration camp survivor wrote that nudism was essential therapy for his wartime injuries.[38] A party member caught during a police raid of a nude bathing spot near Berlin claimed that naked swimming had always been a part of the workers' sport movement. 'In those days [nudists] were thrashed to bits by the rubber truncheons of the fascist police. Such things cannot be allowed to happen in a workers' and peasants' state.'[39] One particularly tenacious group, fighting to preserve their bathing spot on the outskirts of Berlin, argued that 'nudism is an integral part of our party, an old tradition ... our Soviet friends also practise nudism'.[40]

Petitioners were not afraid to target the regime's weak spots. Accused of Nazi sympathies, one group retorted that this was a 'cheap' tactic, similar to those used by the enemies of socialism who claimed that the Free German Youth – the party's youth wing – was the Hitler Youth in different coloured shirts.[41] In any case, nudists were well aware that, in the postwar period, everybody had the right to re-invent themselves. A nudist group at the Zeesener Lake, which had bent with the wind during the Third Reich,[42] insisted in 1954 that 'the new spirit in the camp has nothing to do with the old tradition. Guests from the party and the Free German Youth are helping us to create this new spirit.'[43]

Nudists often stressed that many among their number were communists. One group of 110 members inspected in 1954 had nineteen party members, including two judges.[44] Nudists also enjoyed pointing out the inconsistencies in the ban's enforcement. Even after the ban, some local authorities on the coast continued to authorise nude bathing under the terms of the 1942 law. (However, this decision was reversed after a doctor complained that nudists had attacked him and his wife.)[45] Late in the summer of 1954, it was discovered that the local authorities in a village near Dresden had been running a profitable nudist camp – with the permission of the local council. Almost 1,000 tickets had been sold

---

[38] SAPMO-BArch DY27/1306, Rudolf B, to Kulturbund Feriendienst, 22.6.1954.
[39] BArch, DO1/11.0/HVDVP Nr 898, p. 93, Brandt, DVP Potsdam, to HVDVP, 22.8.1955.
[40] LAB, C. Rep 303–26, Nr 221, p. 15, VP (Volkspolizei) Mitte to VP Berlin, 13.8.1954.
[41] BArch DO1/11.0/HVDVP Nr 898, p. 37, 'Memorandum', Sport-Gemeinschaft 'Freiheit', Berlin, 15.11.1951.
[42] Chronik des Sportgeländes am Zeesener See (n.p., 1998).
[43] LAB, C. Rep 303–26, Nr 221, p. 16, Bericht über die Besprechung mit dem Partei-Aktiv der Sektion Touristik, 4.8.1954.
[44] Ibid., p. 14, VP Mitte to VP Berlin, 13.8.1954.
[45] BArch DO1/11.0/HVDVP Nr 898, p. 73, Rostock DVP to HVDVP, 4.11.1954.

over the course of the summer, and guests included doctors, professors, police officers, and workers. All four men involved in running it were members of the SED.[46] Such inconsistencies made life hard for those who tried to enforce the ban, as outraged nudists argued that nudism was allowed in their hometowns or on other parts of the coast.

The nudists' most successful tactic, however, was civil disobedience. Not only did they continue to swim and sunbathe in the nude, but they also deliberately subverted and ridiculed state attempts to enforce the ban. As the Rostock police commented dryly in 1954: 'After the ban had been made public, some holidaymakers put a tie around their necks and went swimming like that. They wanted to show that they were not swimming naked, but had something on.'[47] Other holidaymakers removed signs banning nude bathing or defaced them with caricatures portraying local politicians as stuck-up, prudish bureaucrats. By 1955, one year into the ban, the situation had, if anything, got worse. Up to 250 people a day were bathing nude at Ahrenshoop and up to 550 on the island of Hiddensee.[48] The policing of the ban became increasingly heavy-handed: hundreds of people were fined, the police patrolled the beaches day and night, and the names of 254 people who had signed a petition against the ban were sent to their local police authorities. But it was clear that the ban was unenforceable. Many nudist beaches set up a watch system that warned bathers of an approaching police officer, so they could slip on their bathing costumes.[49] Embarrassingly for the police, many of these nudists were party members or state officials.[50]

There was something playfully subversive about the nudists' actions, which sought to emphasise the harmlessness of their hobby and the disproportionate bullying tactics being used against it. But if their strategy on the beaches was to draw attention to the silliness of the situation and ridicule the police's attempts to enforce the ban, they were also expressing a deadly serious rejection of the regime's authority. As well as simply disobeying the law, people were not afraid to make their protest heard and defend what they saw as their individual right to bathe as they pleased.

After two chaotic summers and a barrage of complaints, the state was forced to admit defeat. A new law was passed in the spring of 1956,

[46] *Ibid.*, p. 72, Dresden DVP to HVDVP, 28.8.1954.
[47] *Ibid.*, p. 75, DVP Rostock to HVDVP, 4.11.1954.
[48] *Ibid.*, p. 94, Steingräber, DVP Rostock, to HVDVP, 24.8.1955.
[49] According to Klaus Ender, this look-out system survived until well into the 1960s: interview with Klaus Ender, 16.1.2004.
[50] LAG, Rep. 202/1, Nr 12/008, p. 188, 'Betr. Polizeiverordnung zur Regelung des Badewesens', 11.8.1954.

superseding both the National Socialist legislation still on the statute
books and the ad hoc ban of 1954.[51] Under the new legislation, local
authorities were allowed to allocate beaches for nude bathing. Small
groups, such as families, were permitted to bathe naked together, but
on no account in groups of more than ten. Crucially, it remained illegal
to form nudist organisations.[52] Like the earlier guidelines, the new law
made a clear distinction between nude bathing, which was permitted,
and organised nudism, which was not. This legislation remained in
place until the end of the East German state in 1990. But, like the
ban which preceded it, it proved impossible to enforce. As Germany's
economic recovery progressed and more people had the time, money,
and permission to travel to the seaside, the Baltic coast became more
crowded, pushing nudists and non-nudists closer together. Nudists,
used to setting up camp on an isolated stretch of beach, increasingly
came into contact with passers-by, many of whom were witnessing nudism for the first time. Their success in overthrowing the ban also gave
nudists a new confidence. Having taken on the regime on its own terms
and won, they continued to push the boundaries of the legislation – and
of the designated nudist areas.

At the Prerow campsite, there were reports of widespread nudity, to
the point of people shopping in the nude.[53] In 1960 the Rostock regional
council decided that the number of beaches available for nude bathing
should be reduced and that nudism on campsites should be brought
to an end.[54] Attempts to ban nude bathing in Prerow altogether were
shelved after tourists' protests forced the local authorities to allocate
a 500-metre stretch of beach for nudists. Holidaymakers immediately
moved the signs to treble the length of the nudist beach, and a police
inspection in mid July 1960 noted: 'Naked life takes place not just on
the beach, but between the tents too.'[55] The inspectors were greeted
with 'loud howling', designed to alert other nudists to their presence,
and the long-suffering policemen wrote in their report: 'As we left the
camping site, some people sang "dress up warm now", which was probably aimed at us. But we didn't allow ourselves to be provoked.'[56] Prerow

[51] Anordnung zur Regelung des Freibadewesens, Vom 18 Mai 1956, *Gesetzblatt I*, 50, 6 June 1956, pp. 433ff.
[52] SAPMO-BArch DY27/3318, 'Entwurf. Begründung zur Verordnung über die Regelung des Badeverkehrs'.
[53] LAG, Rep 202/1, 12/008, p. 28, 'Einschätzung der Badesaison 1959'.
[54] *Ibid.*, p. 137, Auszug aus dem Beschluß des RdB vom 9.2.1960.
[55] *Ibid.*, p. 199, VP Rostock, 'Betr. Freibadewesen in den Kreisen Ribnitz und Wolgast', 16.7.1960.
[56] *Ibid.*

was to become legendary as a bastion of East German nudism, with the unofficially sanctioned nudist campsite a particular draw.[57]

Nudism in the 1960s

In 1959, the local authorities estimated that about 13,000 people had taken part in nude bathing in the Rostock region. By 1960 their number had risen to 20,000 (out of a total of 1.7 million holidaymakers).[58] By the start of the 1960s, it was clear that any SED hopes that nudism would remain confined to a few isolated beaches had been misplaced. Who were these nudists, and why was nudism expanding at such a rapid pace? In the summer of 1966, two researchers surveyed more than a thousand holidaymakers in nudist campsites on the Baltic coast. This survey permits a rare glimpse into the world of the GDR nudist. Not only do the questionnaires shed light on the irrepressible popularity of nudism in the GDR, they also give us a glimpse of nudists' self-understanding. What are particularly interesting are the ways they defined themselves in relation to the East German state and its values. Not only did nudists see themselves as socialist, in many ways they considered themselves to be more progressive than the regime, whose opposition to nudism was portrayed as old-fashioned, prudish, and reactionary. Their sense of themselves as socialist subjects was a strong one: although the questionnaire's authors stressed its anonymity, many nudists made a point of adding their names and addresses even though no section was provided for this purpose.

Of fifty-six respondents who gave a date for their first nudist experiences, thirty-seven of them were within the period 1956–62.[59] Of course it is possible that respondents were reluctant to admit that they had been breaking the ban before 1956. However, local authority records show a huge increase in demand for nudist camping spots in this period, reinforcing the impression that many came to nudism post-1956. The results of the main survey appeared to back up the regime's claim that nudism was a middle-class activity: 46.3% of men and 25.5% of women questioned were members of the intelligentsia, whereas only 19% of male and 11% of female respondents described themselves as workers.[60] However, the figures for parental background tell a slightly different story: over half (54.9%) came from a working-class background, with

[57] See Thormann, ' "Schont die Augen der Nation"', p. 45.
[58] LAG, Rep. 200, 8.3.2., Nr 27, p. 45, Bericht über den Ablauf der Badesaison 1960 und Schlußfolgerungen für das Jahr 1961 und im Siebenjahrplan.
[59] *Ibid.*, Nr 98, questionnaire responses, 1966.
[60] All percentages refer to the total sample of 1,000.

only 6.6.% born into the intelligentsia.[61] It seems that many of those surveyed were first-generation white-collar workers, who had benefited from the social mobility of the first two decades of socialist rule. This contradicts at least partially the party's picture of nudists as bourgeois intellectuals. Other evidence indicates that working-class Germans may not have been as opposed to nakedness as the SED imagined: photographic evidence from 1952 shows farmers bathing naked after a day in the fields,[62] and the Mecklenburg police reported as early as 1951 that workers from Wismut and their families were making enthusiastic use of a nudist beach in Graal-Müritz, despite the fact that it was three kilometres beyond the normal beach.[63] Nudity was nothing new to the miners of Wismut, who often worked in the nude due to the high temperatures underground.[64]

The vast majority of those surveyed had gone to the nudist beach on the recommendation of friends, acquaintances, and colleagues out of curiosity, or simply because they had stumbled across it.[65] A veterinarian wrote of his conversion to nudism: 'At first out of curiosity, but then out of conviction, because I was so inspired by the people on the nudist beach'.[66] This is not to say that the pre-war traditions of German nudism played no role at all. A number of respondents mentioned that either they or their families had been involved in nudism prior to 1945. But the majority were what might be termed 'opportunistic nudists', who, in the words of one enthusiast, 'saw it – tried it – liked it'.[67] Starting as casual nude bathers, they had been won over by the unique atmosphere of the nudist beach and become committed nudists. In contrast to the West, nudism was a very accessible activity. Anyone – so long as they were naked and were prepared to adhere to certain codes of behaviour – could go to a nudist beach. There was no need to join a club, send off for information, or pay a membership fee. By banning nudist organisations and nudist camps, the regime kept nudism out in the open. But this ban also had the unintended consequence of opening nudism up to a much wider potential public who were, for a combination of reasons, willing to give it a try.

---

[61] LAG, Rep. 200, 8.3.2, Nr 98, p. 3, summary report on the survey.
[62] Bundesarchiv Bild 183-15844-0026, In der Produktionsgenossenschaft 'Thomas Müntzer' 11.8.1952.
[63] BArch DO1/11.0/HVDVP Nr 898, p. 33, Hövelmans, Mecklenburg DVP to HVDVP, 13.10.1951.
[64] *Neue Berliner Illustrierte* 25/1952, pp. 34–35.
[65] LAG, Rep. 200, 8.3.2, Nr 98, graph: 'Wie zur FKK gekommen?'
[66] *Ibid.*, p. 30, questionnaire response, 1966.
[67] *Ibid.*, p. 65, questionnaire response, 1966.

The most commonly mentioned reason for favouring nudism was health, cited by 79.8 per cent of respondents.[68] The questionnaire had been issued by the Sports Medicine Centre in Rostock, and it may be the case that respondents felt this answer was expected of them (unaware that the researchers themselves were sceptical about the health benefits of nudism). Nonetheless, some respondents waxed lyrical on how healthy nudism had made them. One teacher claimed that neither she, her husband, nor their three children had had a cold since their first experiences of nudism seven years previously.[69] A common refrain in this context was liberation from the wet swimming costume: not a trivial matter in the pre-Lycra days of heavy fabrics. Many East Germans wore hand-knitted swimsuits, which must have felt very unpleasant when saturated with seawater. In the notorious winds of the Baltic coast, it was undoubtedly pleasanter and quicker to allow your naked body to dry without soggy swimwear. Nudism was also seen as more hygienic: campers welcomed the chance to wash themselves thoroughly without the obstacle of a swimsuit.[70]

Best of all, nudism was extremely inexpensive. Nudists emphasised the fact that they were spared the price of expensive swimwear, underlining the thriftiness of their hobby as well as implicitly rebuking the regime's pricing policy. (Two respondents also mentioned the prohibitive cost of women's swimwear: 90 marks for a bikini and 150 marks for a one-piece swimsuit.[71] If those prices were correct, it must surely have been tempting to go naked.) Such remarks also suggested a pleasing and socially responsible frugality; nudism could be enjoyed without putting the state's limited economic resources under any more strain.

However, nudist and regime conceptions of health were not identical. Some respondents described nudism as an antidote to the strains of modern urban life. The majority of those surveyed lived in towns and cities.[72] There was of course a tradition of nudism at lakes in the vicinity of large cities such as Leipzig and Berlin, and many of those who had 'discovered' nudism while on holiday at the coast wished to continue their newfound hobby on summer weekends.[73] Some inland nudist provision already existed near Zwickau, Dessau, and Leipzig.[74]

[68] *Ibid.*, p. 13, questionnaire response, 1966.

[69] *Ibid.*, p. 25, questionnaire response, 1966.

[70] *Ibid.*, pp. 78, 28, questionnaire responses, 1966.

[71] *Ibid.*, pp. 51, 49, questionnaire responses, 1966. For comparison, the average gross salary in 1965 was 633 marks: *Statistisches Jahrbuch der Deutschen Demokratischen Republik 1990*, p. 52.

[72] *Ibid.*, graph, 'Herkunftsbezirke der FKK-Urlauber'.

[73] *Ibid.*, graph: 'Kritische Bemerkungen der FKK-Urlauber'.

[74] *Ibid.*, pp. 32, 37, 39, questionnaire responses, 1966.

Significantly, all these beaches were in southern East Germany, which was furthest from the sea, most heavily industrialised, and had the most workers.[75] One frequent visitor to the Zwickau beach, a 32-year-old seamstress, wrote that her weekend nudism gave her 'true rest after a week full of work'.[76] The idea that nudism allowed workers to rest and recuperate may have been calculated to reassure the authorities, but nudist discourses about its health benefits also contained an implicit critique of some aspects of socialist modernity. A kindergarten worker from Karl-Marx-Stadt wrote that a nudist holiday gave her and her family a chance to 'clean out their polluted lungs',[77] and a 52-year-old doctor declared 'there is no better prophylaxis against the illnesses of civilisation!'[78] The idea that nudism was a health-giving antidote to the ill effects of modern urban life was not the only ideological hangover from the Weimar nudist movement. Smoking was also banned or limited to restricted areas at a number of nudist bathing spots.[79]

Numerous respondents described nudism as 'natural', and others eulogised 'the feeling of closeness with nature'.[80] For one man, 'the combination of tent, sea, and nudist beach probably guarantees the most intensive experience of a sea holiday'.[81] The vast majority of nudists surveyed were campers who saw the simplicity of the facilities on offer at designated nude beaches as a plus. In the emerging socialist leisure culture, this put them in a minority. Most East German campers were eager to make life under canvas as cosy and comfortable as life at home. As well as stocking up on the latest camping gear, they put pressure on the tourist authorities to provide modern facilities and shopping opportunities.[82] The nudists of the 1960s, it seems, fell into the smaller category of nature enthusiasts, who enjoyed roughing it and feared that

[75] The southernmost districts of Dresden, Erfurt, Gera, Halle, Chemnitz, Leipzig, Suhl, and Cottbus accounted for 46.1% of the GDR's landmass, but 60.6% of its population and 71.9% of its industrial workers: *Statistisches Jahrbuch der Deutschen Demokratischen Republik 1990*, p. 65.

[76] LAG, Rep. 200, 8.3.2, Nr 98, p. 32, questionnaire response, 1966.

[77] *Ibid.*, p. 67, questionnaire response, 1966.

[78] *Ibid.*, p. 52, questionnaire response, 1966.

[79] LAG, Rep. 200, 8.3.2 Nr 9, pp. 93–94; Friedrich Hagen, *Baden ohne. FKK zwischen Mövenort und Talsperre Pöhl* (Leipzig and Berlin: VEB Tourist Verlag, 1982), p. 40. On smoking in the GDR, see Hong, 'Cigarette Butts and the Building of Socialism in East Germany'.

[80] LAG, Rep. 200, 8.3.2, Nr 98, p. 10, questionnaire response, 1966.

[81] *Ibid.*, p. 23, questionnaire response, 1966.

[82] See Scott Moranda, 'The Dream of a Therapeutic Regime: Nature Tourism in the German Democratic Republic, 1945–1978', unpublished Ph.D. dissertation, University of Wisconsin–Madison (2005).

overdevelopment would tip the fragile balance between enjoying the countryside and destroying it.[83]

Siegfried Lachmann, who began visiting Prerow in the early 1960s, described the 'naturalness' (*Natürlichkeit*) as the most striking thing about the nudist beach:

One time I watched two people, pensioners, I think they were between 75 and 85, so very, very old people. Very tanned, really dark brown, they must have spent months there ... and completely old bodies, not sporty at all. And – but it was so natural, the way they moved, came out of the water, dried each other off, and then sat down in the deck chairs they had brought with them, the way they treated each other so carefully, everything really slow, that made a big impression on me as a young man, how you can move around on this beach. Without any bashfulness ... I'll never forget it.[84]

For Lachmann, 'naturalness' was not just about contact with nature, but also an unabashed and unselfconscious attitude towards the body. What seemed particularly striking was the fact that people with ageing, slack bodies were able to take their clothes off without shame or embarrassment. Many nudists concluded that this openness about the body helped to break the link between nudity and sex. Nudism, it was argued, was not an excuse to ogle the unclad forms of the opposite sex. On the contrary, nudism de-eroticised the body, unlike swimwear, which ratcheted up sexual tension by fetishising the parts it concealed. By allowing its proponents to see nakedness as natural, and by severing all associations with sexual activity, nudism encouraged respectful and equal relationships between the sexes. Lachmann's account, for example, stresses the tenderness of the relationship between the two elderly bathers.[85] Those surveyed in the mid 1960s argued similarly:

The view of another person's body allows decent people no room for erotic feelings.

It is of great value to socialism that nudism prevents any unclean erotic fantasies.

---

[83] For more on the relationship between nudism, industrialisation, and nature, see David Bell and Ruth Holliday, 'Naked as Nature Intended', *Body & Society* 6 (2000), 127–140.

[84] Interview with Siegfried Lachmann, 22.03.2004.

[85] The argument that sexual attraction had no place on the nudist beach has, of course, been crucial for nudists worldwide in their struggles to gain respectability and acceptance. See Ruth Barcan, *Nudity: A Cultural Anatomy* (Oxford: Berg, 2004), p. 172; Martin Weinberg, 'Sexual Modesty, Social Meanings, and the Nudist Camp', *Social Problems* 12 (3) (1965), 311–318; Chad Ross, *Naked Germany*, ch. 7; George Mosse, *Nationalism and Sexuality: Respectability and Abnormal Sexuality in Modern Europe* (New York: Howard Fertig, 1985), p. 51.

Here the woman is not an object of desire, she is a comrade, there is no bikini to excite you.[86]

Nudists contrasted the atmosphere on their sections of beach and camping sites with what they saw as the over-sexualised popular and youth culture of the 1950s and 1960s. A number of respondents referred to the need for nudism as an antidote to commercialised sexuality available even under socialism such as striptease or prostitution at the Leipzig exhibition.[87] Many saw nudism as an escape from the generational conflicts of the postwar period: the nude beach was a rock'n'roll free zone, an oasis for those who wanted to go on holiday to relax and commune with nature, rather than to have noisy fun. While a member of the Erfurt leadership of the SED wrote in 1955, 'naked bathing in the sea can never be wrong and cannot offend anybody', what did offend him was the behaviour of young campers: 'I don't think it is right when 17-year-old boys sleep together with 15-year-old girls in a two-person tent.'[88] Such tensions seem to have got worse as time went on: in the 1966 survey, a 37-year-old engineer cited as his main motivation for nudism the fact that 'rioting young men stay far away'.[89]

One of the attractions of nudism was that it offered the company of like-minded adults, most of them on holiday with their spouses and children. Nudists saw their campsites as an oasis of moral, social, and material order. Even two police officers sent to clamp down on a well-known nudist camping spot were forced to admit that it was cleaner than other campsites in the area.[90] Herr L had fond memories of the camp patrols in Prerow in the 1960s. 'There was silence after 10 o'clock at night! And if there was noise anywhere, three or four men would come along and say "Quiet, or you'll have to leave" … That was such great solidarity, you felt very very much at home there.' Sixties nudists often used words such as 'comradeship'[91] and described the nudists as a 'collective',[92] 'community',[93] or 'one big family'.[94]

Often, this was a means of stressing the asexual nature of nudism. One of the most highly prized values of the nudist community was

[86] LAG, Rep. 2008, 8.3.2., Nr 98, pp. 30, 23, 14, questionnaire responses, 1966.
[87] Ibid., pp. 14, 18, 16, questionnaire responses, 1966.
[88] BArch DY27/3320, Schmarje to Kneschke, 13.9.1955.
[89] LAG, Rep. 200, 8.3.2., Nr 98, p. 63, questionnaire response, 1966.
[90] LAG, Rep. 202/1, Nr 12/008, p. 200, VP Rostock, 'Betr. Freibadewesen in den Kreisen Ribnitz und Wolgast', 16.7.1960.
[91] LAG, Rep. 200, 8.3.2., Nr 98, pp. 30, 40, 49, questionnaire responses, 1966.
[92] Ibid., pp. 50, 37, questionnaire responses, 1966.
[93] Ibid., pp. 33, 37, questionnaire responses, 1966.
[94] Ibid., p. 38, questionnaire response, 1966.

sexual self-discipline.[95] One man praised 'the necessary self-control and everybody's clean behaviour' as what he liked most about nudism.[96] Another respondent mentioned: 'moral cleanliness, indecent behaviour only ever in the case of novices, who are immediately taught better'.[97] Nudists, it seemed, formed a self-policing community based on shared values such as discipline, cleanliness, and (sexual) self-control.[98] The nudists of the 1960s were also broadly sympathetic to socialism – in fact many of them had been the beneficiaries of the postwar reconstruction. But this did not mean an uncritical acceptance of its values: many used their hobby to articulate a critique of socialist consumerism, urbanisation, and the sexualisation of youth culture. Their vision of a simpler, healthier socialism, based on family values, closeness to nature, self-discipline, and sexual restraint, found an outlet in the communities of the nudist beaches.

Race and the naked body

However, we should beware of concluding that all nudists at this time shared such values. While many saw their hobby as a way of decom-modifying the body and combating the over-sexualisation of society, there was also a strand within the nudist movement that adorned and decorated the body. Participants in the Cameroon parties on the Baltic coast used toothpaste, cocoa, shells, feathers, and seaweed to make costumes for elaborate festivals which imitated African 'tribal rituals' (or an East German imagining of them).

The evidence about the nature of these parties is fragmentary.[99] Concerned officials, responsible for the trade union holiday home in Prerow, reported widespread 'cultural barbarism' in the summer of

---

[95] For a similar phenomenon amongst American nudists, see Weinberg, 'Sexual Modesty, Social Meanings, and the Nudist Camp'.

[96] LAG, Rep. 200, 8.3.2., Nr 98, p. 42, questionnaire response, 1966.

[97] *Ibid.*, p. 16, questionnaire response, 1966.

[98] In some cases these values were officially codified. A nude bathing spot near Leipzig, authorised by the Zwenkau town council, was equipped with an exhaustive set of rules: naked bathing was compulsory, dogs, smoking, and photography were banned, children were allowed entry only with the permission of their parents, and six 'suitable friends of free body hygiene' were authorised to ensure that these rules were abided by (LAG, Rep. 200, 8.3.2., Nr 9, p. 94; 'Geländeordnung', 1957). The nude beach at the Parsteiner Lake in Brandenburg had a similar set of rules right into the 1980s, discouraging single male visitors and allowed smoking only in a designated area (Friedrich Hagen, *Baden ohne*, p. 40).

[99] On the Cameroon parties, see Judith Kruse, 'Nische im Sozialismus', in *Endlich Urlaub! Begleitbuch zur Ausstellung im Haus der Geschichte der Bundesrepublik Deutschland, Bonn. 6. Juni bis 13 Oktober 1996* (Cologne: DuMont Reiserverlag, 1996), pp. 106–111; Benno Pludra, *Haik und Paul* (Berlin: Verlag Neues Leben, 1956).

1953. According to their account, nudist groups were gathering under the monikers 'Cameroon', 'Abyssinia', and 'Zambezi', setting up camps, and holding elaborate festivals that culminated with the election of a 'tribal chief'. The celebrations were described as 'scandalous' and 'downright sadistic':

> Harmless walkers, including 62-year-old men, were assaulted, undressed, thrown in the water, and then tied to the red-painted 'stake'. Young, painted girls then carried out 'belly dances' in front of these 'prisoners'.[100]

Clearly such accounts need to be taken with a pinch of salt. The officials admitted frankly that they were concerned not just about the ideologically dubious nature of such parties, but about their negative impact on more 'socialist' leisure pursuits. Attendance at trade union-organised academic lectures and opera performances was at an all-time low, as holidaymakers preferred to join in the less regimented fun of the Cameroon parties.

But there is no reason to believe that the hedonistic nature of these parties was a figment of the official imagination. Photographic evidence shows crowds of fifty or more, all naked or wearing seaweed loincloths, watching 'tribal' dancing around a 'totem pole' (note the conflation of African and Native American cultures).[101] A wide range of ages appear to have taken part, from young children to people in their fifties. The crowds seem, however, to have been made up predominantly of men and women in their twenties and thirties.[102] These parties must have involved elaborate preparation, with participants fashioning complicated costumes and long necklaces of shells, and going to some lengths to acquire products to paint their bodies. Officials in Prerow complained that local shops were completely sold out of toothpaste and shoe polish (the former used for 'tribal' markings, the latter for 'blacking up').[103] It is hard to avoid the impression that the Cameroon parties were motivated in part by a desire to break out of the staid norms of 1950s East Germany. The revellers' costumes and games resembled childhood games of cowboys and Indians. There was also a carnivalesque quality to the celebrations, particularly the selection of a 'tribal chief' and a 'human sacrifice', and the rough treatment of disapproving outsiders.

[100] BArch DR1/8390, pp. 117–118.
[101] Kruse, 'Nische im Sozialismus', p. 110.
[102] See the photographs in Thomas Kupferman, *FKK in der DDR. Sommer, Sonne, Nackedeis* (Berlin: Eulenspiegel Verlag, 2008), pp. 112–113.
[103] Thormann, ' "Schont die Augen der Nation!" ', p. 47.

But the wild and uninhibited aspect of the Cameroon parties also had a more adult subtext. One photograph in particular suggests that official reports of 'young painted girls' had some substance. In it, a young girl, her brown body decorated with concentric white circles, stands at the centre of a circle of admiring onlookers, wearing only a necklace and loin cloth made of mussel shells.[104] What is interesting here is the way in which ornamentation is used to draw attention to the breasts and nipples, emphasising the body as a site of sexual pleasure, both for the participants and the audience. Of course, the use of toothpaste and cocoa or boot polish also drew attention to the skin as a marker of racial difference. Cameroon had been a German colony between 1884 and 1916, and 'Cameroon' and to 'cameroon' may have been used as slang terms for nudism before the First World War.[105] As we have seen, the authorities were deeply uncomfortable with this 'ethnic drag', which raised uneasy memories of Germany's very recent history of racism and deadly discrimination.

However one chooses to interpret them, the Cameroon parties were a much rowdier and bawdier form of nudism than that which emphasised health, nature, and family. A few questionnaires in the 1966 survey also hint that not all nudists were motivated by clean living: a 22-year-old teacher, on holiday from Erfurt with her fiancé and best friend, wrote she liked nudism because it minimised the saltwater damage to one's swimwear. For her, the best thing about the nudist beach was 'the handsome men' and the worst thing was people with unattractive figures.[106] A 19-year-old student stated frankly that the good thing about nudism was that nobody, particularly girls, could hide their true figure.[107] Such bawdiness would have been anathema to traditional nudists.

The nudist boom

Attitudes such as these were to become increasingly common as nude bathing became more popular among the population at large. Nina Hagen's 1974 hit 'Du hast den Farbfilm Vergessen' ('You Forgot the Colour Film') listed the nudist beach as just one amongst many holiday

[104] 'FKK in der DDR. Aufstand der Nackten', *Spiegel-Online*, 10.6.2008, einestages.spiegel.de/external/ShowTopicAlbumBackground/a2127/13/10/F.html#featuredEntry.

[105] Thormann, ' "Schont die Augen der Nation!" ', p. 47.

[106] LAG, Rep. 200, 8.3.2., Nr 98, p. 72, questionnaire response, 1966.

[107] *Ibid.*, p. 57, questionnaire response, 1966.

photographs ruined by her hapless boyfriend's failure to remember the right film for the camera.

> Me in a bikini
> Me at the nudist beach
> Me in a cheeky mini skirt
> And the countryside in reach
> But – how awful – I cry with all my might
> Scenery and Nina, and it's all in black and white.[108]

A liberal attitude towards nude bathing would have been common in Hagen's bohemian circles. But it was surprisingly widespread amongst her audience too. The 1960s and 1970s saw a dramatic upsurge in support for nude swimming. By the early 1970s, 62% of young workers and 75% of students said that they were either in favour or somewhat in favour.[109] From the 1960s onwards, nudism began to appear in newspaper and magazine articles.[110] The TV show *Longshot Leader* (*Außenseiter Spitzenreiter*), watched by half of all East German households, sent its naked reporter-in-chief to the nudist beach to answer a reader's enquiry about how first-timers should behave.[111] Nude bathing reached the big screen too: as we have already seen, *Sieben Sommersprossen*, released in 1978, featured a teenage couple swimming and frolicking naked together.

The first publication dedicated to nude bathing appeared in 1982.[112] Its initiator, the 'Tourist' publishing house, argued that nude bathing had become such a popular activity that a guidebook on the subject was long overdue. By listing inland freshwater beaches, as well as the better-known coastal bathing spots, it was hoped to provide some relief for the by now hopelessly overcrowded beaches of the Baltic coast. Interestingly, another motivation was that West German nudist publications had begun to give details of East German beaches where nudism was permitted. A home-grown publication would provide a counterbalance and, possibly, an attractive export to the Western market.[113] Despite the publishers' matter-of-fact justification, the book was still

---

[108] 'Ich im Bikini und ich am FKK/Ich frech im Mini, Landschaft ist auch da – ja/ Aber, wie schrecklich, die Tränen kullern heiß/Landschaft und Nina und alles nur schwarzweiß.'

[109] ZA S6144: Partner I – Junge Arbeiter 1973, p. 10; ZA S6143: Partner I – Studenten 1972, p. 15.

[110] E.g. 'Warum baden Sie ohne?', *Neue Berliner Illustrierte* 32/1965, 30–31.

[111] 'Nackt bis aufs Tonband', *Berliner Zeitung*, 29.09.2003, 16.

[112] Friedrich Hagen, *Baden ohne*.

[113] BArch DR1/2762, p. 26, Verlagsleiter Tourist Verlag, 'Betr. FKK-Führer', 12.8.1981.

seen as risqué enough to necessitate the personal seal of approval of
Klaus Höpcke, the GDR's 'book minister',[114] and the author was pre-
vailed upon to remove passages that sang the praises of nudism too
enthusiastically.[115] This did little damage to the book's popularity: the
first edition of 100,000 was rumoured to have sold out in four weeks.[116]
Three reprints and a second edition followed.[117] By 1989, the book had
sold a total of 650,000 copies.[118]

State-approved guidebooks were a sign that nudism had moved from
being seen as a threat to forming an integral part of socialist society.
There can be no doubt that in approving such the state was respond-
ing to the popularity of nudism. How can we explain the leap from the
minority nudism of the 1960s to the near-ubiquitous nude bathing of
the 1980s? And why did the state come to accept it? Some degree of
speculation is inevitable here. The lack of a paper trail in the 1970s and
1980s seems to suggest that the regime simply gave up trying to control
nudism. As with youth policy, it was easier to let people do what they
wanted so long as it did not represent a threat to the stability of the
state. Policy towards nudism after 1956 may have been spectacularly
unsuccessful in preventing people from going to the nudist beach – but
it had minimised the problem of nudist groups.

Given the broader changes in attitudes towards sexuality in the late
1960s and early 1970s, it is perhaps not surprising that nudity, once
vilified by the state as immoral, was co-opted by the regime and recast
in a specifically East German light. A relaxed attitude towards nudity was interpreted as a signifier of East German progressiveness and
modernity. Some of this impetus came from East German sex educationalists. Like traditional nudists, they rejected a direct link between
nudity and sex, but insisted on the importance of exposure to the naked
body as a prerequisite for a healthy adult sexual identity. As early as
the 1950s, Rudolf Neubert had indicated to readers of his *Das neue
Ehebuch* (*New Marriage Book*) (for a time the standard sex advice book
available to East Germans) that naked swimming was acceptable in the
right context.[119] The *Wörterbuch der Sexuologie* (*Dictionary of Sexology*)
assured its readers that 'nudism and naked bathing have nothing to do

[114] *Ibid.*, p. 29, 'Kurzerhand' an Höpcke, 22.7.1981.
[115] *Ibid.*, p. 47, 'Verlagsgutachten', 6.2.1982.
[116] Kruse, 'Nische im Sozialismus', p. 111.
[117] Friedrich Hagen, *FKK Zwischen Ostsee und Vogtland* (Berlin and Leipzig: Tourist Verlag, 1987), p. 5.
[118] Thormann, '"Schont die Augen der Nation"', p. 82.
[119] Neubert, *Das neue Ehebuch*, pp. 243–245; Rudolf Neubert, *Fragen und Antworten zum 'Neuen Ehebuch' und zur 'Geschlechterfrage'* (Rudolstadt: Greifenverlag, 1960), p. 216.

with sexuality'.[120] Both books were published by the non-state owned Greifenverlag, which had a pre-1933 history of sympathy with both the nudist movement and the Weimar sex reform movement.[121] But such references to nudism were passed by the censor without a murmur and soon became a part of the sexological mainstream. The 1982 book *Jugendlexicon Jugend zu zweit* (*Young Couples*) described nude bathing in sympathetic terms and included a picture of a young family swimming naked,[122] while *Liebe und Sexualität bis 30* (1984) recommended that small children should become familiar with nudity at home and in the kindergarten.[123]

Building on such expert opinions, images of East German families at ease with their own nudity were used as propaganda for the modern, socialist state and the leisure opportunities it gave its citizens. A news agency picture of a young family running naked through a lake in the Lausitz mining region (Figure 6.2) was given the caption: ' "Mama, Papa and I prefer to swim without [swimsuits]." From year to year the two nudist beaches in the Seftenberg recreation area ... win it popularity with young and old.'[124] Here, the opportunity to swim in the nude is presented as the gift of a progressive regime to its subjects, one which fitted in well with the paternalistic pro-natalism of East German family policy. (The well-known, if unofficial, gay nudist beach at the Müggelsee in Berlin failed to make it into official guidebooks.)[125]

While in the 1950s the SED had seen nudism as a throwback to the dark days of the recent past, indelibly associated with Nazism, social democracy, and moral decay, by the 1970s and 1980s, nude bathing had been refigured in official discourse as a symbol of a young, forward-looking East Germany. Perhaps the most striking example of this was to be seen in 1976 at the opening of the monumental Palace of the Republic in the heart of East Berlin. The building was to house the East German parliament, as well as provide leisure facilities for the population. The spacious foyer held a number of works of art, commissioned under the rubric 'Are Communists Allowed to Dream?' This quote was attributed to Lenin, but it is hard to know what he might have thought of the exhibition's centrepiece, an enormous canvas by the artist Hans

[120] Karl Dietz and Peter Hesse, *Wörterbuch der Sexuologie und ihrer Grenzgebiete*, 4th edn (Rudolstadt: Greifenverlag, 1971), p. 118.
[121] See Wurm *et al.*, *Der Greifenverlag zu Rudolstadt 1919–1993*, pp. 35, 47–49.
[122] Lykke Aresin and Annelies Müller-Hegemann (eds.), *Jugendlexikon Jugend zu zweit*, 3rd edn (Leipzig: VEB Bibliographisches Institut Leipzig, 1982), pp. 89–90.
[123] Friedrich and Starke, *Liebe und Sexualität bis 30*, p. 109.
[124] 'Mama, Papa und ich baden am liebsten ohne', 15.8.1983.
[125] Ulrich Berkes, *Eine schlimme Liebe. Tagebuch* (Berlin and Weimar: Aufbau, 1987), p. 83.

Figure 6.2: 'Mama, Papa, and I prefer to swim without [swimsuits]', Senftenberg, 1983.

Vent entitled *Menschen am Strand* (*People on the Beach*), which depicted seventeen bathers, some of them in the nude.[126]

Nudism was also part of a growing tourist culture, central to the attempt to woo domestic consumers' loyalty to the GDR. Managing consumer expectations was one of the greatest challenges facing East German economic policy, and nudism was no exception. In 1965, the baker Otto G wrote to complain that his application for a place at the nudist campsite in Ückeritz had been turned down for the second year running. Part of his grievance stemmed from the fact that the family had spent 2,000 marks on camping equipment. To add insult to injury, a group of particle physicists had been allocated a generous number of camping places, only one-quarter of which had been taken up. Herr G felt that his family, who worked 12–14-hour days in the bakery, had a right to their holiday of choice. 'If the bakers don't fulfil the plan, there'll be nothing to eat for the particle physicists – or for you', he wrote belligerently.[127] In the first three weeks of 1965, as the process for allocating holiday places for the year began, there were 45,000 applications for a place at the Prerow campsite – which could hold a maximum of 17,500 campers over the entire season.[128] The only way to manage this demand – and the furious complaints of those who were denied a place – was to allow nudism to spill out into other campsites. By the 1980s at the latest, the authorities had made their peace with the fact that some holidaymakers liked to camp as well as swim in the nude.

There is, however, evidence that, as nudism became more popular, the ethics of the nudists of the 1960s – cleanliness, sexual self-control, family values – were no longer in fashion. The popularity of nude bathing spots beside motorways suggests that a preoccupation with nature had been replaced by the desire for a refreshing dip.[129] The nudists of the 1960s had seen the simplicity of their holidays – camping, washing in the sea, and relieving themselves in the bushes – as part of their appeal. But as Honecker's 'unity of social and economic policy' led to significant increases in living standards, so too did consumer expectations rise.

[126] Bärbel Mann and Jörg Schütrumpf, 'Galerie im Palast der Republik. Auftraggeber: Ministerium für Kultur', in Monika Flacke (ed.), *Auftrag: Kunst 1949–1990. Bildende Künstler in der DDR zwischen Ästhetik und Politik* (Berlin: Deutsches Historisches Museum, 1995), pp. 245–260.
[127] LAG, Rep. 200, 8.3.2, Nr 56, p. 22, Otto G, an RdB Rostock, Abt. Erholungswesen, 8.2.1965.
[128] *Ibid.*, p. 47, Karsten, Abteilungsleiter Erholungs- und Bäderwesen, RdB Rostock, to Günther S, 4.2.1965.
[129] Siegfried Lokatis, 'Baden ohne', in Siegfried Lokatis and Simone Barck (eds.), *Zensurspiele. Heimliche Literaturgeschichten aus der DDR* (Halle: Mitteldeutscher Verlag, 2008), pp. 131–133; Thormann, '"Schont die Augen der Nation"', p. 109.

The tourist authorities abandoned their attempts to encourage campers to 'rough it', installing running water and toilet facilities at campsites.[130] Many were converted to nudism by their positive experiences of the culture and comradeship of the nudist beach. But twenty years later, a distinctive nudist culture was a thing of the past: the coastline was so crowded that nudists and swimsuit wearers were packed side by side. As Ina Merkel points out, this represented a remarkably relaxed attitude towards public nudity, but it also signified the end of the community and values propagated by the nudists of the 1950s and 1960s.[131] Nudism was no longer referred to as 'Free Body Culture' (*Freie Körperkultur*) but simply 'FKK'. The rigid distinctions between clothed and nude and the disgust at those who wore bathing costumes were things of the past. Students surveyed in 1978 appear to have been motivated by the goal of an all-over tan and the fact that nude bathing was perceived as fun, but were happy to bathe with or without swimsuits.[132]

Despite the best efforts of nudists and sex educationalists alike, nudity remained firmly linked to sex, both in the attitudes of the authorities and in the popular imagination. Younger nude bathers in the 1970s and 1980s were both more body-conscious and more aware of the sexual potential of the nudist beach. The pop punk band Juckreiz (the name translates as 'itchiness') recorded a song called 'FKK' in 1983. Despite its catchy and cheery chorus ('Here comes the bus, hurrah, hurrah, we're going to the FKK'), the song painted a rather seedy picture of the nudist beach as a place of 'much too much sexiness' ('Erotik viel zu viel'). Lead singer Marion Sprawe described voyeurs 'lurking behind the fence/waiting for a dalliance', and the song continued:

> Girls playing volleyball
> Plump balls everywhere
> Up and down they jump
> And the men are staring
> You can hear them murmuring
> The sight makes me sick [*macht mich schlapp*].

It is also striking that, as the state co-opted nudism, it became increasingly sexualised and commercialised. The celebrations to mark Berlin's 75th anniversary are a good example of this. While the parade of ships included a vessel of both male and female nudists (marked with a sign

[130] Moranda, 'The Dream of a Therapeutic Regime'.
[131] Cf. Merkel, 'Die Nackten und die Roten', 104.
[132] G. Schliephake, 'Einige Tendenzen bei der Einstellung von im Jugendalter stehenden Personen zur Freikörperkultur (gen. FKK)', *Ärztliche Jugendkunde* 71 (1980), 375.

reading 'FKK starts here'), a float in the official procession through the centre of the city bore topless women. As it passed the platform on which the great and the good of the GDR state were seated, Erich Honecker was seen to react with delight. His wife, Margot, seemed less impressed. In the TV footage the women who paraded past the Honeckers appear to be fully naked. However, photographs of the parade show that the 'nudists' in the procession were not nude, but merely topless. Furthermore, rather than representing nudists, they were in fact 'presenting consumer goods and leisure activities of the capital' – hence the fishing rods, fishing nets, and parasols with which their float was festooned.[133] Other pictures of the parade show a preponderance of scantily clad women, amongst them the first Miss (East) Berlin. It is hard to avoid the conclusion that the partial 'nudists' in the parade were there for decoration, not to further the old-fashioned values of nudism.

Conclusion

How, then, should the popularity of nudism be interpreted? Some scholars have seen it as a 'little freedom' in an otherwise repressive regime.[134] Uli Linke has even described it as 'a localized counterdiscourse to the state [and] a nonviolent means of resistance'.[135] This goes too far. The spirited and in many cases co-ordinated opposition to the ban of 1954 was certainly a form of direct resistance, and one of the infrequent occasions that East Germans were able to overturn a piece of government policy by means of peaceful civil disobedience. But opposition to the ban did not mean opposition to the regime: many of those who refused to comply were not only loyal to the state, but party members too.

There is some truth in Linke's observation that nudism offered an escape from the uniforms, work clothing, and status symbols of everyday life.[136] By the 1970s and 1980s, nude bathing had become part of mainstream GDR culture. Family snapshots give a real sense of the beach as a site of pleasure: not only enjoyment of the sand and sea, and the company of family and friends, but of the sexual body too.[137] Taking

---

[133] Bundesarchiv Bild 183-1987-0704-042, 4.7.1987/Berlin: Jubiläum/Festumzug/Zwei Badenixen beim Sonnenbaden präsentieren Konsumgüter und Freizeitangebote der Hauptstadt als Zentrum von Produktion und Wissenschaft.
[134] Kruse, 'Nische im Sozialismus', p. 111.
[135] Uli Linke, *German Bodies: Race and Representation After Hitler* (New York: Routledge, 1999), p. 72.
[136] *Ibid.*   [137] Kupferman, *FKK in der DDR*.

your clothes off was first and foremost a form of escapism from the daily world of work and duty, a chance to relax, play games, and get to know your neighbours on the beach.[138] Beyond this, it seems impossible to identify a single meaning of nudism – it meant very different things to those who had experienced Weimar nudism, families in 1960s, teenagers on their first holiday without their parents, and gay men who frequented the FKK beach at the Müggelsee.

What light does nudism shed on the East German sexual revolution? It is a remarkably clear example of social change against the wishes and intentions of the regime. Its popularity must be seen as a direct result of popular activism. The pioneering nudists of the 1950s overwhelmed the state's restrictions and ultimately opened up nude bathing to a much wider public. The state's decision to ban nudist organisations was counter-productive, as keeping nudism public gave many more people the opportunity to try it out. Thanks in part to the restricted leisure opportunities available, it quickly became a national sport. Unlike many of the developments discussed in this book, East German nudism was an indigenous phenomenon. What is striking, however, is how rapidly the state's initial qualms turned first to tolerance and then to co-option. Not only was the regime unwilling to allow unobserved and uncontrolled nudist activity, it was quick to take the credit for its citizens' growing ease with their own nudity and to tie it into an emerging narrative of 'progressive' socialist sexuality. The result was a society in which nudity was common, but nudism lost any critical potential.

Finally, what conclusions can be drawn about the impact on attitudes towards sexuality? There can be no doubt that many East Germans had a relaxed attitude towards the naked body, which went beyond the beach. Interviewees such as Frau C and Herr P, who had grown up in the 1960s and 1970s, remembered nudity in the family home as a routine part of their childhoods. However, we should be cautious about assuming that nudity was a universal norm in East German households. In 1979, 38% of young people surveyed agreed completely or partially with the statement 'my mother avoided nakedness in my presence', and the figure rose to 49% in the case of paternal nudity.[139] Even amongst families who bared all, nudity was not always entirely voluntary. Lutz Thormann vividly describes his embarrassment as a pre-teenager as his mother forced the family to remove their clothes and confiscated

---

[138] Thormann stresses the importance of holiday and leisure time as an escape from the regimented norms of the East German workplace: Thormann, '"Schont die Augen der Nation"', p. 38.

[139] ZA S6145: Partner II 1979/80, pp. 60, 61.

the bathing trunks he had secretly brought with him.[140] Pre-pubescents and teenagers, of course, were painfully aware of the sexual power of the naked body. But as we have seen, adults themselves did not always subscribe to the nudist ethos of sexual self-restraint.

It is certainly true that many East Germans were relaxed about the public display of the naked body. But it is extremely difficult, if not impossible, to measure the impact of widespread nude bathing on sexual behaviour. What is beyond doubt is that it was a highly visible marker of attitudes towards the body, which has contributed to a widespread perception of a discrete East German sexual identity. But it would be a mistake to see nakedness only in the context of nudism alone – as has often been the case in narratives which claim that there was something natural and untainted about East German sexuality. As we shall see in the next chapter, the loosening of state controls on the depiction of the nude body also allowed the emergence of a sexualised consumer culture, designed to compete with that of the West, but which nevertheless retained a distinctively East German flavour.

[140] Thormann, '"Schont die Augen der Nation"', p. 1.

7   Picturing sex: East German erotica

In some ways, it is surprising that East German erotica existed at all. Throughout the existence of the GDR, the authorities were consistent in their condemnation of the commodification of sex. Under communism, it was argued, sex was about love, not money. Furthermore, the liberation of women that had taken place since 1949 was thought to be incompatible with the sale of the female body. Relationships in the East were to be 'clean' and 'decent', based on admiration, mutual respect, and family formation. Pornography, prostitution, and casual sex were all seen as symptoms of capitalist society, which had no place in the East. After German reunification, this interpretation lived on as a key element of the thesis that presents East German sexuality as unsullied by the demands of capitalism. The non-commodification of sex has come to be seen as a positive, praiseworthy aspect of East German life, and an integral and important part of the discreet charm of actually existing socialism. This prelapsarian idyll, it is argued, was brought to an end only by the influx of West German pornography and erotic goods in the wake of the *Wende* (the events that led up to German reunification).

Such narratives tend to ignore the presence of nude photographs, sexually titillating books, the public display of women's bodies, and even striptease in the East German public sphere. They also omit to mention that West German sex culture was welcomed by some East Germans with open arms.[1] How do we explain these erotic objects and events, and what can they tell us about East German sexuality? Do they challenge or reinforce the idea of a distinctive and egalitarian East German sexual culture? This chapter will discuss the production of erotica, how its existence was justified, and the ways in which the population responded to it. Erotica acts as a valuable reminder that sex is not just about private interactions between individuals – it can also be commodified, circulated, and sold. As this chapter will show, such images

---

[1] Wierling, 'Vereinigungen'.

of sexuality reveal both pragmatic regime attitudes towards sex and the limits of gender equality in East German society.

Nude photography in the 1950s

As we have already seen, the early years of communist rule were marked by anxiety about any display of the naked body. In the early years of the Cold War, nude photographs were often associated with the licentious freedoms of the West German market economy. A cartoon published in 1952 showed Germany divided not just by a border but by attitudes towards women, sex, and the family (Figure 7.1) In the East, wholesome young couples took part in folk dancing, while mothers collected their children from newly built *Kindergärten*. In the West, naked women sat atop piles of rubble, prostitutes tempted customers into bars of ill repute, and newsstands sold pornographic magazines. Such material, it was felt, could and should not be sold in the East. A discussion in a specialist journal for photographers referred repeatedly to the perils of West German nude photography, 'kitschy stereotypes', which were 'poison for young people, there cannot be enough warnings against them'.[2] 'Dubious magazines from over there' were condemned as 'downright pornography', which had no place in socialism.[3] The main objection to such photographs was that they were intended to excite sexual feelings in the viewer – this was ruled to be inappropriate and inadmissible.

These 1950s debates concluded that nude photography in the East was permissible only if it drew the viewer's attention solely to the asexual beauty of the human form. Would-be nude photographers were advised to proceed with extreme care. Only by adhering closely to certain rules and guidelines could they hope to control the potentially dangerous power of the naked body and achieve the goal of 'grace, dignity and cleanliness'.[4] In order to achieve an asexual aesthetic, models should be photographed outside, preferably 'playing sport and happy games'.[5] This should ensure there were plausible grounds for their nudity, and that the viewer would admire the beauty of the human body rather than using the photographs for sexual stimulation.

Coding the nude photograph as 'natural' and 'clean' distanced it from any suspicion of sexual indecency. In attempting to divorce nudity and sexuality, East German photographers were following some important precedents. The aesthetic 'alibi' for the nude was as old as the genre

---

[2] K.-H. Grasselt, 'Gedanken zur Aktfotografie', *Fotografie*, June 1953, 175.
[3] Gerhard Vetter, 'Zum Thema Aktfotografie', *Fotografie*, June 1954, 165.
[4] Hans Steinbach, 'Akt-Fotografie und Akt-Malerei', *Fotografie*, June 1950, 157–158.
[5] Vetter, 'Zum Thema Aktfotografie'.

Figure 7.1: 'There are two paths'. Cartoon in *Neue Berliner Illustrierte*, 13/1952, 38.

itself,[6] which traditionally used conventions to defuse any suggestion of raw sexuality.[7] But to argue that East German nude photography, even in its early years, was asexual would be unconvincing. The lines between nudism's allegedly sexless acceptance of the naked body, the artist's aesthetic appreciation of a nude model, and the mild titillation of soft pornography were blurry. The East German authorities were also aware of the seductive power of sex. Advertisements featuring semi-clad women appeared as early as 1952 and were to remain a feature of East German life.[8] The first specifically erotic consumer good, *Das Magazin*, appeared on the market in the wake of the Workers' Uprising of June 1953. Incensed by a 10% rise in work norms, which combined with price rises amounted to a total wage cut of 33%, workers in Berlin had taken to the streets. The protests soon spread throughout most of the country, and by the afternoon of 17 June, 400,000 people were involved.[9] The SED leadership was forced to go into hiding, and the uprising was put down only with the help of Soviet tanks. It was clear that a rapid improvement in living conditions was necessary if the population were to be won over.[10] In order to ensure the long-term survival of the state, it was vital to persuade East Germans that their standard of living could reach that of their friends and family in the West. Reminded that austerity and ideology alone were not enough, the Central Committee increased the money supply and authorised the production of more consumer goods, including a new entertainment monthly called, simply, *Das Magazin* ('The Magazine').[11]

Das Magazin contained little overt news or politics: as part of its mixture of cultural features, travel and cookery pieces, short stories, and fashion items, it carried a nude photograph in every issue.[12] Readers

[6] On pornographic alibis, see Marcus Collins, *Modern Love: An Intimate History of Men and Women in Twentieth-Century Britain* (London: Atlantic, 2003), pp. 135–139.

[7] John Berger, *Ways of Seeing* (Harmondsworth: Penguin, 1972), pp. 53, 60; Lynda Nead, *The Female Nude: Art, Obscenity and Sexuality* (London; Routledge, 1992), pp. 2, 10, 14.

[8] See for example the advertisement for Mildana soap in *Neue Berliner Illustrierte* 12/1952, 6, in which the model's nipple is clearly visible.

[9] Gareth Pritchard, 'Workers and the Socialist Unity Party of Germany in the Summer of 1953', in Patrick Major and Jonathan Osmond (eds.), *The Workers' and Peasants' State: Communism and Society in East Germany Under Ulbricht 1945–1971* (Manchester: Manchester University Press, 2002), p. 112.

[10] On 1953 as a turning point for East German consumer culture, see Katherine Pence, ' "You as a Woman Will Understand": Consumption, Gender and the Relationship Between State and Citizenry in the GDR's Crisis of 17 June 1953', *German History* 19 (2001), 218–252.

[11] SAPMO-BArch DY30/JIV2/3A/382.

[12] For a more detailed discussion of *Das Magazin*, see Josie McLellan, ' "Even Under Socialism, We Don't Want to Do Without Love" '. See the memoirs of its former

were also treated to erotic short stories, racy articles about marriage and infidelity, and irreverent opinion polls with titles such as 'Wann ist ein Flirt kein Flirt mehr' ('When Is a Flirt More than a Flirt?').[13] Significantly, *Das Magazin* was aimed at both men and women, taking nude photography out of a male-only niche and placing it firmly in the mainstream. Werner Klemke's distinctive cover art, featuring curvaceous, beautiful women and girls, set the tone of the publication: playful, pleasure-seeking, cultured, and aesthetically aware. As early as June 1960, the magazine's cover featured a pretty blonde witch flying through the night sky clad only in fishnet stockings and red high heels.[14] In March 1968, a male insomniac counted Rubenesque women instead of sheep.[15] Klemke's covers often featured blissful couples, whose happiness was clearly based on a strong physical bond.[16] He could be extraordinarily suggestive – the Christmas issue of 1973 featured a kissing couple, naked but for a gold star tied over the man's genitals, and a mask tied over the woman's, giving the impression of an artificial penis and pubic hair.[17] Clearly pleased with this motif, Klemke followed it in February 1974 with a cover in which a man, confronted with a naked woman, appears to wear a large pink dildo on his nose (Figure 7.2). Only Klemke's humor and charm saved such covers from overt smuttiness or official censure.

Unsurprisingly, readers welcomed this new publication as a relief from the daily diet of politics in other newspapers and magazines. *Das Magazin* offered an easy sense of escapism: as one reader put it, 'a glass of champagne at the end of the working week'.[18] Copies were passed from hand to hand and were eventually bound into volumes for future reference. Readers reported using the covers to wallpaper their homes,[19] and one man wrote, 'I collect the nudes, my wife collects the recipes.'[20] By 1965, production had climbed to 425,000, reaching its highpoint of 565,000 in 1981.[21] Even this was not enough to

editor Manfred Gebhardt, *Die Nackte unterm Ladentisch. Das Magazin in der DDR* (Berlin: Nora, 2002); Evamarie Badstübner, '"Zeig', wie das Leben lacht und liebt ...": Die Unterhaltungszeitschrift *Das Magazin* und ihre Leser zwischen 1954 und 1970', in Evamarie Badstübner (ed.), *Befremdlich anders. Leben in der DDR* (Berlin: Dietz, 2000), pp. 432–470; Evamarie Badstübner, 'Auf 80 Seiten um die Welt. *Das Magazin* zwischen 1954 und 1970', in Simone Barck, Martina Langermann and Siegfried Lokatis (eds.), *Zwischen 'Mosaik' und 'Einheit'. Zeitschriften in der DDR* (Berlin: Ch. Links, 1999), pp. 189–201.
[13] *Das Magazin*, February 1961, 23.   [14] *Das Magazin*, June 1960.
[15] *Das Magazin*, March 1968.
[16] E.g. *Das Magazin*, November 1975, which showed a newly wed couple approaching their wedding bed, on which the figure of a prone woman was outlined in flowers.
[17] *Das Magazin*, December 1973.   [18] *Das Magazin*, February 1962, 3.
[19] *Das Magazin*, July 1962, 2.   [20] *Das Magazin*, May 1961, 2.
[21] BArch DC9/9028.

Figure 7.2: Werner Klemke: *Das Magazin*, February 1974, cover illustration.

meet demand, and it remained a much sought-after publication, often available only under the counter or – for the lucky ones – by subscription. Despite *Das Magazin*'s popularity, the regime was unwilling to increase its print run further, due both to the GDR's endemic paper shortages and to the fact that its production costs were heavily underwritten by the state: its original 1954 cover price of 1 mark was never raised.

Gender and the nude

It is sometimes claimed that *Das Magazin*'s monthly nude was the only such erotic material available in the GDR. In fact, books of nude photography were printed on a regular basis from the late 1950s and, from the 1960s, nude photographs began to appear in a number of different publications, including the satirical *Eulenspiegel*, the photo journal *Fotografie*, the youth magazine *neues leben*, and even the *Armee Rundschau*.[22] Nude photographs were often reproduced on the inside covers of magazines, or as stand-alone illustrations, rather than as part of an article: a clear sign that they were for decoration rather than intellectual contemplation. Indeed, as more nudes were published, discussion of their aesthetic worth dried up almost completely. How did this change take place, and how were pleasures of the flesh reconciled with the party's earnest efforts to build socialism?

Utilising such photographs was an integral part of the regime's post-1953 strategy of social pacification. Desirable consumer goods were crucial if the sceptical population were to be won over to socialism. But this is not to say that nude photographs represented a total triumph of economics over politics. There were also sound political reasons for their publication. Public moralising did not rule out the sexual altogether. In fact, the early East German nude did much to reinforce the heteronormative sexuality that was central to the construction of socialism and socialist subjects.[23]

The young women – and they were almost invariably women – in these photographs were often photographed by the sea, in the dunes, or sunning themselves on the rocks. The pretence that they had not stripped off for the photographer's lens was reinforced by the fact that they were often looking away from the camera or splashing in the sea. Photographers prided themselves on the fact that their models were not obviously made up, and often bore visible body hair. Former professional nude photographer Klaus Ender described the ideal model as 'a nice girl; this was after all a GDR girl and GDR citizens had to be nice'. Asked what would have been classified as unacceptable, he replied: 'If she had smoked, if she had been heavily made up, if she had had a lot of jewellery on. I mean, naturalness was the trump card. ... And that's how the girls had to be, they had to be nice ... they had to be

---

[22] For a more detailed account of the history of nude photography, see Josie McLellan, 'Visual Dangers and Delights: Nude Photography in East Germany', *Past and Present* 205 (2009), 143–174.

[23] Jennifer Evans, 'The Moral State'.

aesthetically pleasing.'[24] Such wholesome outdoorsy snapshots actually
dovetailed rather well with the regime's pursuit of a reproductive sexuality, based around heterosexual monogamy.

The view that East German nude photographers created an 'honest
picture of women'[25] has gained ground since the *Wende*. The painter
Willi Sitte introduced a recent collection of nude photographs thus:

> They [the models] seem self-reliant, self-confident, poised. Emancipated.
> GDR women did not see themselves as an object – they asserted themselves
> as subjects ... They seem relaxed. Free. Equal [*gleichberechtigt*]. Equal with the
> person behind the camera too ... [These photographs] tell us where we once
> were, where we are today, and where we need to get to.[26]

This is an unashamedly nostalgic view – for Sitte, nude photographs
transmit a simple message about the triumphs of gender equality in the
GDR and the ways in which these gains have been eroded since 1989.
This is echoed by the East German sex educationalist Jutta Resch-
Treuwerth, in her afterword to the same volume, where she contrasts
the 'naturalness' of the East German models with the 'taut breasts
and sterile-shaven genitals' of Western nudes.[27] It is easy to understand why East German erotica has been interpreted as innocuous and
female-friendly, particularly given the lack of the overt power relations
of Western pornography.[28] But despite the fact that these photographs
featured 'natural'-looking women with pubic hair, the underlying mes-
sages about gender were and remain anything but progressive.

Nude models were, as a rule, young, female, pretty, slim, sexualised,
and in thrall to both the camera and the erotic gaze of the beholder. These
women were almost invariably depicted as the malleable objects of both
the camera's and the viewer's gaze. Models were usually photographed
in passive poses, sunbathing, looking into the distance, or otherwise
being obviously directed by the photographer. In many cases, the viewer
is invited to participate in an act of voyeurism, peeping from behind a
tuft of marram grass at a seemingly unaware young woman (Figure 7.3).
Models were often pictured out of doors, both presenting their bodies as
something natural and timeless, and contrasting their soft, fecund curves
with cliffs, sand, rock face, tree trunks, or driftwood.[29]

[24] Interview with Klaus Ender, 16.1.2004.
[25] Claus Rose, 'Kulturpolitik für ein ehrliches Frauenbild. Die Aktfotos von Walter Streit', *Fine Art Foto* 2 (2004), 22–27.
[26] Willi Sitte, 'Auf Widersehn, du Schöne', in *Schön Nackt. Aktfotografie in der DDR* (Berlin: Das Neue Berlin, 2009), p. 9.
[27] Jutta Resch-Treuwerth, 'Ungeschminkt', in *Schön Nackt*, pp. 189–190.
[28] See Herzog, *Sex After Fascism*, p. 205; Harsch, *Revenge of the Domestic*, p. 295.
[29] See Gerhard Vetter, *Studien am Strand* (Leipzig: Fotokino Verlag, 1968), for examples of both of these motifs.

Figure 7.3: Photograph from *Das Magazin*, 1965.

It is also striking that despite the argument that East German nude photography enabled or at least reflected a deeper and truer intimacy than was possible in the West, these photographs very rarely depicted couples. Any potential intimate interaction was left to the viewer's imagination – making him or her a crucial participant in the creation of the work's meaning. This act of active imagination was a key part of the nudes and is reflected in both male and female readers' eagerness to enter into correspondence with publishers and editors. In early 1982, *Das Magazin* printed a double spread of twenty-four nude photographs – all featuring women – that had been published in the previous two years. Readers were asked to vote for their favourite.[30] A staggering 34,000 replied, with responses coming from as far away as the People's Republic of Mongolia.[31] Their responses give a sense not just of the popularity of the nude, but also of how readers looked at and related to it. Many had formulated their response with family, friends, or work colleagues. In good socialist style, some submitted a collective response, including a Monday bowling club and a group of medical researchers from Magdeburg. The winning photograph depicted two young, slim women, with flowing dark hair (Figure 7.4). One looks mildly into the camera, while the other looks down and to the right of the viewer. This photograph was ranked first by almost one-third of respondents, and was placed in the top three by over half. The second- and third-placed photographs both depicted reclining women, one looking away from the camera and one with her eyes closed. Interestingly, all three were colour studio shots, marking a decisive move away from the black-and-white outdoor scenes that had been a staple of 1960s nude photography. However, more experimental or artistic images, like a striking black-and-white nude by the female photographer Eva Mahn, did not feature in the rankings at all. All in all, it seems that East German readers continued to favour the 'natural look'. The models in the top three photographs were all young, slim, and conventionally pretty. One reader, Hellmuth L, was chided for his remarks that 'one should show only aesthetically pleasing women's bodies, most of us are married to or going out with average ones'. But while he may have been uncomfortably frank, the idea that the nude should reflect desires rather than reality seems to have been near-universal.

Brigitte Sellin, the picture editor of *Das Magazin*, later reflected that readers' letters repeatedly requested pictures of 'a sexy, slightly voluptuous woman, who shouldn't look too self-confident … Time and time again we found that attempts to portray a self-confident woman failed, despite the fact that this was far more representative of East German society.'[32] She concluded many East German readers had little appetite for experimentation. Even photographs in which the model appeared too glamorous were greeted with suspicion. 'Many readers didn't have much time for the sort of aesthetic that works so well for the likes of Helmut Newton. That would have seemed somehow decadent, from another world rather than from Thuringia or Saxony. That would have scandalised the readers a bit.'[33] The nude model had to be approachable

[30] 'Zur Begutaktung', *Das Magazin*, January 1982, 37–39.
[31] 'Zur Begutaktung', *Das Magazin*, May 1982, 65–67.
[32] Interviewed in Uta Kolano, *Nackter Osten* (Frankfurt an der Oder: Frankfurter Oder Editionen, 1995), p. 37.
[33] *Ibid.*

Figure 7.4: The winning photograph from *Das Magazin*'s readers' poll, May 1982.

and accessible so that the reader could imagine him- or herself as a participant in the scenario.

What is interesting is that both men and women saw female bodies as a symbol of sex, pleasure, and eroticism. Two-thirds of respondents were men: Reinhard K wrote that he was using the 'temporary absence of his wife' to assess the pictures. But some women were eager to make their voices heard in this debate. Ingrid F admitted regretfully that, on this issue, 'I don't agree with my husband for once', and submitted her own response. The women of Brigade 'Aurora' in Teltow went so far as to describe the decision making process:

> The great January nude debate
> Was a capital way to spend our break.
> After oohing and aahing with much gusto
> At the bosoms and derrieres on show,

Our men checked with serious faces
All the girls on all the pages
To make sure aesthetic-erotic attraction
Remained to their full satisfaction.
But when it came to the ranking – without fail,
It was we women who tipped the scales.[34]

Their comic verse contains a number of intriguing contradictions. These women were eager to point out their participation in the judging process – and indeed the fact that their opinion had carried the day. The tone is one of indulgent tolerance, which gently mocks and even infantilises male desire. But the fact that it is women's bodies that are being put on show and evaluated for their attractiveness is ignored. Indeed, some women emphasised that they were able to judge the erotic charge of a nude as well as any man. 'A nude photograph *must* radiate eroticism', insisted Birgit S, a sentiment seconded by *Das Magazin*'s editorial staff. There is evidence elsewhere that women enjoyed looking at female nudes. One 'avid female reader' from Berlin wrote to *Das Magazin* in 1968 to complain that the nude photograph in the previous issue did not show enough of the model's figure.[35] Nude photographs certainly offered women the chance of identification with the young, beautiful object of desire at the centre of the photograph.[36] For some, they must also have held the possibility of pleasurable and private same-sex fantasies. Was there a sense in which they stood for the enjoyable escape of sex and intimacy? Did some women like to compare their own bodies to the idealised ones of the nudes? Or was there a painful element to such comparisons, as women counted their own flaws? How and why women read these photographs remains a matter of speculation, but the fact that they did so is undeniable.

Women's interest in female nudes may have been in part a response to the dearth of male equivalents. The male nude remained a rarity, even as the female nude, propelled by the consumerism and increasing prosperity of the mid to late 1960s, spread beyond the niche of *Das Magazin* to other publications. This particular shortage caused much grumbling

[34] Zur Begutaktung', *Das Magazin*, May 1982, 65; 'Der Januar "Zur Begutaktung"-Knüller/war für uns *der* Pausenfüller!/Nach viel genüsslichem ah und oh/beim Anblick von Busen und Popo/begutakteten unsere Männer mit Kennermiene/diese und auch jene Biene,/ob sie mit ihrem aesthetisch-erotischem Reize/bei genauerem Hinsehen auch nicht geize!/Ob Platz oder Sieg – keine Frage,/Wir Frauen waren das Zünglein an der Waage.'
[35] *Das Magazin*, November 1968, 3.
[36] Annette Kuhn, *The Power of the Image: Essays on Representation and Sexuality* (London: Routledge, 1985), p. 11.

among female consumers. Hopes raised by the inclusion of a black male nude in the June 1954 edition of *Das Magazin* were to be disappointed. Despite dogged lobbying on the letters page, the next male nude did not appear until February 1975. Such images were in such short supply that the photo editor had to persuade her dentist to pose for her.[37] Male and female readers reacted enthusiastically to the resulting picture, jokily suggesting that it was part of the East German contribution to the UN's International Women's Year. But many felt it did not go far enough, objecting to the fact that the model's hand coyly covered his groin. An all-women work brigade regretted that the photograph was missing 'a certain something' and, in a rare public glimpse of same-sex desire, a male hairdresser exhorted the editorial staff to be more daring: 'In for a penny, in for a pound!'[38] Seven female readers spoke for many more when they versified on the letters page:

> Dear *Magazin*,
> Showing a man
> Without his full span
> Is really rather unfair
> If you expect the masses to stare!
> We seven Saxons hope and pray:
> Next time take the hand away![39]

In a society where public nudity was increasingly common, the dearth of full frontal male nudity seemed increasingly incongruous. But even such heartfelt appeals fell on deaf ears. Photographers and publishers clearly felt the male nude was inappropriate and unnecessary. Until the 1980s, nude photographers remained almost exclusively male, and their models almost exclusively female. Klaus Fischer's *Aktfotografie* (*Nude Photography*), published in 1978 as a practical guide to the subject aimed at the amateur photographer, gives an interesting insight into the dynamic between photographer and model. Although Fischer pays lip service to the concept of the model as 'partner' in the photographic process, it is clear who is in charge. Photographers, he warns, must be careful not to let an 'active, temperamental, and self-confident model' take control of a session. Inexperienced models, on the other hand, should be put at their ease, for example, by encouraging them to brush

---

[37] Kolano, *Nackter Osten*, p. 41. The photograph can be seen in *Das Magazin*, February 1975, 20.

[38] *Das Magazin*, April 1975, 3.

[39] *Das Magazin*, April 1975, 3. 'Liebes Magazin, zeigst du den Mann/Nicht mit allem Drum und Dran,/kannst Du ihn auch weglassen,/so interessiert er nicht die Massen!/Wir sieben Sachsen hoffen froh und munter:/Im nächsten Heft ist die Hand herunter!'

their hair in front of a mirror: their 'natural, more or less unconscious vanity' will overcome their shyness.[40]

The power relations between male photographer and female model are thrown into even sharper relief by the occasional photographs of naked men that started to appear in the magazine *Fotografie* in the 1970s and 1980s. Unlike the nude photographs of women, these were seldom sexual and did not obey the conventions of the nude. Men were generally photographed in a situation where it made sense for them to be naked, such as swimming or showering after work. Unlike female nudes, who were always at the centre of the photographer's and the viewer's gaze, naked men were mostly photographed in groups, where horseplay or a private joke meant that their attention was focused on each other rather than on the camera lens. The photographer was observing and documenting the scene rather than creating it. To echo John Berger, men act and women appear.[41] These photographs of naked men were not composed around the spectator. Nonetheless, they were no less gendered than their female equivalents, projecting an idealised masculinity based around work, strength, and a desexualised male solidarity. The ideal nude was beautiful, and male and female beauty were conceptualised in very different ways. Men were active, purposeful, and strong. Women were passive, pliant, and vulnerable – a marked contrast to the central role of women in the GDR economy, and the stream of images portraying women at work in traditional male pursuits.

Male nudes – rather than photographs of naked men – rarely existed because they were difficult to fit into the photographic conventions of the nude: passive, sexualised, in thrall to the camera and the spectator. Portraying men in this way was fraught with difficulty, not least due to the spectre of homoeroticism. A photograph published in the February 1985 edition of *Das Magazin* was a rare example of a male nude which resembled the female examples of the genre.[42] The model leaned languidly against a wall, hands behind his back, and his naked body at the very centre of the image. His crossed legs, and coy glance away from the camera were reminiscent of female nudes – but prompted a very different reaction from male readers. Peter S described the picture as 'very aesthetic and appealing, not begging for sex [*sexheischend*].

---

[40] Klaus Fischer, *Aktfotografie* (Leipzig: Fotokinoverlag, 1978), pp. 45, 46. Cf. Berger, *Ways of Seeing*, p. 51: 'You painted a naked woman because you enjoyed looking at her, you put a mirror in her hand and you called the painting Vanity, thus morally condemning the woman whose nakedness you had depicted for your own pleasure. The real function of the mirror ... was to make the woman connive in treating herself as, first and foremost, a sight.'

[41] Berger, *Ways of Seeing*, p. 47.   [42] *Das Magazin*, February 1985, 64.

As a man I must emphasise that.' Hans B on the other hand, was disgusted. 'A naked man – impossible! Typically feminine, languishing away – what the hell [*was soll das*]? This feeble figure is not in the least bit appealing.'[43] It is striking that both men felt that a nude should be appealing – despite the fact that they disagreed as to whether this aim had been achieved in this particular photograph. Both also called upon gender norms: while Hans B felt it was 'impossible' for a man to appear naked without appearing 'feminine' and 'feeble', Peter S felt impelled to underline the fact that the male model's dignity remained intact and that his own appreciation of the image was sexless. While the female subjects of nude photography were unmistakably passive objects of sexual fantasy, male bodies were clearly more problematic.

Eroticisation in the 1970s and 1980s

Nude photographs, then, did much to establish carefully prescribed boundaries for gender and sexuality, and in particular to reinforce claims for a uniquely East German sexuality. These boundaries were not fixed. By the 1970s, as East German sexual mores began to shift, the state was increasingly open to the idea that images and objects could stimulate sexual feelings. Official justifications of erotica – for example the reports produced to justify the publication of a collection of nude photographs – often drew on the importance of ease with the body for the development of a healthy (hetero)sexuality. In recommending the publication of Fischer's *Aktfotografie*, Siegfried Schnabl (author of *Mann und Frau Intim*) suggested that nude photographs – particularly of couples – could be used as sex therapy for people suffering from 'prudishness, false feelings of shame, and frigidity', to help them get in touch with their natural sexual feelings. He even went so far as to claim that such photographs could have a 'not-to-be-underestimated immunisation effect against the influence of capitalist porn'.[44] Unlike the writers of the 1950s, Schnabl saw a sexual reaction to nude photographs (even, he implied, masturbation) as natural and normal. Rather than sexual feelings being something to be denied, they were considered to be an integral part of the socialist personality, which needed to be explored and developed. The differentiation from the West, however, persisted. East Germany claimed to be the 'better Germany' in the realm of intimacy, enabling its citizens to enjoy healthy sex lives while protecting them from the destructive influences of Western sexuality. What was meant by 'socialist morality' had changed considerably, but it remained an important concept.

---

[43] *Das Magazin*, April 1985, 3.   [44] BArch DR1/3082a, pp. 336, 340.

In reality, however, East German erotica was increasingly beginning to resemble the softer side of 'capitalist porn'.[45] As nude photography became more common, it also became much more commercialised and self-consciously 'erotic'. Gradually, the influence of Western nude photography began to permeate East German nudes, edging out the earlier emphasis on 'naturalness' – both of the body and of its location in the landscape. Later nudes displayed an altogether more come-hither attitude, often looking directly into the camera lens and disporting themselves in more sexually provocative ways.[46] Photographers such as Klaus Fischer and Günter Rössler started to introduce accessories into photographs, so that women's naked bodies were displayed through wet muslin or on a shag-pile rug. Semi-clothed models gave the impression of pre- or post-coital disarray. Awkward sexual symbolism, such as a flower held over the pubic area or a model holding a spurting hose left the viewer in little doubt as to the photographer's intention. The editorial staff of *Das Magazin* had a subscription to *Playboy*: not only did they draw on its photographs for inspiration, they were also not averse to bootlegging the more suitable images for reproduction in their own pages.[47] In 1984, this visual traffic reversed, when German *Playboy* published a ten-page spread of Rössler's photographs under the title 'Girls of the GDR'.[48]

In the final fifteen years of the GDR's existence, sexual images and texts began to seep into broader public life. Books such as Fischer's offered lavish and glossy nude photographs in the guise of an advice manual for amateur photographers.[49] The East German publishing industry increased its production of erotic literature – including the *Kama Sutra*, *Fanny Hill*, and the Chinese novel *Chin P'ing Mei*.[50] The East German film industry, better known in the West for its social criticism, had a sideline in erotic slides. These slides were designed for private home screenings, where purchasers could amuse themselves by looking at pictures of naked women.[51] East German television got in on the act too, with *Erotisches zur Nacht* (*Erotic at*

---

[45] On the erotica industry in West Germany, see especially Elizabeth Heineman, 'The Economic Miracle in the Bedroom: Big Business and Sexual Consumer Culture in Reconstruction West Germany', *Journal of Modern History*, 78 (2006), 846–877.
[46] See Kuhn, *The Power of the Image*, p. 41, on the power of the 'come-on'.
[47] Brigitte Sellin interviewed in Kolano, *Nackter Osten*, p. 41.
[48] Tobias Höhn, 'Der erotische Akt im Sozialismus', *Stern*, 6 January 2006, www.stern. de/fotografie/fotografie-der-erotische-akt-im-sozialismus-552665.html.
[49] Fischer, *Aktfotografie*.
[50] Mallanaga Vatsyayana, *Das Kamasutra* (Leipzig: Reclam, 1987); John Cleland, *Die Abenteuer der Fanny Hill* (Leipzig and Weimar: Kiepenheuer, 1987); *Kin Ping Meh*, 2 vols. (Leipzig and Weimar: Kiepenheuer, 1983).
[51] DEFA-Color-Sonderbildband Nr 953, 'Durchblicke'.

Night), soft pornography imported from France.[52] Even striptease, until now emblematic of the exploitation and gender inequality of the West, began to become an acceptable form of entertainment at factory works outings in the mid 1980s (Figure 7.5).[53] Female nudity was also used to mark important dates in the East German calendar: paintings of naked women were used to decorate *Fasching* (carnival) celebrations,[54] and, as we have seen, the parade to mark the 750th anniversary of Berlin in 1987 included bare-breasted women. Many of these products – particularly the slide shows, television programmes, and striptease, consciously emulated what was available in the West. By the 1980s, sex – usually embodied in the shape of a naked young woman – was being used unashamedly as mass entertainment. Hardly surprising, as this had been the underlying rationale behind erotica all along. Right from the start, East German erotica had addressed male heterosexual desires to the exclusion of almost anything else.

As well as entertaining and transmitting fundamental ideas about gender, erotica also had a number of important economic functions. From the 1950s onward, state-owned publishing houses produced pin-ups and glossy books of nude photographs for the lucrative overseas market.[55] This was a simple matter of hard currency procurement. Even books that were also licensed for sale in East Germany had a significant proportion of their run earmarked for export. As early as 1958, one-third of the 30,000 copies of Helmut Burkhardt's *Aktfotografie* (*Nude Photography*) were destined for the export market.[56] By 1980, this was enough of an open secret for the popular East German author Inge von Wangenheim to publish a novel about it. *Die Entgleisung* (*The Derailment*) took as its starting point the moment a train came off the tracks in a small Thuringian village. Its cargo, books of erotic photographs, printed in the GDR but destined for the Swedish export market, quickly disappears – with hilarious results. Supposedly based on a real incident, the novel sent up the hypocrisy of the party and the old-fashioned morality of country folk in equal measure, and was a huge success with East

---

[52] Torsten Wahl, 'Zärtliche Zofen', *Berliner Zeitung*, 7 July 2003, 16.

[53] Günter Rössler interviewed in Kolano, *Nackter Osten*, pp. 57–58.

[54] See the photograph by Harald Hauswald in Häußer and Merkel (eds.), *Vergnügen in der DDR*, p. 168.

[55] On the production of pin-ups in the 1950s, see BArch DR1/7794, Jüttner an Volkskammer, 21.3.1958; BArch DR1/822, Deutscher Buchexport an VVV (Vereinigung Volkseigener Verlage) Leipzig 13.4.1955. For an early example of a book produced solely for export, see *Internationale Aktfotografie* (Leipzig: Fotokinoverlag, 1966).

[56] BArch DR1/3916, pp. 58–59.

Figure 7.5: Ute Mahler, 'Strip Show in the House of Culture, Henningsdorf, 1988'.

German readers.[57] Von Wangenheim's account concluded that this sort
of (s)export was nothing to get alarmed about. But her novel elides the
contradictions between the GDR's condemnation of the commodification of sex and its willingness to sell sexual material for profit.

East German producers of erotica were not blind to such moral
dilemmas. Take the example of the 'bibliotheca erotica', a series of
eighteenth- and nineteenth-century erotic classics produced by the
Kiepenheuer publishing house. The 'erotic library' was economically motivated – indeed the idea had originated in the printing works
rather than the publisher's editorial offices.[58] Roland Links, the head
of Kiepenheuer, admitted that the possibilities of the lucrative export
market (and resulting hard currency) had been central to the decision
to produce the series.[59] The books were published in small editions,
but at a high price – between 75 and 100 marks, placing them firmly
in the luxury bracket. By 1988, however, Links was beginning to question the rationale behind the series. Yes, it had proved an 'excellent
breadwinner'.[60] But, he admitted in a letter to the Ministry of Culture,
he could not honestly say that any of the books in the series were 'great
literature', and he feared he had 'not yet found an oracle that tells me
exactly where the boundary between literature and pornography lies'.[61]
This crisis of confidence was prompted by the explicit content of the
next book in the series, *Josefine Mutzenbacher: Lebensgeschichte einer
Wiener Dirne* (*The Life Story of a Vienna Whore*), which included under-
age sex, child prostitution, rape, and homosexuality.[62] Links' solution
was to suggest a limited edition of 5,000, and a retail price of 200 marks,
almost one-third of the average white-collar monthly wage.[63]

Pricing potential purchasers out of the market was unusually elit-
ist: East Germany prided itself on being a 'land of reading' (*Leseland*),
where literature was available to all. But packaging the work as a luxury
good, stressing its literary credentials, and keeping circulation low was
the only possible way to justify its explicit content. Setting the price
high was supposed to limit its potential audience to bibliophiles and
collectors. At the same time, the luxurious nature of the books, and the
fact that such publications were in short supply, meant that a market
was guaranteed, whatever the price. In fact, 'pricing out' the consumer

[57] Inge von Wangenheim, *Die Entgleisung* (Halle: Mitteldeutscher Verlag, 1980). My
    copy, published in 1985, is the seventh edition.
[58] BArch DR1/3704a, p. 480.   [59] BArch DR1/3884a, p. 457.
[60] BArch DR1/3704a, p. 480.   [61] *Ibid.*, pp. 480–481.
[62] *Josefine Mutzenbacher* was banned in the Federal Republic until 1990.
[63] BArch DR1/3704a, p. 374. In 1988, the average monthly net wage of a worker was
    899 marks, and that of a white-collar worker without a degree 688 marks. See Jeffrey
    Kopstein, *The Politics of Economic Decline in East Germany, 1949–1989* (Chapel Hill:
    University of North Carolina Press, 1997), p. 159.

was unlikely to have been effective in a comparatively cash-rich, goods-poor society like the GDR.

Underground and amateur erotica

In any case, the East German populace was well aware of the value of erotica. A lively unofficial trade in professional and amateur photos ran parallel to the regime's activities, with books changing hands for hugely inflated prices.[64] Erotica was not only a popular leisure activity, but also a means of gaining access to scarce services such as car repair and plumbing.[65] Christoph Dieckmann describes how, as they reached adolescence, boys' trading currency of choice changed from matchbox cars to pornography. Keen to expand his collection of *Mosaik* comics, he got hold of some 'porno-pictures', but carelessly left them lying around at home. His mother, a pastor's wife, discovered them but, to Dieckmann's surprise, showed some understanding of their economic worth. She reacted 'unexpectedly mildly', recommending only 'trading them in as quickly as possible'.[66]

Smuggled erotica was particularly highly prized, possessing the double allure of the West and the sexual. Despite the fact that it was forbidden to bring or send pornography into the country, East Germans and their West German relatives went to great lengths to smuggle *Playboy* and other erotic goods across the border.[67] Not all were successful: border guards had strict instructions to seize anything untoward.[68] The following list of seized goods demonstrates the variety and novelty of erotic goods making their way into the GDR:

> Pornographic material:
> 1 card game
> 1 Super-8 film
> 5 figurines (monk, devil, and others)
> 5 journals
> 16 magazines
> 4 books.[69]

[64] Ulrich Backmann, 'Als die Bilderwelten zusammenstürzten', in *Die nackte Republik. Aktfotografien von Amateuren aus 40 Jahren Alltag im Osten* (Berlin: Das Magazin Verlagsgesellschaft, 1993), n.p.
[65] Günter Rössler interviewed in Kolano, *Nackter Osten*, p. 52; Backmann, 'Als die Bilderwelten zusammenstürzten'.
[66] Dieckmann, *Die Liebe in den Zeiten des Landfilms*, p. 41.
[67] See for example Christian Härtel and Petra Kabus (eds.), *Das Westpaket. Geschenksendung, keine Handelsware* (Berlin: Ch. Links, 2000).
[68] BArch DL203/04-07-05 (Ka: 294a), Stauch an Beater, 17.2.1966.
[69] *Ibid.* (Ka: 294), Abteilung Zollrecht, Übergabe-/Übernahme-Protokoll, p. 7 (probably 1979).

For some, smuggling was a means of getting hold of material that was completely unavailable in the East. This was particularly true for gay men and lesbians. Copies of West German magazines were smuggled in throughout the 1970s and 1980s, alongside directly sexual material, like the postcard depicting gay sex to be found in the archives of the Stasi.[70] In a country where homosexuality was all but invisible in the public sphere, these objects were politically as well as sexually charged: as we have already seen, information on the Western gay liberation movement was a crucial influence on the East German gay and lesbian scene.

Making one's own erotica was also a popular occupation. At the height of the nudist ban of the 1950s, photographs taken on the nudist beach had been seized by the police.[71] But by the mid 1960s, amateurs were being encouraged to send their nude photographs to *Das Magazin* for publication.[72] Small ads were used to buy and sell nude photos, as well as to find models willing to pose naked.[73] As naked bathing grew in popularity, the opportunities to take nude photographs grew still further.

Official attitudes towards such activities were, at times, remarkably tolerant, even with regard to material that went well beyond the sort of photographs published in the press. Making or possessing pornographic pictures for one's own amusement was not a criminal offence. Article 125 of the Strafgesetzbuch forbade only the 'distribution of pornographic material', stating that those who distributed such material or 'otherwise made it publicly available' were liable to a range of punishments, including a prison sentence of up to two years.[74] The ways in which this law was interpreted depended very much on one's understanding of 'publicly available'. Officials in the supreme court tended to define the private sphere rather generously. Even in the early 1970s, it was argued that it was not necessary to prosecute such cases, so long as pictures had circulated only amongst family, friends, and colleagues. Distribution of pornography should become criminal only if it involved passing such material on to unknown individuals or young people under the age of consent.[75] Such an expansive interpretation was probably a result of the fact that such laws could be highly

---

[70] BStU, MfS, HA XX/9 Nr 1976, p. 1; BStU, MfS, HA IX/Fo/1086 Bild 1.
[71] BArch DO1/11.0 HVDVP Nr 898, pp. 76, 85.
[72] 'Wir besuchten die Bildreaktion des MAGAZIN', *Fotografie*, June 1964, 230.
[73] E.g. *Fotografie*, February 1966, 79.
[74] Strafgesetzbuch der Deutschen Demokratischen Republik, 12 January 1968.
[75] BArch DP2/457, 'Problemdiskussion zum kriminellen Gehalt der Verbreitung pornographischer Schriften', n.d.

unpopular. In 1972, a man in Freiberg was fined 400 marks for show-ing 'pornographic pictures' to four colleagues during their morning break. Following his conviction, several of his colleagues voiced amaze-ment that this was classified as criminal behaviour, a view that was also expressed in a number of petitions. A supreme court official noted with concern that such cases were 'stacking up' in several regions, perhaps because of the increase in traffic between the GDR and the West.[76] To prosecute them all would have made the state seem heavy-handed and intolerant, at a time when Honecker was keen to persuade East Germans that even under socialism there should be 'no taboos'.

Such progressive attitudes were not always shared by the regional courts. In 1985, the district court in Bautzen sentenced a defend-ant to one year in prison for taking pornographic photographs at his birthday party, which pictured his wife, his step-daughter and her boyfriend, and another couple. He had also taken photographs during a threesome involving himself, his wife, and another man. In both cases, the photographs had been shared with those involved and sent to an interested third party.[77] The supreme court official involved in scrutinising this case was troubled by a number of aspects, not least the Bautzen court's definition of what made a picture pornographic. The regional court had concluded that a picture could be classed as pornographic only if 'genitals are to be seen', a definition which was rejected as 'far too narrow'. The Berlin official was also troubled that 'in public' (*Öffentlichkeit*) was interpreted in different ways in the con-text of different laws. 'He who expresses racist views in front of his partner and his best friend commits no crime ... but if he shows them pornographic pictures he is a criminal? In my opinion that is a dis-tortion of the law!'[78] The paper concluded that showing pornographic pictures at a birthday party or at work was not an offence, nor was exchanging such pictures within a circle of friends. Such attitudes were clearly shared by the population. Herr S remembered 'really vul-gar' photographs circulating in the army and, by the time the Wall came down, 30 per cent of the population admitted to having been shown illegally smuggled West German pornography at their place of work alone.[79]

While the regime may have been happy – in most cases – to turn a blind eye to the circulation of smuggled or home-made pornography,

[76] *Ibid.*
[77] BArch DP 2/457, 'Zu einigen Problemen der Verbreitung von pornographischen Schriften', 21.2.1986, pp. 2–3.
[78] *Ibid.*, p. 5.
[79] Werner Habermehl and Kurt Starke, *Sexualität in der DDR* (n.p., 1990), n.p.

it went much further when it came to the production and exhibition of more traditionally 'artistic' nude photography. Amateur nude photography was steered by the Kulturbund (League for Culture), which organised nude photography weekend courses, first for professionals and later for hobby photographers. It even held a conference on the subject in 1984.[80] The Potsdam branch of the Kulturbund was particularly active in this field, organising a series of exhibitions around the theme 'Nude and Landscape' throughout the 1980s.[81]

Some of the amateur nude photographs that survive speak eloquently of the fun to be had in producing erotica, as couples posed for each other and for the camera's self-timer. Many amateurs reproduced the motifs of mainstream nudes: female models, soft-focus lenses, and dreamy outdoor settings.[82] Such themes predominate, but were by no means universal. Some home-made photographs went well beyond what the functionaries of the Kulturbund had in mind. Gay erotica seized by the Stasi shows a sense of mischievous *Eigen-Sinn* (autonomy) as a young man with a twinkle in his eye poses in a Roman-style toga with a bowl of fruit, before moving on to more overtly sexual positions (Figure 7.6).[83] Other photographers were clearly driven by financial motives. A dealer in Leipzig showed me a vast collection of pornographic photographs produced and printed in the GDR. They had been printed in multiple copies, obviously with the intention of selling them on (and clearly in violation of paragraph 125). This particular photographer's oeuvre was a curious hybrid of East and West – the pictures were posed in recognisably East German interiors, with no attempt to conceal rather mundane wallpaper and furnishings. Equally, the models did not try to emulate the stars of *Playboy*, and often had heavy body hair and practical haircuts. Yet the photographs made much of risqué lingerie – presumably smuggled from the West – and depicted far more explicit motifs than the usual fare, up to and including sex toys and penetration. Perhaps the 'East German' flavour of the images was intentional, to allow the viewer to plausibly imagine himself participating in the action? It is impossible to know, but interesting to note that these photographs have retained their value and are still traded privately and on internet auction sites.

[80] Roger Rössling, 'Plainair über Aktfotografie', *Fotografie*, April 1980, 122–123. Cf. BLHA, Rep. 538, Kulturbund, Bezirksleitung Potsdam, Nr 234 and Nr 220 on events in 1980 and 1984; BLHA, Rep. 538, Kulturbund, Bezirksleitung Potsdam, Nr 229, Auswertung der DDR-offenen Konferenz zu Fragen der Aktfotografie.

[81] For more on this, see McLellan, 'Visual Dangers and Delights'.

[82] For a collection of amateur photographs, see *Die nackte Republik*.

[83] BStU, MfS, HA XX/Fo/1367, Bild 37, Bild 16, Bild 73.

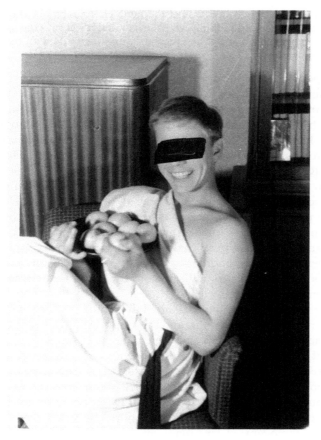

Figure 7.6: Homemade gay erotica, seized by the Stasi.

Challenging the mainstream nude

While the erotic rewriting of homemade pornography took place in private, by the 1980s the conventions of the mainstream nude were also being challenged in public. Both amateur and professional photographers started to produce nude photographs that consciously critiqued the conservative gender politics of officially sanctioned erotica and contrasted them with the realities of life in East Germany. As Gundula Schulze, who began to develop her own take on nude photography as a student, put it:

The public depiction of women's beauty is not real ... the woman who is pictured has nothing at all to do with the picture, because her daily life and her reality look quite different ... I look at the nude photography in *Das Magazin* and in the newspaper and in film year after year and it's always the same, it's a joke, it's an anachronism and it has absolutely nothing to do with the position of women today.[84]

In retrospect Schulze described her pictures as a corrective to 'the totally mendacious hypocrisy' of the GDR: 'I had the feeling that people wanted to be how they are and not be ruled by an idealised picture which makes them feel inferior.'[85] She began by photographing women of her own age, creating nude portraits that aimed to reflect the lived reality of their lives rather than a fantasy of femininity. Her photograph of Regina, a structural engineer, exemplifies the 'self-confident female' so emblematic of the GDR, yet so consistently absent from the nude genre as a whole (Figure 7.7). Like all of Schulze's nude subjects, Regina is photographed in her own home, surrounded by the accoutrements of middle-class intellectual life: paintings, antique furniture, records, and books. Her pose challenges the viewer to accept her sexuality on her own terms, and her eye contact with the camera – and the viewer – is direct and calm, with none of the sexualised coyness of the conventional nude model.

Schulze's series of portraits expanded to include the very old, the very young, the poor, the overweight, and the amputated. All her nudes share Regina's sense of composure, and even defiance of society's norms. Her portrait of Lothar, perhaps her best-known photo, shows an old, frail man, naked but for a pair of slippers, sitting on the edge of a single bed.[86] Above his bed, he has stuck a series of pin-up pictures of young nubile women, their idealised sexuality drawing attention to the rather different reality of his own life. Schulze's portraits were a reminder that, despite the homogenised fare made available for public consumption, the body could be a site of difference and subjectivity. By foregrounding the nudity of her subjects, she also made the point that the body was not just about sexuality, but about illness, ageing, poverty, independence, and friendship too. Her picture of two young, heavily tattooed men suggests a powerful bond beyond the state-subscribed norms of the work brigade and the sports field (Figure 7.8). Tattoos were associated with criminality, time in prison, and even opposition to the state. Were these men clothed, however, the viewer would have no idea of their private identities – a reminder that much may lie beneath the public façade.

[84] *Aktfotografie, z.B. Gundula Schulze* (dir. Helke Misselwitz, 1983), Bundesfilmarchiv BCSP-6732.

[85] Letter from Gundula Schulze Eldowy to the author, 13.2.2004.

[86] For a reproduction of 'Lothar' and more on this image, see McLellan, 'Visual Dangers and Delights', 165–167.

Figure 7.7: Gundula Schulze Eldowy, 'Regina, Leipzig, 1984'.

Figure 7.8: Gundula Schulze Eldowy, 'Rajk and Matthias, Berlin, 1984'.

Like Schulze, Eva Mahn, another photographer of the 1980s, pointed to the contradictions between women's real lives and the visual culture of femininity. Mahn's critique of mainstream photography originated from her own days as a model for fashion and nude photographs.

'I wanted to do something where women weren't objects ... where they were self-confident and where you could see you couldn't boss them around', she recalled. Mahn was electrified by Helmut Newton's angular, aggressive nudes and was inspired to offer her own alternative to mainstream erotica. For one series of photographs she deliberately chose thin models, in order to go against the grain of the pin-up aesthetic. 'You had to have lovely big breasts and curvy hips and that wasn't my type, because I was thin myself.' Her pictures of these women, often in aggressive or provocative poses, provoked mixed reactions. 'People asked me, are you a lesbian, what kind of women are they? There's nothing there for a man, nothing to hold onto. And so cool, so distant. That's not erotic at all.' By producing photographs that were not designed for the male gaze, featuring self-possessed women who challenged rather than tempted the viewer, Mahn overturned the constraints of the traditional East German nude.

A final example of this complex relationship with Western culture is Erasmus Schroeter's mid-1980s nude, exhibited in a Leipzig underground art gallery shortly before Schroeter's departure for West Germany (Figure 7.9). This image clearly references, but also critiques, Helmut Newton. The use of an older model, her heavy make-up and obviously dyed hair, the use of colour and flash, as well as the tropical foliage, all contribute to a sense of artificiality and invite the viewer to reflect on the constructed and commercialised nature of sexuality. In doing so, it challenged not just the glossy perfection of Newton's work and the mainstream nude's focus on naturalness, but also the documentary aspirations of photographers such as Schulze. Interestingly, even the denizens of Leipzig's alternative art scene found this departure from established genres hard to stomach.[87]

This new brand of photography called the imaginary bodies of socialism to account, pointing out that the young, fecund female bodies to be found in *Das Magazin* were unrepresentative and dishonest. It criticised not only socialist culture, but also the lived reality of gender and sexuality. In some cases, its reach was surprising. Mahn was involved with the work of the Kulturbund, sitting on the jury of the 'Nude and Landscape' exhibition, and Schulze's work was included in the National Art Exhibition in 1988. Members of the public were not just able to view such photographs, they were also involved in taking them. The 'Nude and Landscape' exhibition, which hung amateur and professional photographs side by side, showed male nudes as early as 1982, and by 1988 a number of nudes could safely be described as homoerotic. Beauty,

[87] Conversation with Erasmus Schroeter, 1.12.2007.

Figure 7.9: Erasmus Schroeter, 'Der Rote Sessel', Leipzig, 1984.

'naturalness', and utopian aspirations had been almost completely replaced by realism and social commentary. The 'Nude and Landscape' exhibitions demonstrate how widely non-conformist photography was disseminated. In 1983 the exhibition was attended by 42,000 people, not unimpressive for a small-town event.[88]

---

[88] BLHA Rep. 538, Kulturbund, Bezirksleitung Potsdam, Nr 207, Übersicht über Finanzen 'Akt und Landschaft', 6.7.1982.

Nevertheless, many observers found the severance of the traditional link between the nude and beauty highly problematic. A visitor to the 1988 National Art Exhibition commented on Schulze's photographs, 'I am certainly not prudish, but that was simply vulgar and not aesthetically pleasing in the slightest. There are certainly works of art whose subjects allow little or no aesthetic, but every human body can be beautiful.'[89] For those whose appreciation of the nude had been schooled by the images in *Das Magazin*, the uncompromising photographs of the 1980s made uncomfortable viewing.

Conclusion

What, then, can erotica tell us about East German sexuality? It underlines the way in which the regime was happy to use sex as a social pacifier – in this case, from a very early stage of socialist rule. Despite the regime's misgivings about the moral shortcomings of the nude, such images were to become widespread from the 1960s onwards. The visibility of erotica was an integral part of the transformation of East German attitudes towards sex. What is particularly significant in this case is the way in which sexual goods were bought and sold – in public and in private. As Herr L put it: 'Sex wasn't for sale in the GDR. Well, on a small scale.' Like all consumer goods, erotica had an economic function, but it was also system-stabilising in other ways. It enhanced consumers' leisure time and gave them a precious sense of luxury and indulgence. Especially interesting are the ways in which this sense of the 'good life' was linked to rather conventional ideas of how men and women should look and behave. Erotica throws into sharp relief the persistence of traditional gender norms, at odds with the repeated insistence that women in the GDR were liberated from the sexism inherent in capitalist society. State-produced erotica, with its insistence that men should be strong, active, and purposeful, while women were attractive, passive, and apolitical, showed just how durable gender stereotypes were as well as the extent to which they were shared by both men and women. As we have seen, readers and viewers played a central role in shaping the meaning and setting the boundaries of nude photography.

In this way, erotica underscored the heteronormative and often homophobic nature of East German popular culture. The marginalisation and persecution of gay pornography show how narrow mainstream definitions of sexuality were. But gay and other non-mainstream erotica also shows the impossibility of identifying a single unified East

---

[89] B. Lindner, 'Sozialer Raum: Fotografie', *Fotografie*, March 1989, 83.

German sexuality. While many were happy to enjoy, emulate, and identify with the bodies in mainstream nude photography, others felt alienated and strove to articulate their own vision of the sexual and non-sexual body.

Finally, it is difficult to escape the extent to which the public sphere was responsive to Western trends. Not only did erotica imitate and react to trends from across the border, it also reflected societal norms about consumption and gender not dissimilar to those in the West. The East German authorities condemned West German pornography but state-produced erotica was undeniably influenced by capitalist norms. Not only did objects made their way across the border but also – and more importantly – ideas and visual discourses did too. In the area of erotica at least, East Germany could not claim to have taken a separate path.

8   Conclusion: 'space for love'?

In 1989, with the collapse of the SED regime, East and West Germany began the slow and sometimes painful process of reunification. Curiously, perhaps, perceived sexual differences on either side of the Wall became a significant focus of discussion. At first, East Germans were frequently portrayed as having led lives that were sexually as well as politically repressed. 'Sex at last!' gasped *Die Zeit* in June 1990, reporting the opening of the first sex shop to the east of the German–German border. This, according to the newspaper, was a significant event in the dying days of the GDR, a country whose citizens 'were not allowed to show themselves naked or see the naked bodies of others, except at the nudist beach'. 'The workers and peasants', the article went on, 'could practise voyeurism only under the covers of the marriage bed.' Now, at last, currency reform and impending reunification were giving them the opportunity to make up for lost time.[1] During the *Wende*, accounts such as this were common, presenting sex as one of many areas in which East Germans had to 'catch up' with their Western neighbours. The brave new world of the market economy now offered new erotic opportunities as well as the chance to make good their earlier deprivation.

Indeed, some East Germans did actually experience the *Wende* as a time of sexual as well as political new beginnings. Interest in erotic goods was genuine and widespread. Surveyed in the first half of 1990, 83% of 16–18-year-olds had seen pornographic magazines, and 49% had watched at least one pornographic film.[2] Letters to the West German sexual goods entrepreneur Beate Uhse spoke eloquently of their writers' eagerness for new experiences and their desire to compensate for the privations of the past. For many, the sexual opportunities opened up by the *Wende* symbolised the liberation 'which we have dreamed of

---

[1] Ulrich Stock, 'Endlich Sex! In Leipzig eröffnete der erste Pornoladen der DDR', *Die Zeit*, 22.6.1990, pdf.zeit.de/1990/26/Endlich-Sex.pdf.
[2] Konrad Weller, *Das Sexuelle in der deutsch–deutschen Vereinigung* (Leipzig: Forum Verlag, 1991), p. 90.

for 40 years'.[3] This sentiment was echoed by the 45-year-old Silvia E, who wrote in her diary: 'I would really love to go into a sex shop … I just want to have a look at what they've got, the sexy underwear, the negligees. I want to know if there is anything that could help me get more fun out of my sex life. Everyone is different and has different needs, but in the GDR everything was grey and monotonous.'[4]

Yet, over the course of the following two decades, a very different picture of East Germans and their attitudes towards the body emerged. In this version of events, the GDR had enabled a natural, uncommercialised sexuality, unsullied by the demands of capitalism. Rather than 'sex at last', the sex shops which sprang up across the GDR heralded the end of a unique and felicitous period in German sexual history. Sex and relationships in the GDR, it was argued, were based on mutuality and gender equality and reflected a more relaxed, egalitarian society. As Wenzel Müller put it: 'The East Germans were never so physically close as in the time of the GDR. Although daily life was much more strongly regimented than in the West – the bedroom was a free space which young and old … filled with love and desire.'[5] Such intimacy, it was argued, would have been impossible in the West, where time-poor, pressurised lifestyles encouraged competition rather than closeness. In the East, not only were money worries unlikely to put strain on a relationship, but the laid-back nature of the social sphere also created 'space for love'.[6] Away from the rat race of life in the West, East Germans were freer to flirt, daydream, and take time for their relationships. 'The clocks ran slower in the East', remembered Karin Rohnstock, adding that the lack of choice in the shops allowed greater opportunity for a morale-boosting flirt in the queue to pay.[7]

Sex surveys carried out both before and after the *Wende* played an important role in cementing East Germans' reputation as better lovers. A survey of 1,161 East Germans and 8,293 West Germans, carried out for *Playboy* in the early 1990s came to some surprising results: East German men, it seemed, had longer penises, averaging half a centimetre more than their West German comparators. They were also

---

[3] Wierling, 'Vereinigungen', 149.

[4] Ingrid Sharp, 'The Sexual Unification of Germany', *Journal of the History of Sexuality* 13 (2004), 363.

[5] Wenzel Müller, *Leben in der Platte. Alltagskultur der DDR der 70er und 80er Jahre*, (Vienna: Selbstverlag, 1990), p. 98.

[6] Dietrich Mühlberg, 'Raum für die Liebe. Eine Nachbetrachtung', in Rohnstock, *Erotik macht die Häßlichen schön*, pp. 103–202. Cf. Dietrich Mühlberg, 'Sexualität und ostdeutscher Alltag', *Mitteilungen aus der kulturwissenschaftlichen Forschung* 18 (36) (1995), 8–39.

[7] Rohnstock, *Erotik macht die Häßlichen schön*, p. 9.

likely to have sex more often, with 13 per cent claiming to have sex
'at least' once a day.[8] These statistics, particularly on the comparative
rate of orgasm in East and West, were often manipulated by the media
to make them appear more controversial than they actually were.[9] In
truth, the findings of the postunification sex surveys were inconclusive.
Neither East nor West Germans emerged as sexual victors of the Cold
War. The *Playboy* survey, for example, suggested that, although East
Germans had sex more frequently, West German women were more
satisfied with their sex lives than their Eastern sisters.[10] In contrast to
the findings of research carried out during the lifetime of the GDR,
this survey concluded that East German women were less likely have
an orgasm and that 50% of Eastern men and 57% of Eastern women
doubted their abilities in bed: hardly an unambiguous result in favour
of the East.[11] But this is how it was often presented in the media, creating a lasting impression that, as one woman put it: 'Everybody knows
that East-women have more fun. Orgasm rates were higher in the East,
all the studies show it.'[12]

This romantic narrative of East German sexuality had two root
causes. Firstly, East Germans were rightly insulted by the insinuation
that their sex lives had been boring and staid, and that they had been 'left
behind' by the pace of Western sexual change. Secondly, East Germany
had experienced radical changes in (hetero)sexual norms in the two
decades before reunification. For people who had lived through this
sexual revolution, the suggestion that the GDR had been prudish and
repressed was absurd. Why did this transformation take place? Were
changes in sexual mores enabled from above or forced from below?

Interestingly, our interviewees were left with quite different impres-
sions of the state's attitude to sexuality. Some, such as Frau F, felt the
state had implicitly encouraged and promoted sexuality:

I think that this [sexuality] was an area where things were pretty wild [*wo
es ganz schön zur Sache ging*]. Maybe because you were quite restricted and
hemmed in in other ways. And I think, in terms of love and relationships, quite
a bit went on in the GDR. Yes, I'd say so ... And it was welcomed in principle.
You were supposed to procreate and be fruitful and so on, weren't you? They
actually wanted young people to come together as quickly as possible.

[8] Werner Habermehl, *Sexualverhalten der Deutschen. Aktuelle Daten – intime Wahrheiten*
(Munich: Wilhelm Heyne, 1993), pp. 39–40.
[9] Weller, *Das Sexuelle in der deutsch–deutschen Vereinigung*, pp. 29–30.
[10] Habermehl, *Sexualverhalten der Deutschen*, p. 40.
[11] *Ibid.*, pp. 46, 44.
[12] Dagmar Herzog, 'Post coitum triste est ... ? Sexual Politics and Cultures in Postunification
Germany', *German Politics and Society* 28 (2010), 113.

Here, sexuality is seen not only as compensation for other, absent, freedoms, but also as an integral part of the regime's pro-natalism. Frau V concurred: 'There was a deliberate policy to persuade people to have as many children as possible, and in that respect they simply had to allow certain things.' She went on to expound her theory that the regime had deliberately caused power cuts to encourage people to have sex. Frau N, on the other hand, distinguished between a liberated population, and a prudish regime which 'couldn't deal with sexuality at all ... They had huge problems with it. And the fact that the people were emancipated and just did what they felt was right was something that they tolerated, but the official view of it was very unsophisticated and uptight.' Here, sexual change is something that comes from below, rather than being propagated by the state. In fact, the evidence examined in this book appears to suggest that elements of both were at work.

The regime did loosen its control over sexual matters considerably, moving from a somewhat repressive stance in the 1950s to a far more laissez-faire approach in the 1980s. In the vast majority of cases, however, the state adapted and adjusted to popular behaviour and demands, rather than leading the way towards a sexually tolerant society. The East German regime was pragmatic rather than progressive, and in this area concerned with three key priorities: halting – or at least slowing – the decline in the birth rate, keeping women in paid work, and the international reputation of the GDR. Even with regard to homosexuality, the only area where the state really moved ahead of popular opinion, efforts to educate were prompted by the desire to contain and neutralise autonomous and potentially oppositional activity. In part, the regime was simply adjusting its policies to fit new modes of popular behaviour. As Günter Gaus points out, 'niches' such as nude bathing played an important role as 'vents' that released some of the pressure on the beleaguered public sphere. SED functionaries did not welcome the population's rejection of communist ideology and retreat into the private sphere, but the more pragmatic among them realised that it had its benefits too.[13]

There can be no doubt that many shifts in sexual behaviour were the result of popular pressure from below. This pressure took many forms: in some cases, East Germans consciously lobbied for a change in the law, as in the dogged work of gay activists such as Rudolf Klimmer and those who took on his mantle in the 1970s and 1980s. Nudists too took

---

[13] Günter Gaus, *Wo Deutschland liegt. Eine Ortsbestimmung* (Hamburg: Hoffmann und Campe, 1983), p. 157.

it upon themselves to convince the regime of the legitimacy of their hobby and of their need for representation. Other citizens wrote to the regime seeking a solution for their individual situation: for example, women requesting permission to end a pregnancy. These actions were by no means part of a co-ordinated course of action, but were born out of individual desperation. When such letters arrived in large numbers, they placed significant pressure on the state. However, presented with a request, it was all too easy for functionaries to find reasons why the petitioner's intentions were incompatible with socialism. One of the East German state's great weaknesses was its inability to respond directly to the wishes and demands of its citizens.

For this reason, lasting change was created more often by individuals' actions than by their requests. The attempted ban on nudism was a case in point: while there is no evidence that the regime was won over by the numerous petitions it was sent, it was all but powerless in the face of nudists' civil disobedience. Once the ban was overturned, nude bathing quickly spread as more holidaymakers took it up. This cheerful anarchism of individual behaviour can be seen in other areas too: while marriage and the nuclear family remained central to official rhetoric, more East Germans were having children outside wedlock. The economic and social framework of life under state socialism was crucial here, particularly women's work and financial independence. Because of the importance of the family to socialist society, married couples and parents had the most space to pursue their private lives – both physically and ideologically. This was the area in which the regime was most vulnerable to popular pressure, as in the case of the reform of abortion legislation. It was also the area in which behaviour changed the most noticeably – enabled in part by state policy.

If popular pressure and state pragmatism were key in shaping the East German sexual revolution, international trends were a crucial third factor. The GDR was far from hermetically sealed, and its citizens were surprisingly well informed about developments elsewhere. In some cases, these influences were very direct: the gay and lesbian activists of the 1970s saw themselves as part of a broader gay liberation movement and had extensive links to activists in West Germany and beyond. There is still much more to be said about the lasting impact of the Western 1968 in the Eastern bloc. But it would be a mistake to imagine that East Germans were simply mimicking their Western neighbours. In many ways, East and West Germans (and Europeans) should be seen as reacting to similar socio-economic developments: the growth of the welfare state, increased standards of living (particularly housing), higher levels of education, reduced working hours, and so on.

For all the frustrations of the shortage society, East Germans, particularly those born after 1960, showed certain postmaterialist traits.

When did these changes take place? The first signs of a thaw in attitudes towards sexuality occurred in the wake of the erection of the Berlin Wall, particularly with the publication of the *Jugendkommuniqué* in 1963. The 1960s were a time of emergent trends, as nudism started to establish itself as a mass activity, demands for effective birth control grew, and the birth rate began to drop. But it was the start of the Honecker era in 1971 that really marked the turning point of the East German sexual revolution. The policy of 'no taboos' in culture allowed the release of films such as *Die Legende von Paul und Paula* as well as lesser-known works such as Ulrich Berkes' collection of poetry which – amongst other things – celebrated East Berlin cottaging sites.[14] The World Festival Games marked the beginning of a policy of less overt control over mainstream youth culture. Legislation on abortion and the spread of the contraceptive Pill had an immediate and abrupt effect on the birth rate. The 1970s also saw a freer – although by no means free – movement of people both within and into the GDR, resulting in a better flow of information from the West, and allowing more people to move to urban areas such as Berlin and Leipzig. Concerted efforts to improve the GDR's housing stock not only gave families more space and more privacy, but also left many older and dilapidated apartments empty, enabling the emergence of bohemian subcultures such as Prenzlauer Berg in Berlin.

It goes without saying that all these developments had considerable limitations. Literature and films were still subject to censorship. Tolerance of Western pop and rock had its limits. Youth cultures – like the whole of East German society – found themselves under increased Stasi surveillance. Contact with the West was patchy for those without family or other connections. And all of these trends were less pronounced in small towns and rural areas, where social change was slower to take effect.

But, despite this, most people felt that they had autonomy in their private lives. Should we conclude from this that sex and the family formed a 'niche'? To a certain extent, yes, but not in the often-used sense that it allowed people to escape from the socialist system. Rather, it underlines Günter Gaus' point that 'niches are not external [to the socialist system], on the contrary they are niches inside GDR socialism ... Over the decades more facts, beliefs, and standards of really existing socialism

---

[14] Ulrich Berkes, *Icarus über der Stadt* (Berlin and Weimar: Aufbau Verlag, 1976).

have made themselves at home in private corners than niche dwellers are always aware of.'[15]

Undoubtedly, many East Germans experienced sex and relationships as an escape from the pressures of everyday life and politics. As we have seen, many people's freedom of action did expand, with resultant dramatic changes in sexual behaviour. But this does not mean that sex was a completely 'free space'. As Mary Fulbrook and Paul Betts have pointed out, there was a fundamental intertwining of the public and the private under state socialism. Sexuality was no exception to this. Private life and individuals' life paths were decisively shaped by state structures and institutions, particularly education, housing, military conscription, and the allocation of work. While nobody's choices were entirely unrestricted, this was particularly true for those who stepped outside the norms of socialist sexuality. For gay men and lesbians, people in binational relationships, and those unlucky enough to fall into the Stasi's realm of influence, sexuality was deeply unfree.

Furthermore, although in many cases private life and the family did act as a refuge from the demands of work and everyday politics, it is also important to remember that the private sphere was not always a realm of love, intimacy, and respite. The rising divorce rate and the increasing numbers of people who opted not to marry at all demonstrate the frustrations and limits of the nuclear family. As gay men and lesbians discovered, repression could come from within the family too, and private attitudes towards minority sexualities often lagged behind official legislation and declarations of tolerance.

Finally, we should beware of drawing too neat a line between the values and choices of the population and those of the regime. In the Honecker era, sex became part of the social pact between the state and its citizens. The state granted its citizens a greater degree of free choice in sexual matters: abortion was freely available, divorces were more readily granted, and raising children outside marriage became a quotidian matter. As we have seen, such concessions were often direct responses to popular pressures.[16] This increased autonomy in sexual matters was part of the regime's attempts to pacify the population: if the people could not be won over to socialism, they could at least share in a *Wir-Gefühl* (literally: 'we-feeling'), a sense of being 'at home' in the GDR. As Betts has shown, privacy was a way of creating a sense of

[15] Gaus, *Wo Deutschland liegt*, pp. 156–157.
[16] As Annette Timm writes: '[Marriage counselling] opened up spaces for individuals to help shape the form of government services that developed in part through a process of interaction' (Timm, *Politics of Fertility*, 288).

212 Conclusion: 'space for love'?

community around the commonalities of private life. The *Ostalgie* of the post-*Wende* period pays testament to the success of this strategy. But with inclusion came exclusion. Sex and the family certainly allowed people to escape the politicised public sphere, but on the whole the sexual revolution did little to undermine regime values. Changes in both behaviour and values largely benefited heterosexuals, and the autonomy enjoyed by the majority must be contrasted with the limitations placed on minorities. Those who stepped beyond the norms of socialist society, like the men involved in producing homoerotic material, also stepped outside the protection of the 'niche' and made themselves vulnerable to state persecution.

The East German sexual revolution had three major limitations. First was the lack of fundamental change in gender roles, despite widespread female employment. The East German system was in many ways intensely masculine. For all the visibility of women in the workplace, it was a state founded and led by men. East German women tended to dismiss West German feminism as extreme, claiming that such a movement was unnecessary in the East, where women already enjoyed equal rights. But formal rights were not enough to ensure full equality, as the preponderance of sexist images in the public sphere demonstrated. What stung most for many women was the fact that men's roles had not fundamentally changed and that women were still expected to take on the lion's share of domestic responsibility. The division of household labour was even a problem in the experimental Kommune I Ost. Erika Bärthold remembered ruefully that 'the men didn't apply themselves to the housework and the children enough, then we had a protocol or a meeting of the commune. They would be ordered to do things differently, and then it would break down again.' But she concluded that, despite these difficulties, 'I didn't have a specifically female perspective for a long time.'[17] Similarly, despite their biting commentary on the gender norms of the time, the photographers Gundula Schulze and Eva Mahn distanced themselves from feminism, feeling that the economic independence of Eastern women presented them with an entirely different set of challenges from those of their counterparts in the West.

Secondly, there was no revolution in attitudes towards homosexuality. Despite a slow liberalisation, gay men and lesbians faced a dual problem of homophobia and invisibility. State attempts to engage with these issues were lacklustre, and only in the mid to late 1980s was any significant progress made. In part, this failure to empathise with the problems faced by gays and lesbians was part of an inability and/or unwillingness

---

[17] Quoted in Kätzel, 'Kommune 1 Ost'.

to think about unreproductive sex. Even the most forward-thinking sex guides saw sex as inextricably linked to marriage and childbearing. As Jennifer Evans has pointed out, the GDR regime sent a consistent 'message that full and active citizenship must revolve around (re)productive labor and sexual restraint'.[18] This meant that gays and lesbians remained, at best, marginal to East German society.

Finally, East German sexuality, in policy and in practice, was marked by distinctive racial undertones. Whether in the Cameroon parties on the Baltic coast, the treatment of bi-national relationships, or the use of non-Caucasian bodies in erotica, race and sex were uneasy companions.[19] In part, this was a result of the failure to publicly discuss or process the legacy of the Nazi period. The extraordinary silence surrounding the rapes carried out by Red Army soldiers was one part of this, the consistent rebuffing of attempts to discuss gay victims of Nazism another. The SED's interpretation of fascism as an extreme manifestation of capitalism allowed scant space for reflection on its often contradictory sexual policy and its legacies in postwar Germany.[20] State officials circled uneasily around the topic, feeling uncomfortable with the ethnic drag of the Cameroon revellers, but unable to acknowledge the continuities between Nazi and East German homophobia.

All three limitations can in part be traced to the lack of an independent public sphere.[21] It was all but impossible to accuse a state that had proclaimed itself to be both pro-women and antifascist of sexism or racism. While most of the population enjoyed substantial autonomy in their private lives, East Germans lacked a broader societal context in which questions of sexuality, relationships, and gender could be openly discussed. In the 1980s, the Protestant Church offered a valuable forum for lesbian and gay activists. Indeed the role of the church in this story is a curious one: in the thoroughly secularised GDR, it played little

[18] Jennifer Evans, 'Decriminalization, Seduction, and "Unnatural Desire"', 558.
[19] On race and nude photography, see McLellan, 'Visual Dangers and Delights'.
[20] See here especially Herzog, *Sex After Fascism*, and Elizabeth Heineman, 'Sexuality and Nazism: The Doubly Unspeakable?', *Journal of the History of Sexuality* 11 (1–2) (2002), 22–66.
[21] See Thomas Lindenberger, '"Asociality" and Modernity: The GDR as a Welfare Dictatorship', in Pence and Betts (eds.), *Socialist Modern*, p. 222. 'Precisely because the state strove to suppress autonomous social processes of communication, and thereby simultaneously constructed a closed-off sphere for itself, communication and interaction between the SED and the population were reduced to a set of unquestioned "unpolitical" understandings that blocked the formation of any collective political will. This face had an inclusive, positive side: the regime and the population alike saw the value in striving toward the just access for everyone to values such as material security, prosperity, peace, and family. However, it also had its exclusionary, negative side as well.'

role in broader public debates about sexuality. But in the state's final decade, church premises and publications provided a rare platform for those who felt excluded by the heterosexual norms of East German society. For all its merits, however, the church was no substitute for a fully independent public sphere, not least because of the difficulties in reaching a wider audience. The lack of open debate severely restricted the directions in which both public policy and private behaviour were able to develop. As Donna Harsch puts it: 'Only out of the ferment of social experimentation and public debate might have emerged a genuinely new conception and organisation of consumption, housework, child rearing, leisure, architecture, design or fashion. That was something the party could *not* imagine.'[22] The state was prepared to turn a blind eye to developments in private, but remained implacably opposed to the formation of autonomous groups, be they composed of gay activists or nudists.

As Gaus pointed out, niches were not a peculiarity of East Germany or of state socialism, but were 'the ordinary state of affairs everywhere'. What did distinguish the GDR from its Western neighbours was the absence of freedom of expression. This had profound consequences for those whose sexuality did not fit the norm of monogamous heterosexuality, or who felt restricted by officially prescribed gender roles. In such cases, intimacy and self-fulfilment were hampered most not by a lack of privacy, but by a lack of publicity.

Of course, sexism, homophobia, and racism were by no means unique to East Germany. If anything, they underline the similarities between East German and other sexual cultures. Romantic narratives, on the other hand, stress the singularity of East German sexuality, particularly the uncommercialised nature of East German life and socialism's progressive attitude towards women. But the limitations of these narratives are evident in their refusal to take gender issues seriously and in their willingness to take East German rhetoric of 'gender equality' at face value. Sex is seen purely as something lighthearted, carefree, and fun, rather than a site of power and privilege. The emergence of nostalgia as a master narrative of East German sexuality threatens to eclipse other voices, which tell a rather different story about life in the GDR. It is all too easy to forget that for some – both hetero- and homosexual – life could be lonely, relationships could fail, and sex could be disappointing. The story of East German sexuality includes both repression and romance. Both interpretations accurately describe the experiences of some of the people, some of the time. After 1989, as East Germans

---

[22] Harsch, *Revenge of the Domestic*, p. 197.

faced the new challenges of love in the time of capitalism, it can come as no surprise that they staked a claim to what Christoph Dieckmann has called 'the authentic life in an inauthentic regime [*wahres Leben im Falschen*] ... happy islands in the Dead Sea'.[23]

---

[23] Christoph Dieckmann, 'Kindheitsmuster oder das wahre Leben im Falschen. Dankrede anläßlich der Verleihung des Friedrich-Märker-Preises für Essayisten an den Autor', www.zeit.de/1996/52/kind.txt.19961220.xml.

Appendix: Interview questions

Questions asked in interviews carried out by Angela Brock

These interviews were carried out with heterosexual interview partners. Interviewees were asked for their date and place of birth, places of residence, parents' and grandparents' occupations and parents' year of birth; whether they had brothers and sisters; and their religion, if any. They were also asked for brief details of their education and career path.

How and when did you learn about sex? Was sex discussed openly at home, or was school more important?

When you were a child or teenager, did you read books about sexuality and relationships? Which ones?

Do you remember your first love affair?

When you were a teenager, how did you imagine love and marriage? What did you hope for in this area? Was your parents' marriage something you wanted to emulate?

How much freedom did you have to get to know the opposite sex? What did your parents think of this?

How did you get to know your husband/wife? Was it 'love at first sight'? How and when did you decide to get married? Did the man propose, or was it a joint decision? Or: why did you decide to live with your partner, rather than getting married?

If divorced: why? If not divorced: why do you think your marriage has lasted so long?

Do you have children? If so: did you always want children? How well did family life work? Was childcare good? Who was mainly responsible for the children? How did having children affect your life as a couple?

Did you have the sense that men and women were equal [*gleichberechtigt*] in the GDR? How did that work in your marriage? At work?

To what extent did men's role change, e.g. in the family? (Were girls and boys brought up differently? What about in the workplace?)

Did family life change over the generations? Were there big differences between parents, grandparents, and even stepparents?

What sorts of contraception were you aware of? Where did you learn about them? Which ones did you use, and from which age? Where did you get them? What did you think of the Pill? Did you have any problems with the Pill? How did access to contraception change over time? Which did men/women prefer? Was contraception discussed in sex education? Was your gynaecologist somebody you could talk to about such things?

Were sexually transmitted diseases an issue?

How did/do you feel about nudity and nudism? Was nudity common in your family? Did you go naked at the beach?

Did you come across nude photographs or pornography?

Was sex an issue at work?

Did you know any homosexuals, e.g. in your family, your circle of friends, your workplace? If yes, how were they treated?

How much freedom did you have to start and end relationships? Did you have the impression that you were hindered in your private life by anybody/anything? Do you think that people in the GDR were able to live their private lives without interference?

Did you watch Western TV and read Western books? Did you have an idea of what private life in the West was like, either through visits from the West or from Western media? Did you visit the Federal Republic before 1989? Do you think that Western influence played a role in the development of private life and sexuality in the GDR?

Would you say that the GDR was an open society with regard to sexuality? Could one openly discuss sexuality and relationships in one's circle of friends, in the workplace and in the media? Were there taboos (bordellos, unusual sexual practices, homosexuality)? Did things change over time? (If yes to 'open society': was this always the case, or a later development?) After the borders opened in 1989, did you notice differences between East and West Germany in this area?

Is there a book or film that you think gives a realistic depiction of life in the GDR?

Is there anything else that we haven't discussed which you think is important?

Questions in interviews carried out by Josie McLellan in 2010

These interviews were carried out with gay and lesbian interview partners. As they were part of a research project on gay and lesbian spaces and activism in East Berlin, a somewhat different interview schema was employed.

Interviewees were asked for their date and place of birth, places of residence, parents' and grandparent's occupations and parents' year of birth; whether they had brothers and sisters; and their religion, if any. They were also asked for brief details of their education and career path.

What age were you when you realised that you were gay/lesbian? Would you describe that as a 'coming out', or did that happen later?

When did you move to Berlin?

Where did you live? What did you work as?

What sort of places were important to your life in Berlin? Did you have an official flat or were you a squatter? Streets? Public toilets? Parks? Cafés and bars? Discos? Beaches? Saunas?

Where did you go on holiday?

Did you have contact with the working groups within the church? (If yes: did you participate in memorial visits to concentration camps such as Buchenwald, Ravensbrück, and Sachsenhausen?)

Were you involved with the Sunday Club?

Did you visit the Gründerzeitmuseum in Mahlsdorf?

How did you imagine the West? Did you have contact with visitors from the West? Did you have access to Western literature?

Can/should one speak of a gay/lesbian 'scene' in the GDR?

How did one recognise fellow gays and lesbians?

How much differentiation was there within the gay scene? E.g. were people categorised as 'queens' (*Tunten*)? What did a 'queen' look like? Were people ostracised/excluded by the scene?

How would you describe your circle of friends in the GDR: mostly gay men/lesbians? A mixture of gay men and lesbians? Or a mixture of gay and straight?

Were most people looking for a long-term partner? Once in a relationship, how important was sexual monogamy? Were there places where one could have anonymous sex? Did you come across men who had sex with other men but did not see themselves as 'gay', e.g. married men?

What about the Stasi? (How) did you experience surveillance?

Were sexually transmitted diseases an issue?

How did you find the West German scene after the collapse of the GDR? What happened to the East German scene?

Bibliography

INTERVIEWS

In all cases, I have given interviewees' main occupation(s) over the course of their working lives.

INTERVIEWS CARRIED OUT BY ANGELA BROCK

All interviewees have been fully pseudonymised.
Herr A, sports trainer, born 1957, Greifswald, 12.11.2007
Herr B, electrician, born 1951, Greifswald, 28.2.2008
Frau C, construction manager, born 1958, Orlamünde, 11.11.2007
Herr D, carpenter, born 1953, Berlin, 2.11.2007
Herr E, electrician, born 1963, Greifswald, 28.2.2008
Frau F, teacher and lecturer, born 1959, Eisenach, 12.11.2007
Frau G, skilled worker and administrator, born 1960, and Herr H, instrument
    mechanic, born 1952 (partners), Orlamünde, 10.11.2007
Frau I, railway worker, careworker, born 1952, Orlamünde, 10.11.2007
Frau J, midwife, born 1951, Berlin, 21.2.2008, and Herr J, doctor, born 1933,
    Berlin, 16.2.2008, 21.2.2008, 22.2.2008
Herr K, bus driver and motor mechanic, born 1939, Berlin, 24.1.2008
Frau L, kindergarten worker and teacher, born 1932, and Herr L, engineer,
    born 1932, Berlin, 20.11.2007
Frau M, quantity surveyor, born 1935, Orlamünde, 11.11.2007
Frau N, actor, born 1950, and Herr N, actor, born 1945, Weimar, 25.11.2007
Frau O, data processing technician, born 1949, Krauthausen, 12.11.2007
Herr P, teacher, born 1964, Eisenach, 13.11.2007
Frau Q, kindergarten worker, born 1969, and Frau R, kindergarten worker,
    born 1951 (friends), Magdeburg, 23.2.2008
Herr S, teacher, born 1959, Eisenach, 13.11.2007
Frau T, paediatric nurse, born 1948, Beeskow, 17.2.2008
Frau U, medical secretary, born 1971, Berlin, 16.11.2007
Frau V, teacher, born 1962, Eisenach, 13.11.2007
Frau W, careworker/housewife, born 1949, and Herr W, energy worker, born
    1947, Schwerin, 26.2.2008

INTERVIEWS CARRIED OUT BY JOSIE MCLELLAN

* indicates pseudonym
Michael E., book seller, born 1953, Berlin, 24.6.2010
Klaus Ender, photographer, born 1939, Rügen, 16.1.2004
Peter Faber, actor, born 1954, 30.6.2010
Hans Grüner*, writer, born 1957, Berlin, 23.6.2010
Ingo Kölsch, careworker, born 1959, Berlin, 6.1.2004
Ingo Kölsch, careworker, and Heinrich Vogel*, kindergarten worker, born 1960 (friends), 27.6.2010
Siegfried Lachmann, Cultural League functionary, Potsdam, 22.03.2004
Eva Mahn, photographer, born 1947, Halle, 14.5.2004
Heidi Müller*, civil servant*, born 1963, Hamburg, 29.6.2010
Peter Rausch, film editor, born 1950, Berlin, 28.6.2010
Ursula Sillge, academic and activist, born 1946, Berlin, 26.6.2010

ARCHIVES

Archiv des Aufbau-Verlages, Staatsbibliothek Berlin
Bildarchiv, Bundesarchiv Koblenz (Bundesarchiv Bild) (BArch)
Brandenburgisches Landeshauptarchiv (BLHA)
Bundesarchiv, Berlin (BArch)
Bundesbeauftragte für die Unterlagen des Staatssicherheitsdienstes der ehemaligen Deutschen Demokratischen Republik (BStU), Berlin
Bundesfilmarchiv, Berlin
Landesarchiv Berlin (LAB)
Landesarchiv Greifswald (LAG)
Schwules Museum Berlin
Stiftung der Parteien und Massenorganisationen der DDR, Bundesarchiv, Berlin (SAPMO-BArch)
Zentralarchiv für empirische Sozialforschung an der Universität zu Köln (ZA)

WORKS CITED

FILMS

Aktfotografie, z.B. Gundula Schulze (dir. Helke Misselwitz, 1983).
Bis daß der Tod euch scheidet (dir. Heiner Carow, 1979).
Coming Out (dir. Heiner Carow, 1989).
Der Dritte (dir. Egon Günther, 1971).
Ete und Ali (dir. Peter Kahane, 1985).
Die Legende von Paul und Paula (dir. Heiner Carow, 1973).
Sieben Sommersprossen (dir. Herrmann Zschoche, 1978).
Tag für Tag (dir. Volker Koepp, 1979).

PRINTED PRIMARY SOURCES

Agde, Günther (ed.), *Kahlschlag. Das 11. Plenum des ZK der SED 1965. Studien und Dokumente* (Berlin: Aufbau, 2000).

Anordnung zur Regelung des Freibadewesens. Vom 18 Mai 1956, *Gesetzblatt I* (Berlin: Reichsverlagsamt, 195, 50, 6 June 1956, pp. 433ff.

Aresin, Lykke and Müller-Hegemann, Annelies (eds.), *Jugendlexikon Junge Ehe* (Leipzig: VEB Bibliographisches Institut, 5th edn, 1986).

(eds.), *Jugendlexikon Jugend zu zweit.* 3rd edn (Leipzig: VEB Bibliographisches Institut Leipzig, 1982).

Berkes, Ulrich, *Eine schlimme Liebe. Tagebuch* (Berlin and Weimar: Aufbau, 1987).

Icarus über der Stadt (Berlin and Weimar: Aufbau Verlag, 1976).

Bronnen, Barbara and Henny, Franz, *Liebe, Ehe, Sexualität in der DDR. Interviews und Dokumente* (Munich: R. Piper, 1975).

Brückner, Heinrich, *Denkst Du schon an Liebe?* (Berlin: Kinderbuchverlag, 1975).

Brühl, Olaf, 'Schwulsein 2000: Arschficker oder Arschkriecher? Kleines schwules Glossar eines Außenseiters', in *Schwulsein 2000. Perspektiven im vereinigten Deutschland* (Hamburg: MännerschwarmSkript Verlag, 2001), pp. 163–206.

'Sozialistisch und schwul. Eine subjektive Chronologie', in Setz (ed.), *Homosexualität in der DDR*, pp. 89–152.

Chronik des Sportgeländes am Zeesener See (n.p., 1998).

Cleland, John, *Die Abenteuer der Fanny Hill* (Leipzig and Weimar: Kiepenheuer, 1987).

Council of Europe (ed.), *Demographic Yearbook 2001*, www.coe.int/t/e/social_cohesion/population/demographic_year_book/2001_edition/Germany GDR 2001.asp.

Davis, Jeffrey and Stenger, Karl-Ludwig, 'Lesbians in the GDR: Two Women', *New German Critique* 23 (1981), 83–96.

Dieckmann, Christoph, *Die Liebe in den Zeiten des Landfilms. Eigens erlebte Geschichten* (Berlin: Aufbau, 2002).

Dietz, Karl and Hesse, Peter, *Wörterbuch der Sexuologie und ihrer Grenzgebiete*, 4th edn (Rudolstadt: Greifenverlag, 1971).

Eckart, Gabriele, *So sehe ick die Sache. Protokolle aus der DDR. Leben im Havelländischen Obstanbaugebiet* (Cologne: Kiepenheuer & Witsch, 1984).

Familiengesetzbuch der Deutschen Demokratischen Republik, 20 December 1965, www.verfassungen.de/de/ddr/familiengesetzbuch65.htm.

Fischer, Klaus, *Aktfotografie* (Leipzig: Fotokinoverlag, 1978).

Friedrich, Walter and Starke, Kurt, *Liebe und Sexualität bis 30* (Berlin: VEB Deutscher Verlag der Wissenschaften, 1984).

Gebhardt, Manfred, *Die Nackte unterm Ladentisch. Das Magazin in der DDR* (Berlin: Nora, 2002).

Gesetz über den Mutter- und Kinderschutz und die Rechte der Frau, 27 September 1950, www.verfassungen.de/de/ddr/mutterkindgesetz50.htm.

Gesetz über die Schulpflicht in der Deutschen Demokratischen Republik, 15 December 1950, www.verfassungen.de/de/ddr/schulpflichtgesetz50.htm.

Goettle, Gabriele, 'Sie waren weiss, grün oder rosa ... Frauen erinnern sich', in Staupe and Vieth (eds.), *Die Pille*, pp. 181–192.

Gutschke, Kerstin, *Ich ahnungsloser Engel. Lesbenprotokolle* (Berlin: Reiher Verlag, 1991).

Habermehl, Werner, *Sexualverhalten der Deutschen. Aktuelle Daten – intime Wahrheiten* (Munich: Wilhelm Heyne, 1993).

Habermehl, Werner and Starke, Kurt, *Sexualität in der DDR* (n.p., 1990).

Hagen, Eva-Marie, *Eva und der Wolf* (Düsseldorf: Econ, 1998).

Hagen, Friedrich, *Baden ohne. FKK zwischen Mövenort und Talsperre Pöhl* (Leipzig and Berlin: VEB Tourist Verlag, 1982).

FKK Zwischen Ostsee und Vogtland (Berlin and Leipzig: Tourist Verlag, 1987).

Hauswald, Harald, 'Sex und Saufen', in Häußer and Merkel (eds.), *Vergnügen in der DDR*, pp. 189–196.

Hesse, Peter and Tembrock, Günter (eds.), *Sexuologie*, vol. I (Leipzig: S. Hirzel Verlag, 1974).

Hollitscher, Walter, *Der überanstrengte Sexus. Die sogenannte sexuelle Emanzipation im heutigen Kapitalismus* (Berlin: Akademie Verlag, 1975).

Internationale Aktfotografie (Leipzig: Fotokinoverlag, 1966).

Jaritz, A., 'Die "Sex-Welle" oder Ausverkauf der Moral', *humanitas* 19 (1970), 6.

'Der Jugend Vertrauen und Verantwortung. Kommuniqué des Politbüros des Zentralkomitees der Sozialistischen Einheitspartei Deutschlands zu Problemen der Jugend in der Deutschen Demokratischen Republik, veröffentlicht am 21. September 1963', in *Dokumente zur Jugendpolitik der SED* (Berlin: Staatsverlag der DDR, 1965), pp. 63–96.

Karstädt, Christina and von Zitzewitz, Anette (eds.), *... viel zu viel verschwiegen. Eine historische Dokumentation von Lebensgeschichten lesbischer Frauen in der Deutschen Demokratischen Republik* (Berlin: Hoho Verlag Christine Hoffmann, 1996).

Karsten, Thomas and Ulrich, Holde-Barbara, *Messer im Traum. Transsexuelle in Deutschland* (Tübingen: Konkursbuch, 1994).

Kin Ping Meh, 2 vols. (Leipzig and Weimar: Kiepenheuer, 1983).

Kolano, Uta, *Nackter Osten* (Frankfurt an der Oder: Frankfurter Oder Editionen, 1995).

Kulturbund der DDR, Bezirkskommission Fotografie Potsdam (eds.), *Bildmappe der Ausstellung Akt und Landschaft* (1982).

Kupferman, Thomas, *FKK in der DDR. Sommer, Sonne, Nackedeis* (Berlin: Eulenspiegel Verlag, 2008).

Lambrecht, Christine, *Männerbekanntschaften – Freimütige Protokolle* (Halle: Mitteldeutscher Verlag, 1986).

Lemke, Jürgen, *Ganz normal anders. Auskünfte schwuler Männer* (Berlin: Aufbau, 1989).

Gay Voices from East Germany (Bloomington: Indiana University Press, 1991).

von Mahlsdorf, Charlotte, *Ich bin meine eigene Frau. Ein Leben*, ed. Peter Süß (Munich: Deutscher Taschenbuch Verlag, 1995).

Müller, Christine, *Männerprotokolle* (Berlin: Buchverlag Der Morgen, 1985).

Die nackte Republik. Aktfotografien von Amateuren aus 40 Jahren Alltag im Osten (Berlin: Das Magazin Verlagsgesellschaft, 1993).

Neubert, Rudolf, *Fragen und Antworten zum 'Neuen Ehebuch' und zur 'Geschlechterfrage'* (Rudolstadt: Greifenverlag, 1960).

Das neue Ehebuch. Die Ehe als Aufgabe der Gegenwart und Zukunft (Rudolstadt: Greifenverlag, 1957).

Wie sag ich es meinem Kinde? Ratschläge für Eltern, 9th edn (Rudolstadt: Greifenverlag, 1968).

Plenzdorf, Ulrich, *Die neuen Leiden des Jungen W.* (Frankfurt am Main: Suhrkamp, 1999).

Pludra, Benno, *Haik und Paul* (Berlin: Verlag Neues Leben, 1956).

Protokoll der Verhandlungen des V. Parteitages der Sozialistischen Einheitspartei Deutschlands. 10. bis 16. Juli 1958 in der Werner-Seelenbinder-Halle zu Berlin (Berlin: Dietz, 1959).

Psychosoziale Aspekte der Homosexualität. Gemeinschaftstagung der Sektion Ehe und Familie der Gesellschaft für Sozialhygiene der DDR und der Sektion Andrologie der Gesellschaft für Dermatologie der DDR am 28. Juni 1985 (Jena: Friedrich Schiller Universität, 1986).

Psychosoziale Aspekte der Homosexualität. II. Workshop der Sektion Andrologie der Gesellschaft für Dermatologie der DDR und der Sektion Ehe und Familie der Gesellschaft für Sozialhygiene der DDR am 23. April 1988 (Jena: Friedrich Schiller Universität, 1989).

Rausch, Peter, 'Seinerzeit, in den 70ern', in Setz (ed.), *Homosexualität in der DDR*, pp. 151–159.

Reimann, Brigitte, *Ich bedaure nichts. Tagebücher 1955–1963*, ed. Angela Drescher (Berlin: Aufbau, 2001).

Runge, Erika, *Bottroper Protokolle* (Frankfurt am Main: Suhrkamp, 1968).

Schnabl, Siegfried, *Mann und Frau Intim. Fragen des gesunden und des gestörten Geschlechtslebens*, 5th edn (Berlin: VEB Verlag Volk und Gesundheit, 1972).

Schön Nackt. Aktfotografie in der DDR (Berlin: Das Neue Berlin, 2009).

Semprun, Jorge, *Was für ein schöner Sonntag!* (Frankfurt: Suhrkamp Taschenbuch, 1984).

Stapel, Eduard, *Warme Brüder gegen Kalte Krieger. Schwulenbewegung in der DDR im Visier der Staatssicherheit* (Magdeburg: Landesbeauftragte für die Unterlagen des Staatssicherheitsdienstes der ehemaligen DDR Sachsen-Anhalt, 1999).

Statistisches Jahrbuch der Deutschen Demokratischen Republik 1970 (Berlin: Staatsverlag der Deutschen Demokratischen Republik, 1971).

Statistisches Jahrbuch der Deutschen Demokratischen Republik 1974 (Berlin: Staatsverlag der Deutschen Demokratischen Republik, 1974).

Statistisches Jahrbuch der Deutschen Demokratischen Republik 1990 (Berlin: Rudolf Haufe Verlag, 1991).

Stedefeldt, Eike, 'Zur weiteren Veranlassung. Ein Interview mit dem MfS-Offizier Wolfgang Schmidt', in Setz (ed.), *Homosexualität in der DDR*, pp. 185–202.

Stock, Ulrich, 'Endlich Sex! In Leipzig eröffnete der erste Pornoladen der DDR', *Die Zeit*, 22.6.1990, pdf.zeit.de/1990/26/Endlich-Sex.pdf.

Strafgesetzbuch der Deutschen Demokratischen Republik, 12 January 1968, www.verfassungen.de/de/ddr/strafgesetzbuch68.htm.

United Nations, *Abortion Policies: A Global Review*, vol. III (New York: United Nations, 2002).

Vatsyayana, Mallanaga, *Das Kamasutra* (Leipzig: Reclam, 1987).
'Die Verfassung der Deutschen Demokratischen Republik, 7 October 1949', www.documentarchiv.de/ddr/verfddr1949.html.
Vetter, Gerhard, *Studien am Strand* (Leipzig: Fotokino Verlag, 1968).
Wander, Maxie, *Guten Morgen, Du Schöne* (Berlin: Aufbau Verlag, 2003).
von Wangenheim, Inge, *Die Entgleisung* (Halle: Mitteldeutscher Verlag, 1980).
Weller, Konrad, *Das Sexuelle in der deutsch–deutschen Vereinigung* (Leipzig: Forum Verlag, 1991).
Werner, Reiner, *Homosexualität: Herausforderung an Wissen und Toleranz* (Berlin: Verlag Volk und Gesundheit, 1987).
Wolf, Christa, 'Berührung. Ein Vorwort', in Wander, *Guten Morgen, Du Schöne*, pp. 9–19.
Wolf, Markus (with Anne McElvoy), *Man Without a Face: The Autobiography of Communism's Greatest Spymaster* (London: Jonathan Cape, 1997).
Wollenberger, Vera, *Virus der Heuchler. Innenansicht aus Stasi-Akten* (Berlin: Espresso/Elefanten Press, 1992).

SECONDARY LITERATURE

Andritzky, Michael, 'Berlin – Urheimat der Nackten. Die FKK-Bewegung in den 20er Jahren', in Michael Andritzky and Thomas Rautenberg (eds.), *'Wir sind nackt und nennen Uns Du'. Von Lichtfreunden und Sonnenkämpfer. Eine Geschichte der Freikörperkultur* (Giessen: Anabas, 1989), pp. 50–105.
Badstübner, Evamarie, 'Auf 80 Seiten um die Welt. *Das Magazin* zwischen 1954 und 1970', in Simone Barck, Martina Langermann and Siegfried Lokatis (eds.), *Zwischen 'Mosaik' und 'Einhei'. Zeitschriften in der DDR* (Berlin: Ch. Links, 1999), pp. 189–201.
'"Zeig', wie das Leben lacht und liebt ... "': Die Unterhaltungszeitschrift *Das Magazin* und ihre Leser zwischen 1954 und 1970', in Evamarie Badstübner (ed.), *Befremdlich anders. Leben in der DDR* (Berlin: Dietz, 2000), pp. 432–470.
Bailey, Beth, *Sex in the Heartland* (Cambridge, MA: Harvard University Press, 1999).
Barbagli, Marzio and Kertzer, David I. (eds.), *The History of the European Family*, vol. III, *Family Life in the Twentieth Century* (New Haven: Yale University Press, 2003).
Barcan, Ruth, *Nudity: A Cultural Anatomy* (Oxford: Berg, 2004).
Barck, Simone, Classen, Christoph and Heinemann, Thomas, 'The Fettered Media: Controlling Public Debate', in Konrad Jarausch (ed.), *Dictatorship as Experience: Towards a Socio-Cultural History of the GDR* (New York and Oxford: Berghahn, 1999), 213–239.
Barck, Simone, Langermann, Martina and Lokatis, Siegfried (eds.), *'Jedes Buch ein Abenteuer'. Zensur-System und literarische Öffentlichkeit in der DDR bis Ende der sechziger Jahre* (Berlin: Akademie Verlag, 1998).
Baumgartner, Judith, 'Freikörperkultur', in Diethardt Kerbs and Jürgen Renlecke (eds.), *Handbuch der deutschen Reformbewegung 1880–1933* (Wuppertal: Hammer, 1998), pp. 103–114.

Bazinger, Irene, 'Im Gespräch: Katharina Thalbach. Wir im Osten hatten mehr Sex und mehr zu lachen', *Frankfurter Allgemeine Zeitung*, 21.11.2008, 42.

Becker, Peter and Lüdtke, Alf (eds.), *Akten. Eingaben. Schaufenster. Die DDR und ihre Texte* (Berlin: Akademie Verlag, 1997).

Bell, David and Holliday, Ruth, 'Naked as Nature Intended', *Body & Society* 6 (2000), 127–140.

Berger, John, *Ways of Seeing* (Harmondsworth: Penguin, 1972).

Betts, Paul, 'Alltag und Privatheit', in Martin Sabrow (ed.), *Erinnerungsorte der DDR* (Munich: C. H. Beck, 2009), pp. 314–325.

'The Twilight of the Idols: East German Memory and Material Culture', *Journal of Modern History* 72 (2000), 731–765.

Within Walls: Private Life in the GDR (Oxford: Oxford University Press, 2010).

Biess, Frank, *Homecomings: Returning POWs and the Legacies of Defeat in Postwar Germany* (Princeton: Princeton University Press, 2006).

Böhme, Irene, 'Frei von dieser Angst. Über die Pille in der DDR', in Staupe and Vieth (eds.), *Die Pille*, pp. 171–180.

Brock, Angela, 'The Making of the Socialist Personality: Education and Socialisation in the GDR, 1958–1978', unpublished Ph.D. thesis, University College London (2005).

Brown, Timothy S., ' "1968" East and West: Divided Germany as a Case Study in Transnational History', *American Historical Review* 114 (February 2009), 69–96.

'East Germany', in Martin Klimke and Joachim Scharloth (eds.), *1968 in Europe: A History of Protest and Activism, 1956–1977* (London: Palgrave Macmillan, 2008), pp. 189–197.

'A Tale of Two Communes: The Private and the Political in Divided Berlin, 1967–1973', in Martin Klimke, Jacco Pekelder, and Joachim Scharloth (eds.), *Between Prague Spring and French May: Opposition and Revolt in Europe, 1960–1980* (Oxford and New York: Berghahn, 2011).

Brussig, Thomas, 'Aber der Sex war schöner', *Vanity Fair* [Germany] 17 (2007), 92–99.

Bryant, Dara, 'Queering the Antifascist State: Ravensbrück as a Site of Lesbian Resistance', *Edinburgh German Yearbook 3. Contested Legacies: Constructions of Cultural Heritage in the GDR* (New York: Camden House, 2009), pp. 76–89.

Cocks, Harry and Houlbrook, Matthew (eds.), *Palgrave Advances in the Modern History of Sexuality* (London: Palgrave Macmillan, 2005).

Collins, Marcus, *Modern Love: An Intimate History of Men and Women in Twentieth-Century Britain* (London: Atlantic, 2003).

Cook, Hera, *The Long Sexual Revolution: English Women, Sex, and Contraception 1800–1975* (Oxford: Oxford University Press, 2004).

Dennis, Mike, 'Die vietnamesischen Vertragsarbeiter und Vertragsarbeiterinnen in der DDR', in Karin Weiss and Mike Dennis (eds.), *Erfolg in der Nische? Die Vietnamesen in der DDR und in Ostdeutschland* (Münster: Lit Verlag, 2005), pp. 15–49.

Dickinson, Edward R. and Wetzell, Richard F., 'The Historiography of Sexuality in Modern Germany', *German History* 23 (2005), 291–305.

Dieckmann, Christoph, 'Kindheitsmuster oder Das wahre Leben im Falschen. Dankrede anläßlich der Verleihung des Friedrich-Märker-Preises für Essayisten an den Autor', www.zeit.de/1996/52/kind.txt.19961220.xml.

Dölling, Irene, '"We All Love Paula but Paul Is More Important to Us": Constructing a "Socialist Person" Using the "Femininity" of a Working Woman', *New German Critique* 82 (Winter 2001), 77–90.

Duchen, Claire, 'Occupation Housewife: The Domestic Ideal in 1950s France', *French Cultural Studies* 2 (1991), 1–11.

Engler, Wolfgang, *Die Ostdeutschen. Kunde von einem verlorenen Land* (Berlin: Aufbau, 2000).

Evans, Janet, 'The Communist Party of the Soviet Union and the Woman's Question: The Case of the 1936 Decree "In Defense of Mother and Child"', *Journal of Contemporary History* 16 (1981), 757–775.

Evans, Jennifer, '*Bahnhof* Boys: Policing Male Prostitution in Post-Nazi Berlin', *Journal of the History of Sexuality* 12 (2003), 605–636.

'Decriminalization, Seduction, and "Unnatural Desire" in the German Democratic Republic', *Feminist Studies* 36 (3) (2010), 553–577.

Life Among the Ruins: Cityscape and Sexuality in Cold War Berlin (New York: Palgrave Macmillan, 2011).

'The Moral State: Men, Mining and Masculinity in the Early GDR', *German History* 23 (2005), 355–370.

'Reconstruction Sites: Sexuality, Citizenship, and the Limits of National Belonging in Divided Berlin, 1944–1958', unpublished Ph.D. dissertation, Binghamton University, State University of New York (2001).

Falck, Uta, *VEB Bordell. Geschichte der Prostitution in der DDR* (Berlin: Ch. Links Verlag, 1998).

Feinstein, Joshua, *The Triumph of the Ordinary: Depictions of Daily Life in the East German Cinema, 1949–1989* (Chapel Hill: University of North Carolina Press, 2002).

Fenemore, Mark, 'The Growing Pains of Sex Education in the German Democratic Republic', in Lutz D. H. Sauerteig and Roger Davidson (eds.), *Shaping Sexual Knowledge: A Cultural History of Sexuality in Twentieth-Century Europe* (London: Routledge, 2009), pp. 71–90.

'The Recent Historiography of Sexuality in Twentieth-Century Germany', *Historical Journal* 52 (2009), 763–779.

Sex, Thugs and Rock'n'Roll: Teenage Rebels in Cold War East Germany (Oxford and New York: Berghahn, 2007).

Fenton, Kevin A., Johnson, Anne M., McManus, Sally and Erens, Bob, 'Measuring Sexual Behaviour: Methodological Challenges in Survey Research', *Sexually Transmitted Infections* 77 (2001), 84–92.

Field, Deborah, *Private Life and Communist Morality in Khrushchev's Russia* (New York: Peter Lang, 2007).

Fitzpatrick, Sheila, 'Supplicants and Citizens: Public Letter-Writing in Soviet Russia in the 1930s', *Slavic Review* 55 (1996), 78–105.

Frerich, Johannes and Frey, Martin, *Handbuch der Geschichte der Sozialpolitik in Deutschland*, vol. II, *Sozialpolitik in der Deutschen Demokratischen Republik* (Munich: R. Oldenbourg Verlag, 1993).

Fulbrook, Mary, *The People's State: East German Society from Hitler to Honecker* (New Haven: Yale University Press, 2005).

(ed.), *Power and Society in the GDR, 1961–1979: The 'Normalisation of Rule'?* (Oxford: Berghahn, 2009).

'Putting the People Back In? The Contentious State of GDR History', *German History* 24 (2006), 609–620.

Fürst, Juliane, *Stalin's Last Generation: Soviet Post-War Youth and the Emergence of Mature Socialism* (Oxford: Oxford University Press, 2010).

Gallinat, Anselma, 'Negotiating Culture and Belonging in Eastern Germany. The Case of the Jugendweihe: A Secular Coming-of-Age Ritual', unpublished Ph.D. thesis, University of Durham (2002).

Gaus, Günter, *Wo Deutschland liegt. Eine Ortsbestimmung* (Hamburg: Hoffmann und Campe, 1983).

Giersdorf, Jens Richard, 'Why Does Charlotte von Mahlsdorf Curtsy? Representations of National Queerness in a Transvestite Hero', *GLQ: A Journal of Lesbian and Gay Studies* 12 (2006), 171–196.

Grau, Günter, 'Ein Leben im Kampf gegen den Paragraphen 175. Zum Wirken des Dresdener Arztes Rudolf Klimmer 1905–1977', in Manfred Herzer (ed.), *100 Jahre Schwulenbewegung* (Berlin: Verlag Rosa Winkel, 1998), pp. 47–64.

Hidden Holocaust? Gay and Lesbian Persecution in Nazi Germany 1933–1945 (London: Routledge, 1995).

Homosexualität in der NS-Zeit (Frankfurt am Main: Fischer, 1993).

Lesben und Schwule – was nun? Chronik – Dokument – Analysen – Interviews (Berlin: Dietz, 1990).

'Liberalisierung und Repression. Zur Strafrechtsdiskussion zum §175 in der DDR', *Zeitschrift für Sexualforschung* 15 (2002), 323–340.

'Return of the Past: The Policy of the SED and the Laws Against Homosexuality in Eastern Germany Between 1946 and 1968', *Journal of Homosexuality* 37 (1999), 1–29.

'Sozialistische Moral und Homosexualität. Die Politik der SED and das Homosexuellenstrafrecht 1945 bis 1989 – ein Rückblick', in Detlef Grumbach (ed.), *Die Linke und das Laster. Schwule Emanzipation und linke Voruteile* (Hamburg: MännerschwarmSkript Verlag, 1995), pp. 83–141.

Grossmann, Atina, *Jews, Germans and Allies: Close Encounters in Occupied Germany* (Princeton: Princeton University Press, 2007).

'A Question of Silence: The Rape of German Women by Occupation Soldiers', in Robert Moeller (ed.), *West Germany Under Construction: Politics, Society and Culture in the Adenauer Era* (Ann Arbor: University of Michigan Press, 1997), pp. 33–52.

Reforming Sex: The German Movement for Birth Control and Abortion Reform, 1920–1950 (Oxford: Oxford University Press, 1995).

'"Sich auf ihr Kindchen freuen". Frauen und Behörden in Auseinandersetzungen um Abtreibungen, Mitte der 1960er Jahre', in Becker and Lüdtke (eds.), *Akten. Eingaben. Schaufenster*, pp. 239–257.

Günther, Erwin, 'Geschlechtskrankheiten und AIDS in der DDR', in Joachim S. Hohmann (ed.), *Sexuologie in der DDR* (Berlin: Dietz, 1990), pp. 165–174.

Hackett, David A. (ed.), *The Buchenwald Report* (Boulder: Westview Press, 1995).

Hampel, Heide, 'Reimann, Brigitte', *Neue Deutsche Biographie*, vol. XXI (Berlin: Duncker & Humblot, 2003), pp. 334–335.

Harris, Victoria, 'Sex on the Margins: New Directions in the Historiography of Sexuality and Gender', *Historical Journal* 53 (4) (2010), 1085–1104.

Harsch, Donna, *Revenge of the Domestic: Women, the Family and Communism in the German Democratic Republic* (Princeton and Oxford: Princeton University Press, 2007).

'Society, the State, and Abortion in East Germany, 1950–1972', *American Historical Review* 102 (1997), 53–84.

Härtel, Christian and Kabus, Petra (eds.), *Das Westpaket. Geschenksendung, keine Handelsware* (Berlin: Ch. Links, 2000).

Hau, Michael, *The Cult of Health and Beauty in Germany: A Social History, 1890–1930* (Chicago and London: University of Chicago Press, 2003).

Häußer, Ulrike and Merkel, Marcus (eds.), *Vergnügen in der DDR* (Berlin: Panama, 2009).

Healey, Daniel, *Homosexual Desire in Revolutionary Russia: The Regulation of Sexual and Gender Dissent* (Chicago: University of Chicago Press, 2001).

Heineman, Elizabeth, 'The Economic Miracle in the Bedroom: Big Business and Sexual Consumer Culture in Reconstruction West Germany', *Journal of Modern History*, 78 (2006), 846–877.

'Sexuality and Nazism: The Doubly Unspeakable?', *Journal of the History of Sexuality* 11 (1–2) (2002), 22–66.

'Single Motherhood and Maternal Employment in Divided Germany: Ideology, Policy and Social Pressures in the 1950s', *Journal of Women's History* 12 (2000), 147–172.

What Difference Does a Husband Make? Women and Marital Status in Nazi and Postwar Germany (Berkeley: University of California Press, 1999).

Helwerth, Ulrike, 'Kann man in Hoyerswerda küssen? Die Schriftstellerin Brigitte Reimann (1933–1973)', in Franzisa Becker, Ina Merkel and Simone Tippach-Schneider (eds.), *Das Kollektiv bin ich. Utopie und Alltag in der DDR* (Cologne: Böhlau, 2000), pp. 26–55.

Henderson, Karen, 'The Search for Ideological Conformity: Sociological Research on Youth in the GDR', *German History* 10 (1992), 318–334.

Herrn, Rainer, *Schwule Lebenswelten im Osten. Andere Orte, andere Biographien. Kommunikationsstrukturen, Gesellungsstile und Lebensweisen schwuler Männer in den neuen Bundesländern* (Berlin: Deutsche AIDS-Hilfe, 1999).

Herzer, Manfred, 'Communists, Social Democrats, and the Homosexual Movement in the Weimar Republic', *Journal of Homosexuality* 29 (1995), 197–226.

Herzog, Dagmar, 'The East German Sexual Evolution', in Katherine Pence and Paul Betts (eds.), *Socialist Modern: East German Everyday Culture and Politics* (Ann Arbor: University of Michigan Press, 2008), pp. 71–95.

'Post coitum triste est … ? Sexual Politics and Cultures in Postunification Germany', *German Politics and Society* 28 (2010), 111–140.

Sex After Fascism: Memory and Morality in Twentieth-Century Germany (Princeton: Princeton University Press, 2005).

(ed.), *Sexuality and German Fascism* (Oxford: Berghahn, 2004).

'Sexuality in the Postwar West', *Journal of Modern History* 78 (2006), 144–171.

'Syncopated Sex: Transforming European Sexual Cultures', *American Historical Review* 114 (2009), 1287–1308.

Höhn, Tobias, 'Der erotische Akt im Sozialismus', *Stern*, 6 January 2006, www.stern.de/fotografie/fotografie-der-erotische-akt-im-sozialismus-552665.html.

Holschuh, Albrecht, 'Protokollsammlungen der DDR', *German Studies Review* 15 (May 1992), 267–287.

Hong, Young-sun, 'Cigarette Butts and the Building of Socialism in East Germany', *Central European History* 35 (3) (2002), 327–344.

Hörschelmann, Kathrin, 'Audience Interpretations of (Former) East Germany's Representation in the German Media', *European Urban and Regional Studies* 8 (3) (2001), 189–202.

Jefferies, Matthew, 'For a Genuine and Noble Nakedness? German Naturism in the Third Reich', *German History* 24 (1) (2006), 62–84.

Jeffreys, Sheila, *Anticlimax: A Feminist Perspective on the Sexual Revolution* (London: Women's Press, 1990).

Kaiser, Paul and Petzold, Claudia, *Boheme und Diktatur in der DDR. Gruppen, Konflikte, Quartiere, 1970–1989. Katalog zur Ausstellung des Deutschen Historischen Museums von 4. September bis 16. Dezember 1997* (Berlin: Fannei & Walz, 1997).

Kätzel, Ute, 'Kommune 1 Ost', *Der Freitag*, 20.12.2002, www.freitag. de/2002/52/02521701.php.

Klönne, Arno, 'Das "Ja zum Leibe" – mehrdeutig. Zur politischen Geschichte der Freikörperkulturbewegung', *Vorgänge* 33 (3) (1994), 27–32.

Kochan, Thomas, *Blauer Würger. So trank die DDR* (Berlin: Aufbau, 2011).

'Da hilft kein Jammern. Zwischen Resignation und Aufbegehren: Die Szene lebte die Blues', in Thomas Kochan and Michael Rauhut (eds.), *Bye Bye Lübben City. Bluesfreaks, Tramps und Hippies in der DDR* (Berlin: Schwarzkopf & Schwarzkopf, 2004), pp. 68–82.

Den Blues haben. Moment einer jugendlichen Subkultur in der DDR (Münster: Lit Verlag, 2003).

'Rotkäppchen und der Blaue Würger – Vom Alkohol in der DDR', www. geschichtswerkstatt-jena.de/archiv_texte/vortrag_kochan_alkohol.pdf.

Kopstein, Jeffrey, *The Politics of Economic Decline in East Germany, 1949–1989* (Chapel Hill: University of North Carolina Press, 1997).

Kreyenfeld, Michaela, 'Fertility Decisions in the FRG and GDR: An Analysis with Data from the German Fertility and Family Survey', *Demographic Research*, special collection 3, article 11 (17 April 2004), 275–318.

Krüger, Arnd, Krüger, Fabian and Treptau, Sybille, 'Nudism in Nazi Germany: Indecent Behavior or Physical Culture for the Well-Being of the Nation', *International Journal of the History of Sport* 19 (4) (2002), 33–54.

Kruse, Judith, 'Nische im Sozialismus', in *Endlich Urlaub! Begleitbuch zur Ausstellung im Haus der Geschichte der Bundesrepublik Deutschland, Bonn. 6. Juni bis 13. Oktober 1996* (Cologne: DuMont Reiserverlag, 1996), pp. 106–111.

Kuhn, Annette, *The Power of the Image: Essays on Representation and Sexuality* (London: Routledge, 1985).

Kundrus, Birthe, 'Forbidden Company: Romantic Relations Between Germans and Foreigners, 1939 to 1945', in Herzog (ed.), *Sexuality and German Fascism*, pp. 201–222.

Leinemann, Jürgen, 'Sie hat nichts merken können', *Der Spiegel*, 13.1.1992, p. 35.

Lindenberger, Thomas, '"Asociality" and Modernity: The GDR as a Welfare Dictatorship', in Katherine Pence and Paul Betts (eds.), *Socialist Modern: East German Everyday Culture and Politics* (Ann Arbor: University of Michigan Press, 2008), pp. 211–233.

Linke, Uli, *German Bodies: Race and Representation After Hitler* (New York: Routledge, 1999).

Linse, Ulrich, 'Sonnenmenschen unter der Swastika. Die FKK-Bewegung im Dritten Reich', in Michael Grisko (ed.), *Freikörperkultur und Lebenswelt. Studien zur Vor- und Frühgeschichte der Freikörperkultur in Deutschland* (Kassel: Kassel University Press, 1999), pp. 239–296.

Lokatis, Siegfried, 'Baden ohne', in Siegfried Lokatis and Simone Barck (eds.), *Zensurspiele. Heimliche Literaturgeschichten aus der DDR* (Halle: Mitteldeutscher Verlag, 2008), pp. 131–133.

Mac Con Uladh, Damian, 'Alltagserfahrungen ausländischer Vertragsarbeiter in der DDR', in Karin Weiss and Mike Dennis (eds.), *Erfolg in der Nische? Die Vietnamesen in der DDR und in Ostdeutschland* (Münster: Lit Verlag, 2005), pp. 51–68.

'Guests of the Socialist Nation? Foreign Students and Workers in the GDR, 1949–1990', unpublished Ph.D. thesis, University College London (2005).

Madarász, Jeannette Z., *Conflict and Compromise in East Germany, 1971–1989: A Precarious Stability* (London: Palgrave Macmillan, 2003).

Mann, Bärbel and Schütrumpf, Jörg, 'Galerie im Palast der Republik. Auftraggeber: Ministerium für Kultur', in Monika Flacke (ed.), *Auftrag: Kunst 1949–1990. Bildende Künstler in der DDR zwischen Ästhetik und Politik* (Berlin: Deutsches Historisches Museum, 1995), pp. 245–260.

Marx Ferree, Myra, 'The Rise and Fall of "Mommy Politics": Feminism and German Unification', *Feminist Studies* 19 (1993), 89–115.

McDougall, Alan, 'The Liberal Interlude: SED Youth Policy and the Free German Youth (FDJ), 1963–1965', *Debatte* 9 (2001), 123–155.

Youth Politics in East Germany: The Free German Youth Movement 1946–1968 (Oxford: Clarendon Press, 2004).

McLellan, Josie, *Antifascism and Memory in East Germany: Remembering the International Brigades 1945–1989* (Oxford: Clarendon Press, 2004).

'"Even Under Socialism, We Don't Want to Do Without Love": East German Erotica', in David Crowley and Susan Reid (eds.), *Pleasures in Socialism: Leisure and Luxury in the Eastern Bloc* (Evanston: Northwestern University Press, 2010), 218–237.

'Marianne Motz: "Vision"', *Rundbrief Fotografie* 16 (2) (2009), 3–4.

'Sex, Sociability, and Surveillance: Gay and Lesbian Spaces in East Berlin, 1968–1989', unpublished.

'State Socialist Bodies: East German Nudism from Ban to Boom', *Journal of Modern History* 79 (March 2007), 48–79.

'The Transnational History of East German Gay Liberation', unpublished.

'Visual Dangers and Delights: Nude Photography in East Germany', *Past and Present* 205 (2009), 143–174.

Merkel, Ina, 'Die Nackten und die Roten. Zum Verhältnis von Nacktheit und Öffentlichkeit in der DDR,' *Mitteilungen aus der kulturwissenschaftlichen Forschung* 18 (36) (1995), 80–108.

'Hinterher war alles beim Alten', www.bpb.de/themen/ CQPRCM,0,Hinterher_war_alles_beim_Alten.html.

und Du Frau an der Werkbank (Berlin: Elefantenpress, 1990).

(ed.), *'Wir sind doch nicht die Meckerecke der Nation!' Briefe an das Fernsehen der DDR* (Berlin: Schwarzkopf & Schwarzkopf, 2000).

Mertens, Lothar, *Wider die sozialistische Familiennorm. Ehescheidungen in der DDR 1950–1970* (Opladen: Westdeutscher Verlag, 1998).

Mildenberger, Florian, 'Günter Dörner – Metamorphosen eines Wissenschaftlers', in Setz (ed.), *Homosexualität in der DDR*, pp. 237–272.

Moeller, Robert, *Protecting Motherhood: Women and the Family in the Politics of Postwar West Germany* (Berkeley: University of California Press, 1996).

Moranda, Scott, 'The Dream of a Therapeutic Regime: Nature Tourism in the German Democratic Republic, 1945–1978', unpublished Ph.D. dissertation, University of Wisconsin-Madison (2005).

Mosse, George, *Nationalism and Sexuality: Respectability and Abnormal Sexuality in Modern Europe* (New York: Howard Fertig, 1985).

Mühlberg, Dietrich, 'Raum für die Liebe. Eine Nachbetrachtung' in Rohnstock, *Erotik macht die Häßlichen schön*, pp. 103–202.

'Sexualität und ostdeutscher Alltag', *Mitteilungen aus der kulturwissenschaftlichen Forschung* 18 (36) (1995), 8–39.

Mühlberg, Felix, 'Die Partei ist eifersüchtig', in Rohnstock (ed.), *Erotik macht die Hässlichen schön*, pp. 122–143.

'Informelle Konfliktbewältigung. Zur Geschichte der Eingabe in der DDR', unpublished Ph.D. dissertation, University of Chemnitz (1999).

Müller, Wenzel, *Leben in der Platte. Alltagskultur der DDR der 70er und 80er Jahre* (Vienna: Selbstverlag, 1990).

Naimark, Norman, *The Russians in Germany* (Cambridge, MA: Harvard University Press, 1995).

Nead, Lynda, *The Female Nude: Art, Obscenity and Sexuality* (London; Routledge, 1992).

Niethammer, Lutz, *Der 'gesäuberte' Antifaschismus. Die SED und die roten Kapos von Buchenwald* (Berlin: Akademie, 1994).

Onnasch, Christina, 'Experiment "Kommune 1 Ost" ', *Mitteldeutscher Zeitung*, 14.08.2008, www.mz-web.de/artikel?id=1217833454406.

Oosterhuis, Harry, 'Medicine, Male Bonding and Homosexuality in Nazi Germany', *Journal of Contemporary History* 34 (1997), 187–205.

Pence, Katherine, ' "You as a Woman Will Understand": Consumption, Gender and the Relationship Between State and Citizenry in the GDR's Crisis of 17 June 1953', *German History* 19 (2001), 218–252.

Penn, Shana and Massino, Jill (eds.), *Gender Politics and Everyday Life in State Socialist Eastern and Central Europe* (New York: Palgrave Macmillan, 2009).

Pfister, Elizabeth, *Unternehemen Romeo. Die Lebeskommandos der Stasi* (Berlin: Aufbau Verlag, 1999).

Pforte, Dietger, 'Zur Freikörperkultur–Bewegung im nationalsozialistischen Deutschland', in Michael Andritzky and Thomas Rautenberg (eds.), *'Wir sind nackt und nennen uns Du'. Von Lichtfreunden und Sonnenkämpfer. Eine Geschichte der Freikörperkultur* (Giessen: Anabas, 1989), pp. 136–145.

Poiger, Uta, *Jazz, Rock and Rebels: Cold War Politics and American Culture in a Divided Germany* (Berkeley: University of California Press, 2000).

Port, Andrew I., 'Love, Lust, and Lies Under Communism: Family Values and Adulterous Liaisons in Early East Germany,' forthcoming in *Central European History*.

Poutrus, Kirsten, 'Von den Massenvergewaltigungen zum Mutterschutzgesetz. Abtreibungspolitik und Abtreibungspraxis in Ostdeutschland, 1945–1950', in Richard Bessel and Ralph Jessen (eds.), *Die Grenzen der Diktatur. Staat und Gesellschaft in der DDR* (Göttingen: Vandenhoeck und Ruprecht, 1996), pp. 170–198.

Pritchard, Gareth, 'Workers and the Socialist Unity Party of Germany in the Summer of 1953', in Patrick Major and Jonathan Osmond (eds.), *The Workers' and Peasants' State: Communism and Society in East Germany Under Ulbricht 1945–1971* (Manchester: Manchester University Press, 2002), pp. 112–129.

Rauhut, Michael, *Beat in der Grauzone. DDR-Rock 1964 bis 1972 – Politik und Alltag* (Berlin: Basisdruck, 1993).

Risch, William Jay, ' "Soviet 'Flower Children": Hippies and the Youth Counterculture in 1970s L'viv', *Journal of Contemporary History* 40 (3) (2005), 565–584.

Rohnstock, Karin (ed.), *Erotik macht die Hässlichen schön. Sexueller Alltag im Osten* (Berlin: Elefanten Press, 1995).

Röll, Wolfgang, 'Homosexual Inmates in the Buchenwald Concentration Camp', *Journal of Homosexuality* 31 (4) (1996), 1–28.

Rose, Claus, 'Kulturpolitik für ein ehrliches Frauenbild. Die Aktfotos von Walter Streit', *Fine Art Foto* 2 (2004), 22–27.

Ross, Chad, *Naked Germany: Health, Race and the Nation* (Oxford and New York: Berg, 2005).

Ross, Corey, *The East German Dictatorship: Problems and Perspectives in the Interpretation of the GDR* (London: Arnold, 2002).

Rossow, Ina, ' "Rote Ohren, roter Mohn, sommerheiße Diskussion". Die X. Weltfestspiele der Jugend und Studenten 1973 als Möglichkeit für vielfältige Begegnungen', in Dokumentationszentrum Alltagskultur der DDR (ed.), *Fortschritt, Norm und Eigensinn. Erkundungen im Alltag der DDR* (Berlin: Ch. Links, 1999), pp. 257–275.

Sachse, Carola, *Der Hausarbeitstag: Gerechtigkeit und Gleichberechtigung in Ost und West 1939–1994* (Göttingen: Wallstein, 2002).

Saunders, Anna, 'The Socialist and Post-socialist Jugendweihe: Symbol of an Evolving East(ern) German Identity', *Focus on German Studies* 9 (2002), 43–60.

Schliephake, G., 'Einige Tendenzen bei der Einstellung von im Jugendalter stehenden Personen zur Freikörperkultur (gen. FKK)', *Ärztliche Jugendkunde* 71 (1980), 374–382.

Schüle, Annegret, '"Die ham se sozusagen aus dem Busch geholt". Die Wahrnehmung der Vertragsarbeitskräfte aus Schwarzafrika und Vietnam durch Deutsche im VEB Leipziger Baumwollspinnerei', in Jan Behrends, Thomas Lindenberger and Patrice Poutrus (eds.), *Fremde und Fremdsein in der DDR. Zu historischen Ursachen der Fremdenfeindlichkeit in Ostdeutschland* (Berlin: Metropol Verlag, 2003), pp. 309–324.

Schwarz, Gisline, 'Von der Antibaby- zur Wunschkindpille und zurück. Kontrazeptive in der DDR', in Staupe and Vieth (eds.), *Die Pille*, pp. 149–163.

Setz, Wolfram (ed.), *Homosexualität in der DDR. Materialien und Meinungen* (Hamburg: Männerschwärm Verlag, 2006).

Sharp, Ingrid, 'The Sexual Unification of Germany', *Journal of the History of Sexuality* 13 (2004), 348–365.

Sillge, Ursula, *Un-Sichtbare Frauen. Lesben und ihre Emanzipation in der DDR* (Berlin: Ch. Links, 1991).

Sørensen, Annemette and Trappe, Heike, 'The Persistence of Gender Inequality in Earnings in the German Democratic Republic', *American Sociological Review* 60 (1995), 398–406.

Spitzer, Giselher, 'Die "Adolf-Koch-Bewegung". Genese und Praxis einer proletarischen Selbsthilfe-Organisation zwischen den Weltkriegen', in Hans Joachim Teichler (ed.), *Arbeiterkultur und Arbeitersport* (Clausthal-Zellerfeld: Deutsche Vereinigung für Sportwissenschaft, 1985), pp. 77–104.

'"Nackt und frei". Die proletarische Freikörperkulturbewegung', in Hans Joachim Teichler and Gerhard Hauk (eds.), *Illustrierte Geschichte des Arbeitersports* (Berlin and Bonn: J. H. W. Dietz Nachf., 1987), pp. 174–181.

Starke, Kurt, 'Die unzüchtige Legende vom prüden Osten', in Rohnstock (ed.), *Erotik macht die Hässlichen schön*, pp. 153–182.

'Kinderwagen im Seminargebäude. Die Förderung von Studentinnen mit Kind in der DDR', in Waltraud Cornelißen and Katrin Fox (eds.), *Studieren mit Kind. Die Vereinbarkeit von Studium und Elternschaft. Lebenssituationen, Maßnahmen und Handlungsperspektiven* (Wiesbaden: VS Verlag, 2007), pp. 79–91.

Schwuler Osten. Homosexuelle Männer in der DDR (Berlin: Ch. Links, 1994).

'Stasi mit Sex und Peitschen', *Focus* 11 (2002), www.focus.de/politik/deutschland/stasi-mit-sex-und-peitschen_aid_203726.html

Staupe, Gisela and Vieth, Lisa (eds.), *Die Pille. Von der Lust und von der Liebe* (Berlin: Rowohlt, 1996).

Stuhler, Heidemarie, and Wedl, Juliette, 'Bleibt alles anders? Transformationen im alltag ostdeutscher Frauen', in Heiner Timmermann (ed.), *Die DDR in Deutschland. Ein Rückblick auf 50 Jahre* (Berlin: Duncker & Humblot, 2001), pp. 513–552.

Suri, Jeremi, 'The Rise and Fall of an International Counterculture, 1960–1975', *American Historical Review* 114 (February 2009), 45–68.

Svede, Mark Allen, 'All You Need Is Lovebeads: Latvia's Hippies Undress for Success', in Susan E. Reid and David Crowley (eds.), *Style and Socialism:*

Modernity and Material Culture in Post-War Eastern Europe (Oxford and New York: Berg, 2000), pp. 189–208.

Szobar, Patricia, 'Telling Sexual Stories in the Nazi Courts of Law: Race Defilement in Germany, 1933 to 1945', in Herzog (ed.), *Sexuality and German Fascism*, pp. 131–160.

Therborn, Göran, *Between Sex and Power: Family in the World, 1900–2000* (London and New York: Routledge, 2004).

Thormann, Lutz, ' "Schont die Augen der Nation!" Zum Verhältnis vom Nacktheit und Öffentlichkeit in der DDR', unpublished MA thesis, University of Jena (2007).

Timm, Annette F., 'Guarding the Health of Worker Families in the GDR: Socialist Health Care, *Bevölkerungspolitik*, and Marriage Counselling, 1945–1970', in Peter Hübner and Klaus Tenfelde (eds.), *Arbeiter in der SBZ-DDR* (Essen: Klartext Verlag, 1999), pp. 463–495.

The Politics of Fertility in Twentieth-Century Berlin (New York: Cambridge University Press, 2010).

Toepfer, Klaus, *Empire of Ecstasy: Nudity and Movement in German Body Culture, 1910–1935* (Berkeley: University of California Press, 1997).

von Törne, Dorothea, *Brigitte Reimann. Einfach wirklich leben* (Berlin: Aufbau, 2001).

Trappe, Heike, *Emanzipation oder Zwang? Frauen in der DDR zwischen Beruf, Familie und Sozialpolitik* (Berlin: Akademie Verlag, 1995).

Troeger, Annamarie, 'Between Rape and Prostitution: Survival Strategies and Chances of Emancipation for Berlin Women After World War II', in Judith Friedlander (ed.), *Women in Culture and Politics: A Century of Change* (Bloomington: Indiana University Press, 1986), pp. 97–117.

Two, Hsu-Ming, 'The Continuum of Sexual Violence in Occupied Germany, 1945–1949', *Women's History Review* 5 (1996), 191–218.

Usborne, Cornelie, *Cultures of Abortion in Weimar Germany* (Oxford: Berghahn Books, 2007).

Wahl, Torsten, 'Zärtliche Zofen', *Berliner Zeitung*, 7 July 7 2003, 16.

Waters, Chris, 'Sexology', in Cocks and Houlbrook (eds.), *Palgrave Advances in the Modern History of Sexuality*, pp. 41–63.

Weeks, Jeffrey, *Sex, Politics and Society: The regulation of sexuality since 1800*, 2nd edn (London: Longman, 1989).

Weinberg, Martin, 'Sexual Modesty, Social Meanings, and the Nudist Camp', *Social Problems* 12 (3) (1965), 311–318.

Weitz, Eric D., *Creating German Communism, 1890–1990: From Popular Protests to Socialist State* (Princeton: Princeton University Press, 1997).

Westdickenberg, Michael, ' "Somit würde man die Darstellung abschwächen, daß dogmatisches Verhalten, Karrieristentum, Fehler im Justizapparat gesetzmäßig wären." Die Zensur von Prosaliteratur der DDR in den sechziger Jahren am Beispiel vom Manfred Bielers Roman *Das Kaninchen bin ich*', in Beate Müller (ed.), *Zensur im modernen deutschen Kulturraum* (Tübingen: Max Niemeyer Verlag, 2003), pp. 163–180.

Whisnant, Clayton J., 'Styles of Masculinity in the West German Gay Scene, 1950–1965', *Central European History* 39 (3) (2006), 359–393.

Wierling, Dorothee, *Geboren im Jahre Eins. Der Jahrgang 1949 in der DDR. Versuch einer Kollektivbiographie* (Berlin: Ch. Links, 2002).

'Vereinigungen. Ostdeutsche Briefe an Beate Uhse', *BIOS: Zeitschrift für Biographieforschung, Oral History und Lebensverlaufsanalysen* 20 (special issue, 2007), 146–155.

Winkler, Gunnar (ed.), *Geschichte der Sozialpolitik in der DDR, 1945–1985* (Berlin: Akademie Verlag, 1989).

Wolle, Stefan, *Der Traum von der Revolte. Die DDR 1968* (Berlin: Ch. Links, 2008).

Die heile Welt der Diktatur. Alltag und Herrschaft in der DDR 1971–1989 (Bonn: Bundeszentrale für politische Bildung, 1999).

Wurm, Carsten, Henkel, Jens and Ballon, Gabriele, *Der Greifenverlag zu Rudolstadt 1919–1993. Verlagsgeschichte und Bibliographie* (Wiesbaden: Harrassowitz Verlag, 2001).

Zatlin, Jonathan, *The Currency of Socialism: Money and Political Culture in East Germany* (Cambridge: Cambridge University Press, 2007).

'Scarcity and Resentment: Economic Sources of Xenophobia in the GDR, 1971–1989', *Central European History* 40 (2007), 683–720.

Ziegler, Ulf Erdmann, *Nackt unter Nackten. Utopien der Nacktkultur 1906–1942* (Berlin: Nishen, 1990).

Index

For EU product safety concerns, contact us at Calle de José Abascal, 56–1°,
28003 Madrid, Spain or eugpsr@cambridge.org.

www.ingramcontent.com/pod-product-compliance
Ingram Content Group UK Ltd.
Pitfield, Milton Keynes, MK11 3LW, UK
UKHW020330140625
459647UK00018B/2100